About the Author

MARK HALPERIN is an editor-at-large and senior political analyst at *Time* magazine and a political analyst for ABC News. Prior to joining *Time*, Halperin worked for nearly twenty years at ABC News, where he covered five presidential elections and served as political director from November 1997 to April 2007. In that role, he was responsible for political reporting and planning for the network's television, radio, and Internet political coverage. He also appeared regularly on ABC News television and radio as a correspondent and analyst, contributing commentary and reporting during election night coverage, presidential inaugurations, and State of the Union speeches. Halperin founded and edited the online publication "The Note" on abcnews.com. He is the coauthor of *The Way to Win: Taking the White House in 2008* (Random House, 2006). He is a Harvard graduate, and he lives in New York City.

THE **UNDECIDED VOTER'S GUIDE** TO THE **NEXT PRESIDENT**

THE **UNDECIDED** **VOTER'S GUIDE** TO THE **NEXT** **PRESIDENT**

Where the Candidates Come from, What They Believe, and How to Make Your Choice

MARK HALPERIN

HARPER PERENNIAL

NEW YORK • LONDON • TORONTO • SYDNEY

HARPER ● PERENNIAL

HarperCollins books may be purchased for educational, business, or sales promotional use. For information please write: Special Markets Department, HarperCollins Publishers, 10 East 53rd Street, New York, NY 10022.

FIRST EDITION

Designed by Justin Dodd

Printed on acid-free paper

Library of Congress Cataloging-in-Publication Data has been applied for.

ISBN: 978-0-06-153730-1

07 08 09 10 11 [DIX/RRD] 10 9 8 7 6 5 4 3

To Karen,
Always ready for every tough challenge,
burst of laughter, and new adventure

CONTENTS

Contents

INTRODUCTION

I get the same question all the time: *Who will win the 2008 presidential election?*

Rarely does anyone ask me, *Who would make the best president?*

Bill Clinton has described campaigning for president as a job interview, with the application process composed of unrelenting media scrutiny and a grueling coast-to-coast gauntlet of events and debates. Consider these pages a compilation of the references, dossiers, and supporting material for the major applicants, and yourself part of the national hiring committee. The task is not easy. Sometimes the candidate who appears most qualified is not right for the job, and sometimes a résumé does not adequately convey talent or potential. But I hope this book can help you make the best possible choice based on the best available evidence. It may be your only chance to meet all the candidates, compare them side by side, and make an informed decision before the choice is made for you.

The men and woman maneuvering for the White House are an accomplished and fascinating bunch. They include a war hero, a precedent-setting trial lawyer, a famous actor, a billionaire, and a former First Lady. One saved America's Olympic Games from scandal, another was hailed as a national leader after 9/11. Some grew up with modest means and became self-made millionaires; others were raised in comfort and have become richer still. They are a diverse group, with members of the Mormon and Jewish faiths, an African American, an Italian American, an Hispanic, and a woman.

They have written best-selling books, endured personal tragedy, and gotten themselves into—and out of—hot water. Some have already made history in their political careers, and others will have an opportunity to make history if they reach the Oval Office.

They are all impressive, with interesting stories to tell, and enthusiastic supporters to sing their praises. But presidencies evolve in unexpected ways. Both Bill Clinton and George W. Bush, once in office, followed different executive trajectories than had been signaled during their campaigns, disappointing tens of millions, including many who voted for them. When Clinton and Bush were running for the White House, the focus was often on the external dramas and day-to-day ups and downs of their races. It was difficult to anticipate fully how they would eventually lead the country through the haze of polls, pratfalls, and punditry. In order to assess a potential president, one must look past the clutter to study policy plans and political substance. And it is equally essential to understand the personality behind the record, the spirit animating the rhetoric.

This book will give you a sense of the biographies, careers, and priorities of the candidates competing for 2008. It also will explain and analyze their positions on the most pressing domestic and foreign issues affecting the country. The situation in Iraq and the contours of the war on terror will have an impact on every aspect of the race. How the candidates conduct themselves within that vortex will surely be important. But other policy issues—and the questions of character and readiness—will matter as well.

These pages are based on my nearly twenty years covering presidential elections, roaming the campaign trail, observing and interviewing the candidates, chatting with voters and political strategists, and trying to divine the mood and priorities of the nation. I have also relied on the words of the candidates themselves, as well as on the excellent work of my journalistic colleagues and political research groups.

My chief focus is on the seven people who I believe have the greatest chance to become the nation's forty-fourth president. There are also sections about those who are influencing the campaign by participating in the race, by contributing ideas to the public dialogue, or by waiting in the wings, ready to make a hard charge toward the front-runners at a moment's notice.

This is the first American presidential election since 1928 in which neither the incumbent president nor the vice president is in the competition. In addition, after twenty consecutive years of presidents named "Bush" or "Clinton," the nation faces a choice about extending the dynastic cycle—or not.

Running a presidential race requires energy, ambition, sacrifice, courage, and imagination. Everyone in the presidential field should be commended for their efforts. And in this wide-open 2008 season, there is plenty of time for a candidate—even a trailing one—to win the election by combining good ideas, hard work, and an understanding of what the country needs in a president. Read on to figure out who has the best chance of winning and, more important, who is best suited for the most difficult job in the world.

PART I: **THE REPUBLICANS**

RUDOLPH GIULIANI

The Basics

Name: Rudolph William Giuliani

Born: May 28, 1944,
Brooklyn, New York

Political party: Republican

Spouse: Judith Stish Giuliani,
married May 24, 2003

Children: Andrew, Caroline (with
Donna Hanover)

Religion: Roman Catholic

Education: Manhattan College, B.A.,
1965
New York University School of Law,
J.D., 1968

Career: Law clerk, Southern District,
1968–1970
Assistant U.S. attorney, Southern
District, 1970–1975
Associate deputy attorney general,
1975–1977
Partner, Patterson, Belknap Webb
& Tyler, 1977–1981
Associate attorney general, Justice
Department, 1981–1983
U.S. attorney, Southern District of
New York, 1983–1989
Partner, White & Case, 1989
Mayoral candidate, New York City,
1989 (unsuccessful)

Career (*cont.*): Partner, Anderson, Kill, Olick & Oshinsky, 1990–1993

Mayor, New York City, 1994–2002

Chairman and CEO, Giuliani Partners, 2002–present

Partner, Bracewell & Giuliani, 2005–present

Presidential candidate, 2007–present

IRAQ WAR

High Priority? ☐ *Yes* ☐ *No* ☑ *Maybe*

Record/Position: Long supported the Bush administration's goals and strategy, but has sometimes been critical of the conduct of the war and the failure to pursue terrorists elsewhere.

Quote: "It's unthinkable that you would leave Saddam Hussein in charge of Iraq and be able to fight the war on terror. And the problem is that we see Iraq in a vacuum. Iraq should not be seen in a vacuum. Iraq is part of the overall terrorist war against the United States."

WAR ON TERROR

High Priority? ☑ *Yes* ☐ *No* ☐ *Maybe*

Record/Position: Says it is the number one issue in the election and anticipates a long global battle. Refers often to his record after 9/11 and "the terrorists' war on us." Has supported aggressive interrogation and investigative tools to combat terror.

Quote: "I think the American people in November 2008 are going to select the person they think is strongest to defend America against Islamic terrorism."

GOVERNMENT SPENDING/DEFICITS

High Priority? ☐ *Yes* ☐ *No* ☑ *Maybe*

Record/Position: Cut some spending as mayor of New York, but has not been specific about where he would seek reductions in federal expenditures. Has made a promise to rehire only half of retiring civilian federal workers over the next decade, although he has not provided details. Says entitlement programs must be changed to reduce the deficit, but refuses to lay out a plan for Social Security until after the election, because he says he doesn't want the issue to become "partisan."

Quote: "All spending is discretionary. Read the Constitution. Congress has to appropriate it; the president has to sign it. All spending is discretionary and it has to be looked at from the point of view of, can we afford it now? Is it appropriate to pass it on to the next generation? This is what I did in New York City. I restored fiscal discipline."

ENERGY/ENVIRONMENT

High Priority? ☑ *Yes* ☐ *No* ☐ *Maybe*

Record/Position: Has put forward a plan to reduce America's dependence on foreign energy through a variety of measures, including alternative energy and nuclear power. Had little record as mayor on these issues, but says this is one area in which he supports a major role for the federal government akin to the Manhattan Project. Believes global warming is taking place, but does not support a cap on greenhouse emissions and says the debate over climate change is "almost unnecessary . . . because we should be dealing with pollution anyway."

Quote: "Every potential solution must be pursued—from nuclear power to increased energy exploration to more aggressive investment in alternative energy sources. I believe that America can achieve energy independence through a national strategy that emphasizes diversification, innovation, and conservation."

HEALTH CARE

High Priority? ☐ *Yes* ☐ *No* ☑ *Maybe*

Record/Position: Supports tax benefits for individuals who purchase their own insurance and other market-oriented ways to expand coverage by lowering the cost of insurance, and legal reform to lower doctors' costs. Wants to let people buy insurance across state lines, diluting state control of the industry. Rejects Democrats' proposals for universal coverage and European systems. As mayor expanded programs for uninsured children.

Quote: "America is at a crossroads when it comes to our health care. All Americans want to increase the quality, affordability, and portability of health care. Most Republicans believe in free-market solutions to the challenges we face. I believe we can reduce costs and we can do it through tax cuts, not tax hikes. We can do it by empowering patients and their doctors, not government bureaucrats. That's the American way to reform health care."

TAXES

High Priority? ☑ *Yes* ☐ *No* ☐ *Maybe*

Record/Position: Worked to keep taxes low in New York and pledges to do the same at the federal level. Does not support major tax reform, such as a flat or sales tax system, because he says they would be too difficult to achieve and disruptive to the current economy.

Quote: "The more ways that we can find to put money back into the private economy, the more our economy grows. The money gets used to create jobs."

JOBS/ECONOMY/TRADE/AGRICULTURE

High Priority? ☑ *Yes* ☐ *No* ☐ *Maybe*

Record/Position: Believes the government best fosters job growth by cutting taxes and reducing bureaucracy, as he did in New York City as mayor. Thinks America's future depends on free trade. Has little experience with agricultural issues.

Quote: "America is at its best when we serve as a shining city on a hill, a beacon of freedom and opportunity to people around the world. Our success in this new century depends on reinvigorating our historic mission with determined leadership that gives hardworking American families confidence their future will be better than their past."

ABORTION

High Priority? ☐ *Yes* ☑ *No* ☐ *Maybe*

Record/Position: Personally opposes abortion, but supports a woman's right to choose as a matter of national policy. Says he would nominate judges and justices who strictly interpret the Constitution, but has remained purposefully ambiguous about whether he would be troubled if abortion laws changed—or if they stayed the same. Before he was mayor he was prolife, but as mayor supported government funding for abortion and opposed a ban on partial-birth abortion (a position he has now changed).

Quote: "I hate it. I don't like it. I wish somebody didn't have to have an abortion, and I would recommend anyone that asked me . . . My personal opinion would be have the child and we'll help you. . . . But I do believe ultimately a woman has to make that choice and you have to respect her."

EDUCATION

High Priority? ☐ *Yes* ☑ *No* ☐ *Maybe*

Record/Position: Advocated school vouchers in New York City and mentions them favorably on the campaign trail more often than do most other candidates, but without specifics. Failed in efforts to gain more control over New York's school system.

Quote: "You only get one chance to educate a child, and if you screw it up, then it's very hard to correct it later. [We] should be ashamed of ourselves, that we do not have the political courage to take on the unions, the special interests, and everything else that are holding our children back."

STEM CELL RESEARCH

High Priority? ☐ *Yes* ☑ *No* ☐ *Maybe*

Record/Position: Supports government funding with what he has called "very, very strict limits" on the use of stem cells from human embryos.

Quote: "The strict limits should be that life is not created for the purpose of destroying life and just for the purpose of scientific experimentation."

GAY RIGHTS

High Priority? ☐ *Yes* ☑ *No* ☐ *Maybe*

Record/Position: He supported same-sex civil unions, although as a presidential candidate, has expressed doubts about laws that make them equivalent to marriage. Opposes both gay marriage and a federal law or amendment outlawing gay marriage. Was an outspoken supporter of gay rights as mayor, hiring openly gay people for government jobs, signing legislation recognizing domestic partnerships, marching in gay pride parades, and living with a gay couple during his divorce. Has downplayed the issue as a presidential candidate.

Quote: "I'm pro-gay rights."

GUN RIGHTS

High Priority? ☐ *Yes* ☑ *No* ☐ *Maybe*

Record/Position: Before running for president, was one of the nation's most outspoken advocates of gun control, including as mayor of New York, when he worked publicly with Bill Clinton on the issue. Supported the 1993 Brady Handgun Violence Prevention Act, the 1994 federal assault weapons ban, and federal handgun licensing and registration. Criticized gun manufacturers, as well as southern states, for lax gun sale laws. Now says he believes in the constitutional right to bear arms and thinks states should decide for themselves what kind of gun laws they want.

Quote: "I do not think the government should cut off the right to bear arms. My position for many years has been that just as a motorist must have a license, a gun owner should be required to have one as well. Anyone wanting to own a gun should have to pass a written exam that shows that they know how to use a gun, that they're intelligent enough and responsible enough to handle a gun."

WELFARE/POVERTY

High Priority? ☐ *Yes* ☐ *No* ☑ *Maybe*

Record/Position: Substantially reduced the welfare rolls in New York City. Believes that work, education, and crime reduction are the keys to changing the lives of the poor.

Quote: "Over the last century, millions of people from all over the world have come to New York City. They didn't come here to be taken care of and to be dependent on city government. They came here for the freedom to take care of themselves."

IMMIGRATION

High Priority? ☐ *Yes* ☐ *No* ☑ *Maybe*

Record/Position: Supports comprehensive immigration reform that includes a process to "regularize" undocumented immigrants, but has opposed 2007 congressional efforts he says provide amnesty. Advocates a tamperproof national ID card for foreign students and workers, and a database to check citizenship. Emphasizes learning the English language and border security, although previously has expressed skepticism about the feasibility of controlling the border. As mayor, denounced federal immigration laws as "harsh and unfair," and stopped city employees from reporting illegal immigrants seeking government assistance.

Quote: "It's a typical Washington mess. . . . The litmus test you should have for legislation is: will it make things better? . . . The organizing purpose should be that our immigration laws should allow us to identify everyone who is in this country that comes here from a foreign country."

For all current issue positions, check out http://www.joinrudy2008.com/issues/.

America's Mayor

On September 11, 2001, Rudy Giuliani, the mayor of New York City, was having a breakfast meeting at the Peninsula Hotel in midtown

Manhattan when American Airlines Flight 11 hit the north tower of the World Trade Center. Giuliani rushed downtown, reached Greenwich Village when the second plane hit the south tower, and was on the scene at Ground Zero to witness the horrors (and barely escape injury) when the building collapsed. Covered in debris, he contacted the governor of New York and the White House, and telephoned a local television station to deliver a message to New Yorkers: "My heart goes out to all of them. I've never seen anything like this . . . it's a horrible, horrible situation, and all that I can tell you is that every resource that we have is attempting to rescue as many people as possible . . . Let's pray."

> *"Something I learned a long time ago, also from my father, is that the more emotional things get, the calmer you have to become to figure your way out."* —on how he kept calm after the attacks on the World Trade Center towers

With the city's emergency management center destroyed in the attack, he assembled his team at Police Academy headquarters, where he directed the city response. He held televised press conferences throughout the afternoon and evening, a model of resolute courage. "New York is still here," he said. "We've suffered terrible losses and we will grieve for them, but we will be here, tomorrow and forever . . . Hatred, prejudice, and anger is what caused this . . . We should act bravely and in a tolerant way." President Bush was under Secret Service protection aboard *Air*

Force One and largely unavailable to the public for long stretches, while Vice President Cheney was secured in a Washington, D.C., bunker. Rudy Giuliani was the face of leadership during the worst attack ever on American soil.

In the following days, Giuliani was a constant presence on television, pushing for the reopening of the New York Stock Exchange, insisting that the Yankees World Series games and the New York City Marathon go on as planned, and leading Bush and other world leaders on grim tours of Ground Zero. Inspired by the example of Winston Churchill during World War II, Giuliani displayed resolve and a rarely seen compassionate side, attending countless funerals for lost firefighters and police officers. He inspired the city, the nation, and the world to honor the memory of those who perished. He also sent a clear signal that life would go on, that New York was back in business. By the time he left office a few months later, on December 31, 2001, he had become America's Mayor.

That is the story everyone knows, the story that defined Giuliani as a national hero, earned him international fame (the Queen of England presented him with the Order of the British Empire), and established his reputation as a natural leader in a time of crisis. But that is just one part of his story. In fact, Giuliani received nationwide press attention for many aspects of his professional life long before 9/11.

There was his tenure in Ronald Reagan's Justice Department, where he held the number three position and spearheaded the effort to combat large-scale drug trafficking. There was his high-profile role as New York City's mob-busting, Wall Street–raiding federal prosecutor, which made him enemy number one of the Gotham City criminal. As mayor during the 1990s, he successfully dealt with the staggering problems of crime, welfare, the economy, and quality of life, drawing widespread acclaim. Simultaneously, his role in the city's racial conflicts brought censure and bad publicity—as did his rocky personal life. Finally, his short-lived Senate run against Hillary Clinton in 2000 further elevated his profile as a major political player. Before 9/11 he was seen as a tough, smart, choleric, controversial, acid-tongued hothead who had both cleaned up and ruptured New York City. Today he is seen as one of the leading contenders for the presidency, despite his checkered professional and personal past and his liberal views on social issues. His social positions are problematic because they differ from those of the party's recent presidential nominees and from many Republicans who dominate the nominating process.

A strategist for George W. Bush observed Giuliani stumping for Republican candidates on the campaign trail in 2004, and described voters' reaction as positively electric. Rudy Giuliani, he said, can walk into any bar in America, including in the Deep South, be recognized, get a unanimous standing ovation, and receive eager offers to buy him a drink. Not necessarily the primary qualification to become commander in chief, but a phenomenon that reflects the unique basis for Giuliani's strengths as a presidential candidate—the emotional bond he has with the country.

This will be the first post-9/11 presidential election without an incumbent. And whether or not there is another attack against the United States before November 2008, it is possible that the candidate who gives the strongest impression of being able to fight terrorism just might win the greatest number of votes based purely on that case, much the way Bush had an advantage in 2004.

This is particularly important for Giuliani, who will need to convince much of the Republican base to ignore deep reservations about his liberal views. Before he entered the race, it was expected that Giuliani would challenge the party to become more centrist and tolerant on social issues. For the most part, however, Giuliani has quietly downplayed his differences with the party platform, and has loudly emphasized his conservative bona fides on economic and national security matters. Giuliani has suggested that the election is essentially about the terrorist threat to America, and who can keep the country safe. If the electorate agrees with this reasoning, Giuliani will hold a strong hand in the 2008 race.

> *"In choosing a president, we really don't choose a Republican or Democrat, a conservative or liberal. We choose a leader."*

The people most skeptical of a Giuliani nomination, aside from those who have challenged his 9/11 heroism, have followed his political career closely and believe he lacks the temperament and copacetic personal history— as well as the conservative credentials—to run the gauntlet of caucuses and primaries while being scrutinized by the national media and tested by his political rivals.

A Leader Grows in Brooklyn

Rudy Giuliani was born in Brooklyn, New York, the only child of Harold Giuliani and Helen D'Avanzo Giuliani, and although his family moved to Long Island in 1951 when he was seven, he has adopted that Brooklyn identity as part of his persona, with its gritty, authentic appeal. In high school, he commuted to Brooklyn as a scholarship student at the boys-only Catholic school Bishop Loughlin. He went on to Manhattan College in the Bronx, and then to New York University Law School. Upon graduation, he began his New York–centric career (with some stints in Washington and post-9/11 travel). In his presidential campaign, he has identified himself as a classic Brooklyn boy—resilient, realistic, capable, plain-speaking, unafraid.

Unlike his rival candidates, who court voters by presenting their personal history and family values as a complement to their records and platforms, Giuliani sticks to his national security message, his résumé, and his twenty-first century deeds. Beyond New York, the Yankees, and his current felicity with his wife, Judith Giuliani, the former mayor rarely mentions his private life. Every presidential candidate must decide how to balance the messages of policy ideas, social views, professional record, and biography through advertising, speeches, Web sites, and campaign surrogates. Almost all the other 2008 contenders talk at length about their backgrounds to create a sympathetic intimacy with the voter. Strikingly, Giuliani's presidential candidacy is almost completely devoid of the personal, and he makes scant attempt to contextualize himself in a familiar way. He rarely mentions his family, his children, his faith. In part this may be a reflection of Giuliani's public style, but perhaps a psychologist or a political strategist would offer different theories. Much of his personal past is not overtly helpful to a traditional political campaign. What is helpful is his professional life. As he asserted in his memoir *Leadership*, it was not September 11 that made him a leader, but a lifetime of experience handling courtrooms, criminals, and City Hall.

The Prosecution (Never) Rests

Some might find it difficult to imagine Giuliani as a religious counselor—in 1986, *Time* magazine said he resembled "a quattrocento fresco of an obscure saint"—but he seriously considered the priesthood as a youth before choosing the legal profession. He confided to the Christian Broadcast Network in 2007 that "frankly, in the Catholic Church the vow of celibacy was something I wasn't sure I could keep." And he is a natural attorney—even his style on the campaign trail has a legalistic air, with his deliberately phrased or nonresponsive answers to tricky questions, his sharp delivery, and his uncompromising commentary.

As a prosecutor, Giuliani was a force to be reckoned with in the courtroom. After New York University Law School and a federal clerkship, he became an assistant U.S. attorney in New York's Southern District, where he was unrelenting, quick-witted, and thorough, and made a name for himself prosecuting police, and political corruption cases. Famously, in 1974, during the bribery trial of former Brooklyn representative Bertram Podell, he cross-examined the defendant so assiduously that the man broke down on the stand, stopped the trial, and pleaded guilty. In 1975 he moved to Washington to join the Ford Justice Department as associate deputy attorney general. At this time he switched his political affiliation to Republican, having started off as a Robert Kennedy Democrat. He has said he soured on the Democratic Party after voting for George McGovern in 1972 and then decided the party was too far to the left, particularly on national security matters during the Cold War. He was an independent for several years before joining the Republican Party.

Giuliani spent Jimmy Carter's presidency in private law practice in New York, and in 1981, Ronald Reagan named him associate attorney general, the number three position in the U.S. Department of Justice. He was given extraordinary jurisdiction over much of the nation's law enforcement bureaucracy when he was only thirty-seven. He expanded the FBI's role in drug enforcement, established a dozen special task forces, and garnered extra resources for his team. To the surprise of many, he left Washington in 1983 to return to the Southern District for the job of U.S. attorney. As he explained before returning to New York, "The job I have now is important and interesting, and it was a close decision. But I enjoy being a prosecutor, running cases, and the ability to be more involved as a lawyer. I won't miss the policymaking." He also laid out the four major areas of focus—drugs, organized crime, white-collar crime, and public corruption—and promised that he would try cases himself.

The Southern District was only one of the ninety-four U.S. attorneys offices that Giuliani supervised while at the Justice Department, but it is widely considered the most important federal prosecutor position in the nation, covering Manhattan and its surrounding areas, a hotbed for just the kind of cases Giuliani planned to pursue. But no one in modern times has used the Southern District, or any other U.S. attorney position, to become as nationally well known as did Giuliani. The *New York Times* called him "the most celebrated Federal prosecutor of his generation," while *Vanity Fair* said he was "the most dazzling prosecutor in fifty years."

After just a year in the job, Giuliani's high-profile cases and assertive manner made him a fixture on the news, national as well as local, with appearances on programs such as *Nightline*, *Good Morning America*, and *Today*. He was a reliable, compelling guest: fast with a sound bite, smart with interviewers. Under his management, the U.S. attorney's office had increased the number of indictments by 10 percent, and sustained the conviction rate of 95 percent. He followed his specialized strategy for success: erring on the side of prosecutions, maintaining a cavalier attitude about civil liberties, making demands on his staff for long hours and thorough preparation, and tackling the minor issues as well as the major problems. He assigned task forces to sweep drug-blighted neighborhoods, arrest petty dealers, and try them in federal court. He cracked down on white-collar corruption cases; prosecuted the wealthy, such as financier Marc Rich on tax evasion charges; and demanded stiffer sentences for everybody, as part of his "deterrent effect" approach. Giuliani's hard-line tactics and public profile led many to suggest that he was positioning himself for a political career, but he denied it, and insisted his office was not about "partisan politics." Others felt that his no-nonsense offensive against all criminals, whatever his ultimate objective, improved the city's morale and confidence.

After two years in the job, his celebrity (and television appearances) had increased even more, and he was recognized for his all-out assault on the Mafia. Some skeptics observed that many of the key mob investigations had been launched years before Giuliani's tenure began, and that he was merely carrying on the work of his predecessors. Giuliani ignored his detractors, and was adamant about pursuing the Mafia with a grand flourish, going after the heads of the five leading mob families in a single trial. As he explained, "If we can prove the existence of the Mafia commission in court beyond a reasonable doubt, we can end this debate about whether the Mafia exists. We can prove that the Mafia is as touchable and convictable as anyone. And without their mystery, they will lose power."

Despite all the praise Giuliani received for his bold pursuit of flashy cases and his shrewd attention to minor offenses, he was assailed for his cold-blooded methods and abrasive style. When asked by the *New York Times* in 1986 about criticism from civil lib-

Giuliani prosecuted the police corruption case that was the basis of Robert Daley's book *Prince of the City*, later made into a movie. (Giuliani joked of the film, "I can't believe how well I came off.")

As a prosecutor, he was given an award from the Italian government for battling the Mafia.

ertarians concerned by overzealous wiretappings, and about accusations of being a publicity hound, he barked, "Damn them . . . If I don't tip in favor of law enforcement, who will? . . . My view is: The way you end corruption, you scare the daylights out of people."

Throughout his term, he worked long days, energized the attorneys who reported to him, let loose his competitive instincts and his temper, and had his life threatened because of his aggressive anti-mob agenda. He fought for jurisdiction, fought for credit, and fought against charges of stringent tactics and political ambition. His headline-grabbing cases continued, with victories in the Mafia-related "Pizza Connection" heroin trafficking case, and the ground-breaking "Commission" trial. In 1987, eight Mafia leaders of the so-called Commission, a body that had controlled the mob in major cities throughout the United States since 1931, were convicted. Among those who received hundred-year sentences were Anthony (Fat Tony) Salerno of the Genovese family, Anthony (Tony Ducks) Corallo of the Lucchese family, and Carmine (Junior) Persico of the Colombo family.

Giuliani also focused on Wall Street, where he took down the titans of junk bonds, prosecuting accused insider traders such as Ivan Boesky and Michael Milken. Giuliani's controversial persona was underlined by publicity stunts such as having several Wall Street executives arrested, handcuffed, and dragged out of their offices and off the trading floor in full view of tipped-off television crews. Criticism of such moves escalated when some of the humiliating public arrests resulted in dropped or reduced charges.

Broken Windows

Giuliani remained U.S. attorney for six years, then briefly joined a Manhattan law firm until his first, unsuccessful campaign for mayor in 1989. Polls showed that Giuliani entered the race as a clear front-runner despite being a Republican in a predominantly Democratic city. He ran on his prosecutor credentials, painting a picture of "a city out of control, overwhelmed by crime, crack, and corruption," stressing his managerial experience and leadership qualities, and attempting, somewhat in vain, to soften his image. New York had not elected a Republican mayor in a quarter century, but Giuliani lost by just 3 percentage points. His defeat was attributed to Democrats rallying around their nominee, David Dinkins, and Giuliani's failure to handle controversies, such as when a newspaper reported that his law firm had represented Panamanian dictator Manual Noriega.

Having fallen short in his first try for elected office, he retreated again to a Manhattan law firm, where he made money, studied his campaign errors, and plotted a comeback. Dinkins, meanwhile, was not considered a successful mayor. The city continued its steep decline, while Dinkins fought charges of incompetence and unethical behavior. When the 1993 race came around, Giuliani hired a new team of strategists, who conceived a fresh look. Hip signs read simply "Rudy!" and he donned muted clothes and subtle glasses. Although he instantly launched a biting negative campaign against Dinkins, he maintained a calm facade. His opponents assumed that, under the pressure of the race, Giuliani would explode with anger and turn off voters, but he never did. (In the 2008 presidential campaign, Giuliani's Republican and Democratic rivals are making the same assumption about his perceived erratic disposition.)

Giuliani won by 49 percent to 46 percent, and when he took the oath of office in 1994, he delivered rousing remarks about the city he loved. " 'Only in New York' has too often become shorthand for the despair of a whole generation of Americans," he said. "But I am here tonight to say the days of our despair can come to an end if we have the courage to lift our eyes and raise our spirits . . . I think that fear and doubt and cynicism have been too much of a part of what's been going on in the city."

Biting the Big Apple

When Rudy Giuliani assumed the job as mayor of New York, the world's greatest city was a mess. The streets were grimy, with panhandlers seemingly prowling every corner, and more stalking the subways. Central Park, despite its architectural beauty, was, after dark, a crime scene waiting to happen. Times Square was a wild neon circus with sleazy shops, prostitutes, pickpockets, X-rated parlors, and grubby bars crowding the grand theaters and Art Deco icons. The notorious "squeegee men" accosted cars stalled at red lights to squirt water on the windshield, perform a rapid, streaky wipedown, and demand cash. There were splatterings of graffiti, regular muggings, and frequent violent crimes.

During his eight years in office, Giuliani seized a wild sabertoothed tiger of a city and turned it into a golden Lion King. He was guided in part by the "Broken Windows" theory, derived from a 1982 sociology article and subsequent book that hypothesized that major crimes and problems could be prevented or alleviated by addressing minor ones. Giuliani applied a zero-tolerance attitude toward anything that had a negative impact on the quality of life, from squeegee men to murder. By 2001, the avenues were relatively clean, Central Park was reasonably safe, even at night, and 42nd Street was a tourist's Mecca. Giuliani took on the Democratic-dominated City Council, the unions, the interest groups, the taxi drivers, the street vendors, and the media. He cut taxes, increased the size of the police force, and reorganized the city's government. He cut the budget initially, although he increased spending on education and law enforcement after the economy rebounded. He brought more than half a million people off the welfare rolls, requiring substance abuse treatment and proof of work in return for payments, and transformed the paradigm of what welfare meant before such changes were applied at the federal level.

He developed a contemptuous attitude toward city bureaucracy and the establishment which has shaped his view of the role of government. As he said in 1995, "The biggest and largest special interest group in the city is the intellectual establishment. New York is a great intellectual center that has become one of the most backward parts of America—unwilling to think a new thought . . . The thinking establishment goes into convulsions over the idea that we could ask people on welfare to work, or that we should fingerprint them to prevent fraud. It's almost as if a secular religion had developed in which these are the things that you must believe to be considered an educated, intelligent, and moral person."

Giuliani's primary problem as mayor can be summed up in one chilling phrase: Giuliani Time. In 1997, Abner Louima, a Haitian immigrant, was beaten and tormented by police officers, spurring outcries about recurrent police brutality. Louima claimed that the police officers shouted at him, "this is Giuliani time," along with racial epithets. While he later admitted to inventing the remark, it nonetheless symbolized what many felt was Giuliani's greatest failure: that he allowed racial tensions and his police force to get out of control, and in doing so, revealed himself as insensitive at best, and intolerant at worst. In 1999, twenty-two-year-old Amadou Diallo was gunned down by police in a hail of forty-one bullets near his home in the Bronx; he was unarmed and had no criminal record. Giuliani refused to reprimand the police for their actions. Although the officers were eventually acquitted, Diallo's death prompted a slew of angry protests and arrests, editorial outcries, and public concern over racial profiling and double standards. Giuliani was blamed for fostering a sense of unchecked power in the Police Department, given his kinship with law enforcement, his encouragement of harsh tactics, and an alleged history of inattentiveness to minorities. Many factors contributed to making America's largest city a roiling mass of constant conflict between different ethnic and racial groups and Dinkins, too, had faced several incidents during his mayoralty. But Giuliani's confrontational style surely played its role.

Giuliani's reaction to criticism was to dig in his heels. He repeatedly refused to meet with minority leaders, even some who were elected officials, and he used incendiary language in situations that seemed to beg for calm. As he had in the past, Giuliani showed more talent for making enemies than friends during conflicts, describing those who opposed him as "babies" and "jerks."

> *"They wanted someone who was going to change this place. How do you expect me to change it if I don't fight with somebody? You don't change ingrained human behavior without confrontation, turmoil, anger."*

Giuliani's tenure also was marked by colorful incidents that made national and international headlines, such as his unapologetic ejection of Palestinian leader Yasser Arafat from a Lincoln Center concert during the United Nation's fiftieth-anniversary celebration (an act heartily praised by the local press and the general populace), and his fight with the Brooklyn Museum over what some felt was a religiously perverse exhibit. He even threatened to cut off the institution's funding when it refused to remove the offending works. In these cases and others, Giuliani was perpetually before the television cameras, arguing his position with energy and a take-no-prisoners style. In more general incidents—murders, fires, and accidents—the mayor also was highly visible, rushing to the scene, holding press conferences, and offering guidance. On a more upbeat note, he was a constant salesman for his beloved city, appearing at Yankees games, at award galas, on late-night television chat shows, always pushing the "I Love New York" message.

When Giuliani finished his eight years, New York was by no means a utopia—there was still litter, crime, and major municipal problems (in particular, the troubled education system, which was bogged down by petty power struggles between the mayor and the teachers' unions and local education chancellors). There was a housing shortage, a slowing economy, and a deficit of several billion dollars. Still, there were undeniable successes. The material improvements were themselves valuable, but they had two multiplier effects. First, business leaders with corporate headquarters and satellite offices in New York, from Wall Street to Madison Avenue to the fashion district, appreciated the lower taxes and safer environment in which to operate and live, resulting in an explosion of new investment and economic activity. Many residents of the metropolitan area who lived in well-to-do New Jersey, Connecticut, and New York suburbs, were delighted that it was once again possible to come into the city and enjoy the arts, shops, and restaurants without fearing for their lives and property, and their regard for Giuliani's performance heightened the overall goodwill he received.

Perhaps most of all, Giuliani reversed the impression that New York City was ungovernable, a turnaround that many commentators called the single greatest act of urban renewal of modern times. Columnist George F. Will deemed his tenure the finest achievement of conservative governance in twentieth-century America. To be sure, much of the liberal New York population thought Giuliani was a racially discriminatory, intractable bully who favored the wealthy and white over the disadvantaged and minorities. Some city residents were relieved that Giuliani was term-limited, and were ready to see him go; before September 11, he saw his approval rating measurably decline. But most of the city's residents conceded that Giuliani had handed them back a celebrated, comfortable, strongly functioning home, bolstered by the expectation that New York would continue to thrive. Indeed, Giuliani's administration strengthened New York's deepest foundations, making the city solid enough to withstand a terrorist attack and allow for a speedy recovery from the trauma of September 11. This, arguably more than his four-month post-9/11 stint as valiant guide, was proof of his exceptional ability.

September 11, 2001, was supposed to be primary day in New York City, and voters were to begin selecting Giuliani's successor. After the attacks, the election was rescheduled. Giuliani's handling of the crisis caused a resurgence of his popularity, and he publicly and privately explored the possibility of staying on beyond the December 31 expiration of his term. His plan was never seriously considered, however, and he eventually threw his support to Democrat-turned-Republican (and now an independent) Michael Bloomberg. With the help of a television ad featuring an endorsement from Giuliani, Bloomberg extended the party's control of City Hall.

Fathers and Sons

Rudy Giuliani is a great aficionado of the opera, particularly Italian opera. And such music would provide proper accompaniment to his life, with its simple pleasures, private intrigue, and grand passions.

Harold Giuliani, who ran a Flatbush pizzeria and bar called Vincent's Restaurant, taught his only son to box at age two, and bought him his first tiny Yankee uniform when he was three. (Giuliani recalls being set upon by an angry group of Dodger fans, after which "my mother or father said, 'Well, now you're going to be a Yankee fan' . . . So I kept wearing that Yankee uniform, and I kept getting thrown in the mud.") Giuliani remembers that his father resented the Mafia for tainting the good name of Italian Americans, and that he encouraged his son not to spend too much time helping out at the restaurant, but to focus instead on the goal of college. According to Giuliani, his father "had a lot of rules . . . He instilled in me a sense of discipline about working, about focusing on what is important in life. I was brought up to respond more to tragedy than to joy, so that if somebody is in trouble, I feel an obligation to help him. My mother and father used to say that the best test of friendship is when you show up at hospitals and wakes, not at weddings. Everybody enjoys going to a wedding."

It was not until Giuliani's Senate campaign in 1999 that a bombshell was reported: in 1934, Harold Giuliani robbed a milkman at gunpoint for $128.82 and gave a false name when he was arrested; he served a year and a half in Sing Sing prison. He also had allegedly been involved in a loan shark operation. Giuliani says both he and his father learned a lesson from the experience: "He would tell me, 'Never take anybody else's money, make sure you always pay for things, make sure that you don't make a mistake when you fill out a form, make sure it's accurate' . . . I've driven myself crazy over this all my life. And when any mistake has been made it really bothers me, and I realize more than I did as I was growing up why my father was doing that. I mean, he wanted to make sure that I didn't make the same mistakes that he believed he had made." Harold Giuliani died of prostate cancer in 1981. Rudy Giuliani bought his mother, Helen, an apartment in his building; they remained close until she died in 2002.

Giuliani was not remembered as a ladies' man in his youth; some described him as shy and a bit ungainly. Influenced in part, he has said, by his father's criminal past, he chose law as his profession, and after finishing school in 1968, he married Regina Peruggi, his childhood friend and second cousin. The relationship fell apart during his Washington years and he had the marriage annulled in 1982 on the grounds that he and Peruggi were related by blood. He wed Donna Hanover, a local television anchor, in a Catholic ceremony in April 1984; son Andrew was born in 1986, and daughter Caroline in 1989, during his first mayor's race.

The local media in New York are lively, prurient, and relentless, with an eager eye for melodrama and scandal. When word developed that there were problems in the Giuliani-Hanover marriage, the press followed it with glee, often slipping out of news and into gossip. Headlines from the tabloids were filled with screaming banners of fights, adultery, and bad behavior. Giuliani and Hanover officially separated in the middle of his Senate campaign in 2000. After the mayor announced their break-up to reporters, which was apparently before he told his wife, she held a dramatic press conference outside Gracie Mansion, the stately mayoral residence, at which she complained of shabby treatment, alleged a mistress (a prominent Giuliani staffer and the subject of much speculation), and acknowledged the oft-rumored flaws in their marriage. Giuliani ultimately dropped out of the Senate race in the spring of 2000,

when he was diagnosed with prostate cancer. He underwent radiation treatment and recovered well.

Giuliani's rather caddish reputation was another negative that
was cleansed during his September 11 renaissance; his leadership
after the tragedy made the tawdry
aspects of his personal life seem
small and irrelevant. His soon-to-
be third wife, Judith Nathan, was
his partner at the time of the attack and a comforting presence
at his side during the aftermath.
Under the circumstances, many
New Yorkers and members of the
media seemed comfortable accepting them as "Rudy and Judi."

Not everyone warmed to Judith
Giuliani, however, and Giuliani's
children, Andrew and Caroline,
have kept their distance from their
father and his campaign. This is
quite a switch from the early years,
when little Andrew accompanied
his father during his campaigns for
mayor (Giuliani once took a de-
tour on his way to an event so Andrew could play in a park), and
famously mugged for the cameras at his father's 1994 swearing-in
ceremony. They played golf together (Andrew now aspires to be
a professional golfer), and Andrew was the best man at Giuliani's

Giuliani's ties to the
New York Yankees are
extensive. The word
"fan" (as in "fanatic")
truly applies. He has
attended innumerable
games, kept an original
Yankee Stadium chair
in his office, frequently
dons a Yankee cap,
and is acquainted
with the players and
management. Even if
he won the presidency,
he would root fervently
and unapologetically
for his home team
(although he *might*
allow another team to
visit the White House
should the Yankees lose
the World Series during
his administration).

2003 wedding. But the relationship has since deteriorated. Andrew made headlines in March 2007 when he told the *New York Times*, "There's obviously a little problem that exists between me and his wife. And we're trying to figure that out. But as of right now it's not working as well as we would like." Caroline, meanwhile, attracted some media attention in August 2007 when she listed herself as a Barack Obama supporter on her Facebook page. Rudy Giuliani has declined to discuss these matters specifically, but always refers to his children with warmth and esteem. They are currently leading lives under the radar as college students, Andrew at Duke University and Caroline at Harvard.

Judith Giuliani

The marriage of Rudy and Judith Giuliani has both public and private aspects. As Giuliani campaigns for president, Judith Giuliani (née Judith Ann Stish of Hazleton, Pennsylvania) is a visible presence, focusing her adoring smile and affectionate praise on her heroic husband. She has appeared in magazines and in fashion spreads, and the two sat with Barbara Walters on *20/20* in a vivid and much-discussed interview. Memorably, Giuliani suggested he would consider including his wife in policy meetings: "If she wanted to, if they were relevant to something that, that she was interested in, that would be something that I'd be very, very comfortable with." The Giulianis have not shied away from public displays of affection, touching and kissing regardless of the presence of cameras, and still have the air of newlyweds about them. They married in a very public way, on the lawn at Gracie Mansion in May 2003, with Mayor Michael Bloomberg performing the ceremony. Their formal reception and dinner was attended by four hundred guests, including Yogi Berra, Donald Trump, Henry Kissinger, Vera Wang, Giuliani's two children and Judith's daughter, and a number of notable members of Giuliani's administration, with music performed by Ronan Tynan and Sarah Brightman. At the ceremony, the two happily described their romance to the *New York Times*. Rudy Giuliani gushed, "Our attraction was instantaneous. There was almost something mystical about the feeling." His bride said, "Rudy truly is a romantic," and added, "We simply were two people in love—never mind the extracurricular stuff that went on around us."

They have been reticent about discussing their initial meeting, in part because Giuliani was still married, albeit unhappily. Judith was present during his abbreviated Senate campaign, but remained a discreet presence, and after he formally separated from his wife, supported him as he underwent treatment for prostate cancer. The media hounded her during the uncomfortable denouement of Giuliani's marriage (Donna Hanover, most conspicuously, barred her from the mayor's residence), but after the terrorist attacks, she stepped into the spotlight as Giuliani's public companion. In recent years, they have lived a glamorous, prominent life, enjoying

When Giuliani and Donna Hanover separated, he moved in with his friend car dealer Howard Koeppel and Koeppel's domestic partner, Mark Hsaio, a Juilliard-trained pianist and Department of Cultural Affairs employee. Koeppel described to the *New York Times*'s Frank Rich an idyllic, squabble-free trio, and a household of vigorous conversation and cute nicknames. Koeppel explained, "I could listen to him all day and not be bored with him—not that I agree with everything he says. That's how much I enjoy having him around. Actually, I love him. It's not sexual, it's just mental. I have my preferences, and I don't find him attractive at all."

the New York social scene, jet-setting, their work (she has been in-volved in a number of charitable causes and joined a philanthropic organization), and their marriage. She often accompanies him on his frequent travel for the legal, consulting, and public speaking work that has been his career since leaving office.

These days Judith Giuliani remains subject to the particular scrutiny of the tabloid press. The mainstream media have gotten in on the act, tossing around details of her three marriages (the first of which was an early five-year union that did not come to light until 2007, and the second of which ended with an unfriendly di-vorce in 1994 and produced adopted daughter Whitney Nathan); her career as a trained nurse and surgical supply salesperson (she received bad press when it was revealed she spent four years dem-onstrating medical stapling tools on live dogs—her spokesperson responded only that she had not been involved in procuring the animals); her switch to philanthropic work after meeting Giuliani; and her deliberate efforts to conform to the glossy image of a po-tential First Lady.

Rudy Giuliani, no stranger to the acid pens of his home-town press, has defended her with passion and respect. After the "puppy killer" story, he asked the media to back off. "My wife's career is one of caring for people in very, very deep and funda-mental ways . . . I've actually seen her act as a nurse and do Heim-lich maneuvers and help people who have fainted . . . Attack me all you want . . . There's plenty to attack me about. Please do it. But, you know, maybe show a little decency." As his campaign has progressed, however, Judith Giuliani has had to endure continued attention, some unfavorable.

Although presidential campaigns are always difficult for family members, Judith Giuliani seems enthusiastic, upbeat, and ready for the challenge. Her husband considers her his "closest adviser," and she will likely remain a crucial part of his team and image as the campaign continues.

Areas of Potential Controversy

– His business dealings since leaving the mayor's office, which have included lucrative speaking engagements around the world, legal work, and consulting for some controversial companies and governments.
– 9/11 backlash, with questions raised about his conduct both before and after the attacks, including having placed the city's emergency command bunker in the World Trade Center complex.
– His marriages, especially the tempestuous end of his relationship with Donna Hanover.
– His estrangement from his children.
– His prostate cancer. Although his treatment by radiation was completely successful, there is some chance of recurrence.
– His decision to don dresses and full makeup for comedy routines in front of cameras.
– His decision to live with a gay couple during the breakup of his second marriage.
– Controversy, wrongdoing, and criminality involving some of his close associates, particularly his former police commissioner Bernard Kerik.

Why Giuliani Can Win a General Election

• If Giuliani wins the Republican nomination, he would be hailed by the national media for defying the odds—many political analysts were once convinced he had exactly zero chance of being his party's choice. If selected, he either might change and strengthen his party, or instead be the de facto leader of a divided and embittered one. If it is the former, several reliably Democratic states, such as New York, New Jersey, Connecticut, and California, could be in play for Republicans. At the very least, Democrats would have to expend time and resources to defend them.

- Giuliani has suggested that the conservative movement can best be revitalized by focusing on lower taxes, smaller government, and strong national security. By downplaying the social agenda that has been a major part of the Republican platform under the party's last three presidents, he might be able to expand outreach to independents, suburban voters, and others who have been turned off by the emphasis on a conservative platform.

- In the 2002 and 2004 elections, the Bush White House adeptly used the levers of federal power to enhance the Republican Party's prospects, highlighting (critics would say "exploiting" or "fabricating") national security threats and the Republicans' perceived superiority in dealing with such dangers. Given his platform, image, and record, Giuliani would be able to pair himself with the outgoing administration in such efforts.

- Giuliani has one particularly strong advantage: universal name recognition. On the campaign trail, he is met with intense bursts of weepy applause and sentimental strains of the national anthem usually reserved for sitting presidents.

Why Giuliani Can't Win a General Election

- The more Americans across the country get to know Giuliani, the more likely it is they will be introduced to his temper. He can be mean and provocative, and might provide fodder for negative ads and reproving editorials. For the most part, he has kept his anger in check, and if he can continue to be calm, he will avoid being branded a moody autocrat. But presidential campaigns are highly stressful and frustrating environments, and maintaining equilibrium is always a challenge.

- Giuliani may love America, but he doesn't much care for campaigning. He is a homebody, comfortable in familiar surroundings, attended by friendly faces. He likes his city, his restaurants, his house, his Yankees. He doesn't relish small talk or campaign-speak; when chatting up state leaders, party bigwigs, or voters, he can lose interest fast if the conversation veers from golf or baseball.

- He has never been elected to federal office, a résumé gap that might reveal itself at inopportune moments, such as in debates.

- In a profession that seems to invite flip-flopping, Giuliani's weaving stance on abortion has permanently turned off many evangelicals and other staunchly prolife voters. He says he supports legal abortion, and believes a woman should have the right to decide what to do about a pregnancy, but says it is morally wrong and he is personally opposed to it. He switched his view on whether so-called partial birth abortion should be legal, adopting the more restrictive position, and now says he would not care if *Roe v. Wade* were overturned. Lightning literally struck during a June 2007 Republican debate while he struggled to answer the abortion question, generating nervous laughter and a visual complement to his dilemma.

- Other aspects of Giuliani's past record and current positions might depress the turnout of conservative voters in key states. He has championed gun control (a stance he has since softened during his presidential campaign), gay rights (although he has never supported gay marriage), and immigrant rights (another view he has altered during his White House run). He also notably endorsed Democratic New York governor Mario Cuomo for reelection against Republican George Pataki in 1994, a choice that reverberated throughout his party for years afterward.

- His wavering positions and political history may damage him in a general election, although many moderates and liberals will be comfortable with his social perspective. But Red states won by President Bush might be up for grabs if conservative voters who cannot abide Giuliani's liberal views either refuse to vote or cast their ballots for an alternate candidate.

- While there is no denying that Giuliani's indomitable conduct in the wake of the 9/11 attacks helped the city and the nation through one of the most traumatic moments in America's history, critics have questioned his overall record and its relevance to presidential performance. While some New York firefighters appreciate Giuliani's long-standing rhetorical support and his attendance at their fallen comrades' funerals, others have criticized him for failing to equip them with radios that would have allowed them to communicate more effectively on the morning of the tragedy. They resented his decision to limit recovery efforts at Ground Zero after the initial round of searching for victims was completed. They also have been angered by apparent insufficient testing of the environmental hazards at Ground Zero and a perceived indifference toward the subsequent severe health problems suffered by recovery workers. Some relatives of civilian 9/11 victims have lodged similar

complaints, and have formed groups to dog Giuliani at
public events. The International Association of Fire Fight-
ers union made a video called *Rudy Giuliani: Urban Legend*
to detail their grievances. The media coverage of these
controversies is likely to continue.

- Some have asked if being able to respond to an attack
  involves the same skills as preventing future attacks, and
  argue that Giuliani has limited experience in international
  diplomacy and intelligence operations that would enable
  him to protect the country.

- Far less grave, Giuliani twice appeared in drag. In 1997
  Giuliani made a splash at the Inner Circle, an annual charity event organized by local New York media. The program
  features musical parodies put on by reporters, participation from the cast of the year's most popular Broadway
  show, and typically, a performance by the sitting mayor.
  Giuliani showed up as "Rudia," wearing a blond wig, a
  pink gown, and bright red lipstick. He spoke in falsetto,
  sang "Happy Birthday, Mr. President" Marilyn Monroe–
  style, and flaunted a cigar. The family-friendly Julie
  Andrews, who was starring on Broadway in the cross-
  dressing musical *Victor/Victoria*, appeared with him on
  stage, but even that could not assuage the jarring image.
  To this day, the picture of Rudia is notorious, and might
  now repel members of the more conservative faction of
  his party. (While in costume he joked, "I already play a
  Republican playing a Democrat playing a Republican"
  in a politically charged paraphrase of a line from *Victor/
  Victoria*.) Giuliani resurrected the alter ego in a video
  for the Inner Circle three years later. It costarred Donald Trump, who admired Rudia's beauty and nuzzled his

bosom; the clip is available on the Internet. This is a minor issue on one level, perhaps, but it offers a quirky reminder of Giuliani's less conventional brand of Republicanism, and some conservatives, particularly in the South, bring it up regularly.

- The media still seem uncertain how to cover the former mayor. The New York press is overly familiar with his taut style, spotted professional record, and awkward personal history, but does not quite fathom his celebrified nation-wide image. The national press, meanwhile, understands Candidate Rudy but does not fully grasp his complex and strident hometown reputation. Either way, however, there is much fodder for an engaged press corps.

- He has shown stubborn loyalty to cronies such as former police commissioner Bernard Kerik. Giuliani pushed Kerik for homeland security secretary, a nomination that resulted in embarrassment for the Bush administration when Kerik was forced to withdraw his name because of legal troubles and looming scandal.

- In addition to Kerik, other former Giuliani allies have been accused or convicted of offenses such as the misuse of New York City money and the cover-up of child molesta-tion by priests, while a few associated with his presidential campaign have been involved in sex or drug scandals.

- Also problematic (albeit highly lucrative) have been Giu-liani's business dealings at Bracewell & Giuliani (formerly Bracewell & Patterson, but renamed when he joined in 2005), a Texas-based law and lobbying firm. Bracewell has represented coal-fired power plants (anathema to environmentalists) and other companies that seek looser environmental regulations; Purdue Pharma, the makers of OxyContin who were required to pay more than $600 million in penalties and fines because of false marketing charges and problems with the product; tobacco producer UST; Saudi Arabia; and, for a time, Citgo Petroleum Corporation, which had ties to Venezuelan president Hugo Chávez, who called President Bush "the devil."

- Some believe Giuliani's full record could not survive the scrutiny of a long general election, when the dramatic imagery of September 11 is pushed aside and the newspapers are filled with investigative reports. The reams of unflattering print headlines about Giuliani's previous professional and marital woes could haunt him, and his relationship with his children could continue to be a problem. Other past actions by Giuliani are sure to receive additional scrutiny, including his decision to quit the Iraq Study Group in 2006. He claimed there was an appearance of conflict with his potential presidential run, when other evidence suggested that the meetings were interfering with his lucrative speaking engagements.

The Best Case for a Giuliani Presidency

- Giuliani would not be intimidated by the history and austerity of the Oval Office. He has capably tackled every big assignment throughout adulthood, with absolute confidence and unflagging energy. He knows how to delegate, how to manage his time, how to formulate a plan, and how to get results, even if a little arm-twisting is involved.
- Giuliani is explicitly patriotic, but he is not a xenophobe. It is easy to imagine him traveling the globe, making a good impression, charming allies, threatening enemies,

and commanding respect. That he is already known and esteemed by many abroad, particularly in Europe and Asia, would help repair damaged international relations, and he is certainly scary enough to present an imposing force to America's foes.

- Giuliani often asserts on the stump that the job of mayor of New York is the toughest in the world. This may be an exaggeration (being leader of the free world is unquestionably tougher), but not by much. He whipped the city into shape, and he is comfortable being in charge.

- In his presidential campaign, Giuliani has put together an assembly of longtime aides and mixed them with talented new people rather than relying on an insular group of loyalists as has been his pattern. This makes it less likely that he would build a cabinet filled with cronies.

- He has worked in Washington enough to have an understanding of how things are accomplished, but not so much that he is captive to its provincial ways. Voters who seek change in Washington would get a president who is not afraid to shake things up.

The Worst Case for a Giuliani Presidency

- Giuliani has always been a man of action, confident in his own ability and opinions. If he won the White House, he might be inclined to toss all peripheral advice out the window, and do what he liked. He might revert to his tendency to bring in a staff based on loyalty rather than on merit and experience. His wife might be present at every cabinet meeting. The Yankees would win every baseball game, by national decree. (Some readers might slot this last bit in the Best Case column.)

- To date, he has not been specific about what kind of policies he would pursue as president, and some of America's most pressing problems (Iraq, health care, Social Security, energy, immigration, education) are going to require focused White House leadership to solve.
- Giuliani is prone to destructive and time-wasting feuds, vendettas, and clashes with those he dislikes or distrusts. As was once observed about the former mayor, "It's not Giuliani's tactical sense, but his very nature, that makes him turn everything into a battle, and every battle into Armageddon."
- Critics say that when Giuliani was mayor he demanded absolute loyalty from members of his government and unusual secrecy about government activities. Those two traits are shared by the Bush administration, and some in the country might bristle at the continuation of an increasingly unpopular inclination.
- Giuliani has little direct foreign policy experience. This could be a drawback, as the next administration is likely to be heavily focused on international affairs.

What to Expect If Giuliani Is President

- If Giuliani becomes president, his inaugural address will be filled with references to the war on terror, the fundamental theme of his campaign.
- The administration would probably undergo a longer and rougher adjustment period than Giuliani currently expects.
- Giuliani would aggressively repel what he calls the "terrorists' war against us," with an internationalist agenda on trade and the extension of America's brands around the world. He would manage the Iraq War in part by employ-

ing his forceful and controlling personality, and continue the Bush administration practice of protecting national security at the expense of civil liberties. He likely would make a splashy trip to Italy, land of his ancestors, at some point during his term.

- He would apply the "Broken Windows" theory that served him so well in New York, and would address issues such as immigration, energy, and spending, as well as other quality-of-life problems. His philosophy would be tested in the Oval Office, where the small problems are major and the big problems are global.

- His cabinet would likely include plenty of New Yorkers. Undoubtedly, a few of his old friends and staffers would get senior positions. A Giuliani administration should expect some controversy related to his staff selections.

- At press conferences, Giuliani would establish himself as boss, welcoming journalists but asserting his authority— there might be some fractious exchanges. Expect Yankee jokes on both sides, particularly during spring training, playoff season, and the World Series. If the Yankees won the championship, Giuliani would likely don his baseball cap in the Rose Garden.

- At a time when many Americans seem to be looking for national unity and decrying partisan strife in Washington, a Giuliani administration might invite the kind of conflict that has accompanied his success in public life. He has based much of his presidential campaign on deriding the Democratic Party and its presidential candidates as weak on terror and zealous about raising taxes, and he almost never reaches out in an attempt to unify the parties.

- Giuliani likely would enforce an air of formality, and expect high productivity, a clear chain of command, tidy appearances, and conservative suits.

- Judith Giuliani would take to life as First Lady as enthusiastically as any presidential spouse in the modern era. She would maintain a traditional role, similar to that of Laura Bush, although she perhaps would present herself more visibly and dynamically than does the current First Lady. Her relationship with the press likely would continue to be tense and splintered. Andrew and Caroline also would receive some media attention regarding security, their professional aspirations, and their social lives. The press would follow Giuliani's paternal interactions, and report on rapprochement or continued estrangement.

Giuliani's Own Words

"I've created a lot of my own stereotype."

"For purposes of ethics and of law we elevate human beings by holding them responsible. Ultimately, you diminish human individuality and importance when you say, 'Oh, well, you're not really responsible for what you did.' "

"Part of the challenge of life is doing different things, proving that you can do it, proving to other people that you can do it . . . The point to be made is that everybody has a more complex personality. You don't really know public figures. All you know is the little bit that is presented to you, and then it's usually the repetition of the same thing. Human beings are enormously complicated."

"I started thinking about Churchill, started thinking that we're going to have to rebuild the spirit of the city, and what better example than Churchill and the people of London during the Blitz in 1940." ———on how he found strength after the 9/11 attacks

"People ask, 'have you changed a lot since 9/11?' Actually, I changed more from the prostate cancer. Having to deal with that had a bigger impact and, I think, gave me more wisdom about the importance of life, the lack of control you have over death. It removed some of the fear of death."

What His Supporters Say

"It's like you're with Elvis, for God's sake. This isn't a political response. This is a real emotional response."

—former New York City congresswoman
Susan Molinari, eight years before September 11, 2001,
about walking with Giuliani in a St. Patrick's Day parade

"Nobody believed Giuliani had a heart. He's not supposed to have a heart. He's an animal, he's obnoxious, he's arrogant. But you know what? He gets it done. Behind getting it done, he has a tremendously huge heart, but you're not going to succeed in New York City by being a sweetie. Giuliani has no gray areas—good or bad, right or wrong, end of story. That's the way he is. You don't like it, f___ you."

—former New York City police commissioner Bernard Kerik

What His Critics Say

Giuliani is "consumed with raw power."

—the late legendary Washington lawyer
Edward Bennett Williams, after facing him
in an insider-trading case

Giuliani has "an ambition so consuming that that which sustains it is embraced willy-nilly, that which does not directly feed it is neglected, and that which runs counter to it is earmarked for destruction."   —a 1989 article in the *American Lawyer*
                    based on interviews with fifty judges and lawyers

"It's a cult of personality around the great leader. They don't want anyone to question his decision-making. All they understand is intimidation. Rudy loves to shut you down, cut you to the quick. If he wants your opinion, he'll beat it out of you."
                    —a former aide in 1995 about the way
                    Giuliani ran the mayor's office

Giuliani Facts and Stories

– His closest friends remain those he met in childhood.
– An opera fan from an early age, he started an opera club in high school; his fellow members would troop to the Metropolitan Opera house and sit in the cheap seats.
– As a youth, he considered a career in medicine.
– He made law review at New York University Law School.
– He avoided service in Vietnam through student and work-related deferments and then by drawing a high draft lottery number.
– He was not active in either the antiwar or civil rights movements of his era, and once said of the decade-defining unrest, "Just exactly how I missed it, I can't describe." He also eschewed the decade's enthusiastic drug experimentation.
– For years he has regaled audiences with an amusing *Godfather* imitation, which has offended some Italian Americans who say it perpetuates stereotypes. If elected, Giuliani would be the first Italian American president.

– Giuliani successfully fought prostate cancer in 2000; his father died of the disease in 1981.

– He was named *Time* magazine's person of the year in 2001.

– He has become a millionaire many times over since leaving office, with a big book deal and a multifaceted career as a lawyer, lobbyist, consultant, and public speaker.

– He was portrayed by the actor James Woods in a made-for-television miniseries titled *Rudy: The Rudy Giuliani Story*. Woods called Giuliani "truly an American hero."

– He has hosted *Saturday Night Live*, performed in episodes of *Seinfeld, Mad About You*, and *Law & Order*, and been a guest on talk shows such as *The Late Show with David Letterman*, *The Tonight Show with Jay Leno*, and *The Daily Show with Jon Stewart*. He has appeared in films such as *Anger Management*, *The Out-of-Towners*, and *Eddie*, and in many documentaries about New York, including several about September 11.

– He and his wife divide their time between a $5 million Upper East Side apartment and a $4 million residence on Long Island.

Quirks, Habits, and Hobbies

– Nothing tops his Yankees love, but he likes football and basketball, too.

– He has recently become acquainted with NASCAR; on an Iowa radio program, he said after attending a race, "I became [a fan]. I had not been to a NASCAR race. I'd watched them on television. I'd been in a NASCAR once. I drove around a track once. I love cars. I love sports and I never realized it was such a tremendous, spectacular event. I'm still talking about it."

– He plays golf and tennis, and has given his wife golfing lessons; during a joint radio interview, Judith Giuliani said he was a good teacher and explained, "The key to this game is you drive for the show, and you putt for the dough, so I've been taking putting lessons." Giuliani has said of his love of the sport, "I wouldn't get too excited about how great I am at it, but I really enjoy it. It's a great way to relax . . . I squeeze it in whenever I can, which means I don't get a great deal of time to play and therefore I have it as an excuse. Whenever I don't play well I can say, I don't play enough. It's a great excuse."

– He has said a preferred alternative career would be a "sports announcer."

– He has eaten his fair share of Raisin Bran and likes apples.

– He appreciates a good cigar.

– He told the Associated Press that his worst habit is "talking too much."

– For years he wore his hair in a much-maligned comb-over; a new, sleeker style that he adopted several years ago (apparently at the suggestion of Judith Giuliani), is considered far more flattering.

– He only requires about four or five hours of sleep a night.

– He has described himself as a fan of Theodore Roosevelt, Abraham Lincoln, and former New York City mayor Fiorello La Guardia.

The Undecided Voter's Guide Questionnaire
For what unhealthy food do you have the biggest weakness?

I don't think of any particular food as being unhealthy. It's all a question of moderation and a balanced diet.

In what way would you hope America would most fundamentally change by the end of your time in the White House?

I want to continue to make America better, stronger, safer, and even more hopeful than it is today.

What is your most memorable childhood activity?

Playing baseball and going to baseball games.

What is the biggest single difference between men and women, besides physiology?

It's obvious.

What is your most strongly held superstition?

Wearing cowboy boots during Yankee playoff and World Series games. Second, not mentioning a possible no-hitter after the fifth inning.

Name someone you would like to see in your cabinet, or, at least, tell us what would be most distinctive about your cabinet.

Joe Torre.

What is the worst thing you did as a teenager?

Too long ago to remember.

How are you most different as a person than your parents?

I'm alive and unfortunately I've lost them.

What is your favorite way to relax (besides spending time with your family)?

Playing golf, reading, and watching baseball.

Where is your favorite place to vacation?

Anyplace close to a golf course.

Presidential Announcement

Giuliani made no formal announcement speech.

Read More About Giuliani

Rudolph W. Giuliani, *Leadership* (New York: Hyperion, 2002). A memoir of his experiences on September 11, as well as of his career as an attorney and mayor.

Andrew Kirtzman, *Rudy Giuliani: Emperor of the City* (New York: William Morrow, 2001). A full account of Giuliani's mayoralty by a New York City reporter who covered the administration and was with the mayor on September 11.

Wayne Barrett, *Rudy! An Investigative Biography of Rudolph Giuliani* (New York: Basic Books, 2000). A tough biography of Giuliani's colorful life story.

http://www.joinrudy2008.com/

JOHN McCAIN

The Basics

Name: John Sidney McCain III
Born: August 29, 1936,
　　Canal Zone, Panama
Political party: Republican
Spouse: Cindy Lou Hensley McCain,
　　married May 17, 1980
Children: Doug, Andrew, Sidney Ann
　　(with Carol Shepp McCain)
　　Meghan, Jack, Jimmy, Bridget
　　(with Cindy McCain)
Religion: Episcopalian
Education: U.S. Naval Academy,
　　Annapolis, 1958
Career: Director, Navy Senate Liaison
　　Office, Washington, 1977–1981
　　Sales representative, Hensley &
　　Company, Phoenix, 1981–1982
　　U.S. congressman, Arizona, 1983–1986
　　U.S. senator, Arizona, 1987–present
　　Presidential candidate, 2000
　　(unsuccesful)
　　Presidential candidate, 2007–present

IRAQ WAR

High Priority? ☑ *Yes* ☐ *No* ☐ *Maybe*

Record/Position: Has been among the most outspoken supporters of the Bush vision, but also highly critical of the administration's performance and execution, particularly by former secretary of defense Donald Rumsfeld. Believes that troop withdrawal would endanger America's reputation and security.

Quote: "I know how tough it is for the American people, I know how frustrated Americans are . . . But I also want to tell you that I believe if we fail, the consequences of failure are catastrophic. If we leave Iraq, they are going to follow us home."

WAR ON TERROR

High Priority? ☑ *Yes* ☐ *No* ☐ *Maybe*

Record/Position: Believes the fight against terror is central to the role of the presidency for the foreseeable future. Has been highly critical of some Bush administration incarceration and interrogation policies, especially those involving possible torture.

Quote: "America faces a dedicated, focused, and intelligent foe in the war on terrorism. This enemy will probe to find America's weaknesses and strike against them. The United States cannot afford to be complacent about the threat, naïve about terrorist intentions, unrealistic about their capabilities, or ignorant to our national vulnerabilities."

GOVERNMENT SPENDING/DEFICITS

High Priority? ☑ *Yes* ☐ *No* ☐ *Maybe*

Record/Position: Has been a leading crusader against excessive government spending for many years, especially earmarked projects for specific members of Congress, sometimes called "pork barrel" spending. Says he would seek a line-item veto, would veto bloated-spending bills, and publicize the names of big-spending lawmakers in order to save the taxpayers money. Favors fixing entitlement

programs such as Social Security and Medicare to put them on
sounder footing, but has provided limited details.

Quote: "Taxpayers should be outraged that their hard-earned dollars are
being spent on projects like the National Automotive Center—to the
tune of $12.5 million. One of the research activities conducted by
this center involves a 'smart truck.' I wonder whether the intellect of
this truck will be such that it will not only be capable of heating up a
burrito, but will also be able to perform advanced calculus while
quoting Kirekegaard."

ENERGY/ENVIRONMENT

High Priority? ☑ *Yes* ☐ *No* ☐ *Maybe*

Record/Position: Has put efforts to reduce global warming at the center
of his platform. Has frequently criticized the Bush administration for
not doing more on the issue and has called for a cap on greenhouse
gas emissions. Advocates allowing companies to trade, save, and
borrow emissions credits, and to generate "offset" credits. A strong
proponent of nuclear power and the preservation of national parks.

Quote: "We are convinced that the overwhelming scientific evidence
indicated that climate change is taking place and human activities
play a very large role . . . It's the special interests versus the people's
interests and I still have enough confidence in our system of government that the people's interest will ultimately prevail."

HEALTH CARE

High Priority? ☐ *Yes* ☑ *No* ☐ *Maybe*

Record/Position: Supports tax incentives for individuals to buy health
insurance, more community health centers, health savings accounts,
expanding the State Children's Health Insurance Program, putting
more medical information online, malpractice reform, and greater
availability of generic and imported prescription drugs. Has supported increased spending on health care for veterans. In the past,
has championed a patient's bill of rights. Has not emphasized health
care reform in either his 2000 or 2008 presidential campaigns.

Quote: "For my part, I would simply affirm that the sacrifices borne by veterans deserve to be memorialized in something more lasting than marble or bronze or in the fleeting effect of a politician's speech. . . I am, I assure you, committed to honoring that debt."

TAXES

High Priority? ☐ *Yes* ☑ *No* ☐ *Maybe*

Record/Position: Has at times opposed his party's efforts to reduce taxes, citing concerns about the deficit, and has suggested he does not strongly believe in supply-side economics. Would seek to repeal the Alternative Minimum Tax and extend the Bush tax cuts that are due to expire—many of which he originally opposed.

Quote: "My record is very clear. I have never voted for a tax increase in twenty-four years. That should be sufficient time to convince average Americans of my commitment not to raise taxes."

JOBS/ECONOMY/TRADE/AGRICULTURE

High Priority? ☐ *Yes* ☐ *No* ☑ *Maybe*

Record/Position: Supports free-trade agreements and reform in the agricultural subsidies system. Has objected to a large role for the federal government in creating jobs or steering the economy.

Quote: "Expanding free trade is a way to improve the well-being of all Americans, particularly the working poor. The most basic economic analysis shows that tariffs represent an unfair tax on an already overtaxed public. Reducing barriers to trade is the equivalent of a tax cut for every consumer."

ABORTION

High Priority? ☐ *Yes* ☑ *No* ☐ *Maybe*

Record/Position: Has a strong prolife record as a senator. Supports the overturning of *Roe v. Wade*, many federal restrictions on the availability of abortion, and a constitutional amendment banning most abortions, but wants to change the Republican Party platform to explicitly recognize exceptions for rape, incest, and the life of the mother. Rarely discusses the issue unless asked.

Quote: "At its core, abortion is a human tragedy. To effect meaningful change, we must engage the debate at a human level."

EDUCATION

High Priority? ☐ *Yes* ☑ *No* ☐ *Maybe*

Record/Position: Is skeptical of a large federal role in education policy and spending. Originally supported No Child Left Behind, but has subsequently expressed some reservations.

Quote: "We must work to ensure that our students do not continue down the path of cultural illiteracy and educational under-performance. But how? One major step in the right direction is to take away power from education bureaucrats and return it to those on the front lines of education—the local schools, the local teachers, and the local parents."

STEM CELL RESEARCH

High Priority? ☑ *Yes* ☐ *No* ☐ *Maybe*

Record/Position: Has been a leading Republican champion of federal funding for research, as long as cells aren't created for the express purpose of destroying them. In 2006, supported bills calling for more federal funding for adult stem cell research, a ban on the creation of embryos for research, and providing federally financed research using embryos slated for destruction by fertility clinics.

Quote: "Stem cell research has the potential to give us a better understanding of deadly diseases and spinal cord injuries affecting millions of Americans."

GAY RIGHTS

High Priority? ☐ *Yes* ☑ *No* ☐ *Maybe*

Record/Position: Opposes gay marriages but also a constitutional ban on them unless state courts begin to legalize the practice. Endorsed an Arizona ballot initiative to limit marriage to a man and a woman and supported the 1996 Defense of Marriage Act. Has expressed conflicting views on civil unions.

Quote: "On the issue of gay marriage, I do believe, and I think it's a correct policy that the sanctity of heterosexual marriage, a marriage between man and woman, should have a unique status. But I'm not for depriving any other group of Americans from having rights."

GUN RIGHTS

High Priority? □ *Yes* ☑ *No* □ *Maybe*

Record/Position: As a senator has a mixed record on gun measures, voting for safety locks, gun show checks, and a few other restrictions, but voted against the Brady law and the assault weapons ban. As a presidential candidate, has emphasized his support for the Second Amendment.

Quote: "Neither justice nor domestic peace are served by holding the innocent responsible for the acts of the criminal."

WELFARE/POVERTY

High Priority? □ *Yes* ☑ *No* □ *Maybe*

Record/Position: Has not emphasized a major role for the federal government in reducing poverty. Has voted for welfare reform. Has a mixed record on raising the minimum wage.

Quote: "Welfare and antipoverty assistance is a shared responsibility among federal, state, and local government; the private sector; community- and faith-based organizations. Welfare policy must provide a strong safety net, while promoting work, responsibility, self-sufficiency, and dignity."

IMMIGRATION

High Priority? ☑ *Yes* □ *No* □ *Maybe*

Record/Position: At great political cost, has been a leader among Republicans in favor of comprehensive immigration reform, with a path to legal status for undocumented workers. He is also for increased border enforcement.

Quote: "We can't allow the status quo to prevail. Twelve million people marching around America illegally. Broken borders. No viable temporary worker program for our agricultural workers here. Employers being forced to be in violation of the law because they feel forced to hire people who are here illegally. This issue needs to be resolved."

For all current issue positions, check out http://www.johnmccain.com/ Informing/Issues/.

The Straight Talk Express

"We have so little water in Arizona, the trees chase the dogs."

"Last night I slept like a baby. I slept for two hours and woke up crying. I slept for another two hours and woke up crying."

"Remember the words of Chairman Mao: 'It's always darkest before it's totally black.'"

John McCain likes to tell jokes. Some are clever, some are corny, some are spontaneous, some have been told a thousand times. He has a dry wit, a lively mind, a sarcastic streak, and a sharp tongue. Many of his barbs are aimed at himself, a few go over the line, most lend a refreshing insouciance to his statesman's identity.

As a man who grew up in a decorated military family, and spent five and a half grueling years in a POW camp in Vietnam, humor is his most reliable tool. While he takes governance and politics very seriously, he has an expansive and jaunty view of the world, enhanced by his personal experiences and his bold nature. As a result, John McCain is renowned for his relaxed candor in public and with the press, his tart irreverence in the Senate, and his maverick flair as a presidential candidate.

But there were few fun or humorous moments during the

early days of his 2008 campaign, his second run for the White House.

In 2000, John McCain shook up the Republican presidential nomination race, transported in style on the *Straight Talk Express*, the big blue campaign bus where reporters were invited for free doughnuts and frank repartee. Journalists were duly charmed; McCain even mischievously referred to the media as "his base." He skipped the Iowa caucuses, won the New Hampshire primary to much fanfare, but lost the South Carolina primary, and was subsequently flattened by the streamrolling trifecta of George W. Bush's funding, organization, and inevitability, combined with the Bush campaign's aggressive negative strategy.

McCain's failed presidential bid nevertheless improved his standing as a political player and national figure—he lost the White House but won new fans and increased his power. Over the following years, he assembled an unofficial national coalition of Republicans who respected his military service and conservative instincts; of independents who appreciated his panache, free spirit, and views on campaign finance reform, stem cell research, and global warming; and of Democrats, who felt that in an age of war he was a trustworthy alternative to leaders of their own party. Everyone seemed drawn to his innate charm and populist persona. Republicans sought him out to campaign and raise money for their races, and he was even talked about as a running mate for Democratic presidential nominee and fellow Vietnam veteran John Kerry in 2004.

In the 2008 campaign, well before the voters had their say, John McCain lost control of his public image. He was defined by out-of-favor positions on such issues as the Iraq War and immigration. Everything positive about McCain—the compelling character, fierce rectitude, and heroic sheen that made him one of the most popular and exciting politicians in America—faded, replaced by a crushing sense that his time had passed.

In many ways, McCain is now a man without a party. Republicans in Congress, in the Bush camp, and in the national and state GOP organizations have grown weary of his nonconformist impulses. At one time, they overlooked his sometimes mutinous behavior—his reflexive openness to bipartisan deals, flirtation with the media, and propensity to gratuitously provoke other leading party members, including President Bush, with whom he clashed over taxes, interrogation tactics, campaign finance, ethics, and the environment. As McCain's strength has waned, they no longer have felt the pressure to tolerate his temperamental and stubborn behavior. Some conservatives—leaders and grassroots activists alike—have discounted McCain's largely consistent right-leaning voting record on social issues such as abortion, seizing instead on his occasional errant opposition to their agenda and faulting him for not prioritizing their preferred causes. In an unusually partisan era, where compromise is sometimes seen as treachery, McCain has led bipartisan movements in a highly flagrant fashion.

McCain's staunch support for the Iraq War, including for the increase of soldiers on the ground, has alienated moderates and independents anxious to see the war end at once. As McCain has struggled to redefine himself as the Republican establishment candidate, he has disappointed the once-rapt media, who have complained that his "straight talk" has become stock political-speak and shameless pandering. To some extent, the connection between McCain's stirring biography and the causes he champions has been broken.

McCain, however, is a fighter to the core. As he said in July 2007, after weeks of bad fund-raising news, falling poll numbers, and poignant staff departures, "I have faced a lot tougher times than this in my life. I am going to get out the bus and do the town halls and work 24/7. I am confident I will do well. This is a day at the beach compared to some days I have had in my life." Doubtless this is true; he underwent years of rigorous training at the Naval Academy, half a decade of brutal torment as a prisoner of war, arduous rehabilitation upon his return home, a bumpy entry into the world of politics, political humiliation as a participant in the Keating Five banking scandal, vicious fights on the Senate floor, negative attacks in 2000, and a variety of personal ordeals throughout. McCain is battle-scarred but battle-ready. He is tough, he is confident, and he is daring.

> *"I may not be the youngest candidate in this race, but I'm certainly the most prepared. And I'm prepared to lead this country. I don't need any on-the-job training. I'm ready to do the hard things, not the easy things. And that's what I intend to do."*
>
> —May 13, 2007

The next president will take office in January 2009. He or she will seize the reins of a country beset by war, terrorism, global warming concerns, civic division, and domestic disarray. McCain trusts that his national security credentials, Senate experience, and innate leadership abilities make him the most qualified candidate in the race. Indeed, the weight and breadth of McCain's résumé alone justify that faith.

Not Self But Country

John Sidney McCain III, son of Roberta Wright McCain and John Sidney McCain Jr., was born into an illustrious military family. His father was a four-star U.S. Navy admiral who led Pacific forces in the Vietnam War; his grandfather, John Sidney "Slew" McCain, was a four-star admiral who commanded aircraft carriers in World War II. Both were legendary in the navy for their accomplishments and bravery, and for their impressive father-son success. Senator McCain mentions them sparingly on the campaign trail, but he has written with pride about them in his memoirs, and both men clearly have influenced McCain's attitude toward conduct and duty. McCain's ancestry is of British American stock. Further down on his family tree are Confederate soldiers, Mississippi plantation and slave owners, an aide to George Washington, and the famed fourteenth-century Scottish king Robert the Bruce.

As a child, McCain was hot-tempered, roguish, bright, and popular, having inherited his mother's spirit and his father's swagger. The McCains moved around, typical of a navy family, settling temporarily in the Washington, D.C., area. McCain attended the private school St. Stephen's, and then went to boarding school at Episcopal High School in Alexandria, Virginia. Following in the family footsteps, he enrolled at the Naval Academy. He was an unabashed troublemaker at Annapolis, collecting demerits left and right for his sloppy room, unchecked tongue, and taste for partying. He graduated fifth from the bottom of his class thanks to a lax attitude toward the subjects that bored him, such as math, although he was strong in history and literature. It is in keeping with his personality that he seemed to chafe at the rituals of the academy, with its traditions of hazing, humiliation, and deference. Duty and honor came easily; submission did not. As he once said, "I had more fun at the Naval Academy than most anybody ever should, but I've also got

"Whatever sacrifices you must bear, you will know a happiness far more sublime than pleasure. My warrior days were long ago, but not so long ago that I have forgotten their purpose and their reward."
—October 9, 2001, speech to students at the U.S. Naval Academy

to tell you that I think it was a rebelliousness on my part. I didn't like the regimentation. I thought that a lot of the rules and regulations were incredibly stupid. I was always trying to beat the system." This trait can be seen in his political career—he has been a proud Republican and has defended some of the party's major principles, but he has often broken conspicuously from the GOP line.

After graduation, McCain was commissioned as a naval officer in 1958, and, in 1964, after years of carefree womanizing, he met Philadelphia model Carol Shepp while he was training as a pilot in Pensacola, Florida. They married in her hometown in 1965, and he adopted her two sons, Doug and Andy, from a previous marriage. In 1966 they had a daughter, Sidney. In January 1967, McCain was promoted to lieutenant commander in the Navy, and within a few months, he was off to Vietnam.

McCain had scarcely begun his tour when he was one of the lucky survivors aboard the USS *Forrestal*; more than 130 men were killed and twenty planes were destroyed after a rocket was accidentally launched across the carrier and hit the fuel tank of McCain's plane. He was in the cockpit at the time of impact, but suffered only minor injuries. He then relocated to the *Oriskany* carrier and continued to fly. On October 26, 1967, during his twenty-third bombing mission, his plane was hit by a surface-to-air missile as he flew over North Vietnam near Hanoi. McCain ejected from the plane, broke both arms and his right knee, and was knocked unconscious. Captured by North Vietnamese, he was violently pummeled, had his shoulder broken by a rifle butt, and was bayoneted in the ankle and groin. He was taken as a prisoner of war, held in inhumane conditions, and brought to the Hoa Lo prison camp, grimly dubbed the Hanoi Hilton. His injuries were severe and he might have been left to die in his cell, but because he was the scion of a prominent military family, the news of his plight was reported on the front page of the *New York Times*, and his status as an admiral's son excited his captors. They nicknamed him the "Crown Prince" and began to manage him with more care. His dire injuries were treated, albeit inexpertly, in a hospital, and he was offered early release, a propaganda ploy that he refused according to the American military policy requiring that prisoners be liberated in the order of capture.

His heritage notwithstanding, he endured great suffering at the hands of his guards; at one point under torture he agreed to sign a confession, for which he would later express profound regret (such acquiescence was common for pris-

His 1999 memoir *Faith of My Fathers* was a best seller. It was subsequently made into a 2005 television movie. His most recent book is *Hard Call: Great Decisions and the Extraordinary People Who Made Them*, published in August 2007.

oners under great duress). Over five years, he sustained beatings, periods of solitary confinement, malnutrition, dysentery, and the numerous, incomprehensible forms of abuse employed during the war. Some of his bones were broken again; his shoulder was permanently dislocated from its socket. He was near death on several occasions, and even considered suicide. Photographs from the period show McCain, snowy-haired and emaciated, with limbs shriveled and askew, and an expression of miserable determination on his face. If McCain now appears to hold his arms stiffly, or seems to shuffle slightly as he walks, it is because of his sustained torments. He is still, for instance, unable to raise his arms above his head, and often requires assistance with such basic tasks as brushing his hair or donning a jacket.

Imprisoned, he found strength from two sources—some of his fellow POWs, with whom he developed intense, lifelong bonds, and his love of America, which, he says, was a balm to his spirit and a constant inspiration to adhere to the code of honor and not lose faith. McCain, since beginning his political career, has retained a connection with his military brethren. Many veterans of all ages attend his campaign events in their uniforms; he goes out of his way to thank them from the stage and meet with them privately after he speaks. Those with whom he served, and especially those with whom he was incarcerated, talk about him with respect and devotion, and never fail to recount his loyalty, grit, and moxie. Emotion is important in politics (particularly if it is genuine), and McCain regularly chokes up when recalling his brave comrades in Vietnam, or when referencing the sacrifice of the troops currently serving in Iraq and Afghanistan, and the concerns of their families at home.

After his liberation in 1973, and his long physical rehabilitation, McCain was a changed man. Not, as one might suspect, in temperament (he was always a taut firebrand), nor in spirit (he has insisted that he shook off the strains and agonies of captivity upon his release and never let the trauma haunt or control him), but in personal drive. Having wasted, as he saw it, nearly six years of his life, he was raring to go. He continued to serve in the navy, as a squadron commander and then as a liaison to the U.S. Senate. His injuries slowed him down somewhat, as did his marriage. His wife, Carol, had waited loyally during his imprisonment, and been gravely injured in a car accident in his absence. McCain was no longer committed to the marriage, engaged in infidelities, and eventually sought a divorce; Carol McCain was unhappy with the split, but in recent years has expressed understanding.

In May 1980, a month after his divorce was official, he married Cindy Hensley of Phoenix. She was nearly two decades his junior, and from a wealthy family that owned a lucrative Anheuser-Busch beer distributorship. He retired from the navy in 1981 as a captain, and moved with her to her home state of Arizona, where he immediately began to plan his entry into politics.

McCain's experience as a POW has played a major role in his political career, although he has often said, "I don't want to be the POW candidate. I want to be John McCain from Arizona." But Americans trust and appreciate a hero, and McCain showed extraordinary courage and fortitude during his imprisonment, even though he tends to describe his ordeal with modesty, and to emphasize the bravery of his fellow captives, many of whom he insists suffered far more than he. Both Bill Clinton (who avoided serving in Vietnam through student deferments and connections) and George W. Bush (whose service in the Texas National Guard has prompted accusations of nepotism and evasion) struggled against angry censure in their four presidential campaigns, and even John Kerry, who fought in Vietnam and won three Purple Hearts for his efforts, was pilloried by his political enemies for the brevity of his tour of duty, for his actions as a soldier, and for his antiwar activities once back in the United States. McCain, in contrast, is an indisputable American hero and model of military bravery. When he got into politics, his experiences in Vietnam not only attracted voters but also made him indurate to the relatively tame tribulations of politics; bickering and dirty tricks are trifles compared to the horrors of war. McCain seemed fearless, unbothered by the petty slights of the political game, and buoyed by his newfound impatience. With rare exceptions, throughout his political career he has maintained this sanguine tenacity.

The White Tornado

In 1982, following a brief stint working for his father-in-law at the Hensley & Company liquor distribution business, McCain leaped at an open congressional seat in Arizona's first district, batting aside accusations of carpetbagging and silencing his critics with the humorous and pointed line "The longest place I ever lived was Hanoi." (He was an itinerant navy brat as well as a prisoner of war.) Years later, referring to his hasty entry into Arizona politics, he joked, "I got lost on the way to my own rallies." Once he entered elective politics, McCain never lost a race in Arizona. In 1986, after getting his feet wet with two terms as a U.S. representative, he went for the Senate seat vacated by the conservative icon Barry Goldwater, and

> *"I don't want to be the POW Senator. What I've tried to do is position myself so that if opportunities come along, I'm qualified and ready.*
> *—in 1988*

won. Instantly, he was perceived as a political star. He was a war hero and a smooth talker, and he had important friends in the Republican Party—he had met Ronald Reagan upon his return from Vietnam, and had maintained an acquaintance with Nancy Reagan. George H. W. Bush considered him as a running mate in 1988, and while McCain was not asked to be on the ticket, he appeared at the Republican National Convention with President Reagan.

With stardust on his shoulders, McCain learned the ways of the Senate and directed his attention to the familiar and high-energy areas of defense and foreign policy. The spotlight found him, first for his irrepressible charisma, then under the glare of the Keating Five scandal.

In 1987, Arizona banking executive Charles Keating attempted to use his influence in Congress to keep federal regulators from taking action against him for questionable business practices. The Democrats controlled Capitol Hill at the time, but Keating (who was eventually convicted for wrongdoing in running his savings and loan operation) spread around campaign donations to both parties to make sure he had bipartisan allies.

After the colossal failure of the S&L industry, the press and the public were looking for villains to blame for the huge losses to the government and the plight of the individual victims. Keating became an archetype for the venality of banking executives who broke the rules to enrich themselves. After years of media and governmental investigations, the five U.S. senators who assisted Keating ("the Keating Five") became symbolic of alleged Washington corruption—elected representatives who took campaign donations and gifts from moneyed interests who sought special treatment and favors.

McCain was the only Republican member of the Keating Five (and, along with his wife, a personal friend of Keating), and as the investigations moved painfully forward, Democrats were reluctant to let the Arizona senator off the hook, for fear that the scandal would morph from a bipartisan embarrassment to a condemnation of the Democrats alone. In the end, the Senate ethics committee found that McCain broke no laws but erred by attending two meetings with regulators and his Senate colleagues to appeal on Keating's behalf.

McCain acknowledged bad judgment in agreeing to attend the meetings (although he pointed out that Keating was a constituent who employed many Arizonans). Additionally, financial and personal ties between Cindy McCain's family and Keating, coupled with McCain's own professional (if limited) connection and his status as the lone Keating Republican, kept him at the center of the scandal for several years. There were lengthy newspaper, magazine, and television stories recounting in excruciating detail the overlapping chronologies of how Keating fleeced the unsuspecting, and of his interactions with McCain. The coverage intimated that McCain was guilty, by his actions, inactions, and association. McCain, always so cocky and righteous, was mortified to find his reputation tainted; as he said, "I believe in duty, honor, and country, and I never thought I'd be embroiled in something like this." He undertook his rehabilitation seriously, calling it "like a campaign. A campaign for credibility." The Arizona media were particularly harsh, drawing McCain's wrath and altering forever his relationship with some of the state's leading news organizations.

He belatedly repaid Keating for money spent on joint family vacations, he contritely and candidly admitted to his mistakes, and he gave interviews to all interested media. But McCain was savvy enough to know that regardless of his repeated mea culpas, the episode would blemish his reputation and leave a permanent entry in his biography. As he remarked in an interview with *60 Minutes* and has often reiterated on the campaign trail, "Outside of the prison experience, obviously, it was the most unpleasant experience of my life. There's no doubt about that . . . it'll be on my tombstone, 'One of the Keating Five.' "

The Subversive

The *New York Times* once observed that John McCain's POW experience gave him an "impatience with bureaucratic inertia and ideological purity that goes beyond raw political ambition." After his humiliating experience on the wrong side of the moral divide with the Keating Five episode, McCain embraced senatorial ethics with an intensity some considered overcompensation. While nearly all senators are by nature ambitious and egotistical, McCain placed his principal focus on his own image and moral code, championing causes and supporting policies that fit into his veracious reformer persona, even if it meant clashing with the Republican Party.

In 1997, McCain told an interviewer about power in Washington, "This is a very seductive kind of environment. You are here and you are called a senator. You have an aura of infallibility. You develop a thing where you feel you really are different and should be treated differently. And live by a different set of rules." McCain has indeed lived by different rules, especially for a Republican seeking the presidency. Rather than working the traditional levers of Washington power and the GOP, he has relied on his popular, centrist appeal, with an assist from an adoring media. The *New York Times* once titled a profile about McCain "The Subversive," a term that would never be applied to Richard Nixon, Gerald Ford, Ronald Reagan, Bob Dole, or George Bushes 41 and 43.

Many of the issues McCain has promoted in the Senate work to his advantage as a presidential candidate. When he first came to Washington, he concentrated on relatively minor domestic issues, such as Native American rights and noise pollution in the Grand Canyon, until he became a prominent national spokesman on foreign affairs and reform. On international policy, he was credited with expertise because of his military background and his willingness to confront presidents of both parties. On ethics, special-interests, and campaign finance reform, he propelled changes in the way lobbyists conducted business, campaign money was raised, cigarette companies were regulated, and pork-barrel spending was authorized.

The McCain-Feingold bill brought about the most significant changes in fund-raising laws for federal campaigns since the aftermath of Watergate. Some of the law's provisions have been struck down by the courts, and debate continues on how effective it has been at breaking the tie between special-interest money and political influence. But it is clear that McCain's leadership on the issue raised his profile and endeared him to a number of newspaper reporters, editorial writers, and reform-minded independent voters. It also earned him enduring hostility from many conservatives, who felt it abridged their First Amendment rights, and Republicans, who thought that it would threaten their long-standing fund-raising advantage over the Democrats. To compound matters, McCain's hotshot airs and sarcastic taunts on the Senate floor and behind the scenes further alienated members of his own party.

When McCain ran for president in 1999, despite his status as one of the more celebrated senators in the country, and the best-selling author of a memoir about his POW history, he still needed to boost his name recognition. With George W. Bush a clear front-runner, and the rest of the Republican field quite weak, McCain generated a semblance of a real race. Bush was the establishment leader; McCain was the insurgent. Bush lacked national security credentials; McCain was overflowing in international experience.

Bush was evasive with the media; McCain invited anyone with a press pass for chummy on-the-record tea and tête-à-têtes. Bush ran a national campaign; McCain zeroed in on symbolic first-in-the-nation New Hampshire.

> *"I'm not running for president to be someone. I'm running to do something."* —on his 2000 run

The race was rough, with negative attacks and scathing rhetoric; during a February 2000 Republican debate, McCain commented, "This is probably the nastiest campaign that people have seen in a long time. But look, I'm enjoying it. This is a great and exhilarating experience . . . I'm Luke Skywalker getting out of the Death Star." Bush snapped back, "You're playing the victim here. Remember who called who untrustworthy."

McCain lost his temper on several occasions during the nomination season, allowing his opponents to define him as angry and equivocal. He later said, "One of the things that happened . . . is that I became angry, and I let my anger show. It got me off message, got me kind of off stride. And people don't like that. What they care about is what you're gonna do for them as president of the United States." The lesson was learned too late (and Bush was far too strong a front-runner, in any case). Religious conservatives and other important groups within the Republican Party massed for Bush, while the GOP establishment circled the wagons. McCain won New Hampshire and racked up a few more contests, but his loss in the South Carolina primary brought his momentum to a screeching halt. He lashed out at Bush's supporters for running a viciously negative campaign in South Carolina (even though his side took its shots at Bush as well), and, just as his campaign was ending, gave a speech that attacked some of the most prominent leaders of the religious right as "agents of intolerance." Once Bush became the nominee, McCain swallowed his resentment and offered his support, out of obligation to the party and canny self-protection. For the next four years in the Senate, McCain deliberately built his bipartisan national reputation while both the Republican and Democratic parties viewed him with cautious respect and uneasy suspicion.

By 2004, with Bush increasingly unpopular and the Iraq War marching steadily into bedlam, some Democrats were eager to claim McCain as their own, and speculated about adding him to the ticket as John Kerry's running mate. The media took a greedy interest in the scenario, and the effort to enlist McCain was protracted and overwrought. In the end, McCain turned down Kerry's invitation to join a unity ticket. But the explanation McCain offered afterward illustrated his awkward simultaneous left-right maneuvering, a problem he has encountered in the 2008 race: "I would have been a man without a country! The Democrats never would have really accepted me, the Republicans would never trust me again." McCain's ultimate loyalty to the Republican Party (had he defected, a Kerry-McCain ticket would indeed have been formidable), combined with his refusal to denounce the Democratic Party, left him in some ways as a beacon of hope and integrity in polarized American politics. In Washington, some considered him an egotistical, volatile rebel, but still recognized his potential.

"Older than Dirt"

America is generally perceived as an ageist country, and age will likely be a factor in the 2008 race. Youthful candidates are presenting themselves as representatives of change, a desirable notion to the many Americans who have expressed unhappiness with the country's direction. McCain, meanwhile, has been pigeonholed as a status quo candidate, particularly because of his views on Iraq. In the past, McCain preened happily over his reputation as an honorable, valiant maverick, but in 2007 he came to be seen as a gruff, myopic, out-of-touch, fossil. Rather than being appreciated for his wisdom and charisma, he was pitied for his lost momentum.

Despite McCain's spry manner, he has suffered several bouts of skin cancer, thanks to a childhood spent outdoors and an adulthood under the strong Arizona sun. He had a melanoma extracted from his shoulder in 1993, revealed when he released medical records in December 1999 (which showed him to be in good mental and physical health); had more lesions removed from his arm and temple in 2000 (along with lymph nodes in his jaw, which left him with a lump of scar tissue); and had a third skin cancer recurrence, in 2002. He now has regular skin checkups and mole removals, coats himself in sunscreen, and boasts a long scar on his face. (He often remarks wryly that he is "older than dirt," with "more scars than Frankenstein.") McCain's resulting pallor, set off by his white hair, can give him a rather spectral air, particularly when he is tired. He has been treated for an enlarged prostate, and suffers from arthritis and other ailments common in men of his years.

His campaign staff and his supporters scoff at this elderly image, stressing McCain's hipness, his magnetism, his vigorous hikes with his twentysomething sons, the vitality and good genes of his globetrotting ninetysomething mother. McCain, in mind and soul, if not necessarily in body, seems a young man, with boyish features, an energetic intellect, and an awareness of contemporary culture (he is a guest on Jon Stewart's show nearly as often as he appears on *Meet the Press*, which is saying something). He's had nary a senior moment nor a misplaced pop cultural or idiomatic reference. But polls suggest that many Americans prefer their presidents to be hardy and exuberant rather than contemporaries of Abbie Hoff-

His mother, Roberta McCain, born in 1912, has often been described as feisty, both in her youth and as a Navy wife. After her husband's death in 1981, she spent part of each year traveling the globe, sometimes with her twin sister, Rowena. She has been supportive of her son's career, but not of his cussing; when he used coarse language in his memoir to describe his prison captors, she warned, "He better never speak like that again, or I'll smack him bald-headed. Of course, he almost already is." Her treatment of the press mirrors the wry banter her son employs; she teased a *Time* magazine reporter, "If I don't like what you write, I'm gonna get you fired. And then I'm going to sue *Time*."

man, Troy Donahue, Albert Finney, Bill Wyman, Don Drysdale, and Ursula Andress. (And if you don't know who those people are, or are uncertain if they are still alive, well, that's the point.) McCain has been through a lot in his long lifetime, and he is not getting any younger.

Cindy McCain

Cindy McCain has always provided a support system for her rambunctious husband, holding down the Arizona fort while he fought his battles in Washington and on the campaign trail. The couple met in 1980 when she was twenty-four, on vacation with her parents in Hawaii. As she recalled, "I was standing at the hors d'oeuvre table, young, shy, not knowing anybody when suddenly this awfully nice-looking navy captain in dress whites was kind of chasing me around the table . . . I loved his intelligence, humor, completely different perspective. Having seen the bad side of life, he didn't take it too seriously. And my parents liked him instantly. John was absolutely an original." The pair were smitten, and their relationship progressed swiftly, despite his marital status and their nearly two-decade age difference (both initially fudged their ages—she added three years, while he subtracted four). Cindy Lou Hensley was quite a catch—young, beautiful, and very wealthy. McCain, who had never earned a significant income in the military, found himself married to an heiress. His first job after retiring from the navy in 1981, following the death of his father, was working for his father-in-law as a public affairs agent for Hensley & Company, a job that allowed him to travel around Arizona to plug both Budweiser and himself in preparation for his successful congressional bid.

Cindy McCain retained her close relationship with her parents, James and Marguerite, and lived near them in the same Phoenix neighborhood. Her father died in 2000, her mother in 2006. Even after John McCain won his Senate seat, Cindy McCain chose not to move to Washington, D.C., but maintained the home base in Arizona, where she continued her work with disabled children; she received her undergraduate degree in education and her master's in special education from the University of Southern California. The McCains had three biological children—Meghan, Jack, and Jimmy—and adopted a fourth, Bridget, from Bangladesh in 1991. Cindy McCain seems to have led a charmed life, with her famous husband, lovely children, good looks, and great wealth (she has a personal fortune estimated at many tens of millions of dollars).

But Cindy McCain has had her share of strife as well. She became addicted to prescription drugs in the late 1980s and early 1990s, provoked by pain from back surgery and the stress of her complicated life as political spouse (John McCain's chagrin over the Keating Five scandal exacerbated her anxiety). Her addiction drove her to steal pills from the Third World relief organization she founded, American Voluntary Medical Team. In 1992, her concerned parents confronted her, and she vowed to stop taking the drugs. John McCain was surprised to learn of his wife's addiction but was sympathetic and supportive. She sought treatment and was not charged for any wrongdoing, although she endured some nasty media attention from the local Arizona press. She told NBC's Jane Pauley in 1999, "I have a lot to offer to this country. I have a lot to offer to my family, and I think I can do good things. I know I can. I have done good things. And the best thing I've ever done is to go into recovery and stay drug-free."

In 2000, she was appalled that her youngest child, Bridget, was used as a pawn in a negative campaign by Bush allies, who spread rumors that she was the result of an adulterous affair. In 2004, at age forty-nine, Cindy McCain suffered a cerebral hemorrhage after neglecting to take her blood pressure medication; the stroke was minor, and she made an excellent recovery. All of these trials have given Cindy McCain a certain fragile air, although she is a uniformly gracious and elegant presence on the campaign trail, and McCain supporters never fail to mention her striking blond looks in their introductions. She is far more visible in the 2008 campaign than in 2000, and while she does not offer opinions on policy or politics, she is a close observer of the

> Cindy McCain describes her husband as "a remote-control freak. Once he gets hold of the remote control, forget it. If you want to watch something else, you're out of luck."

organizational workings of her husband's campaign, and has plenty of ideas about how he should be presented to the voters. When describing her husband, she does not address the details of his political platform, but keeps it simple and direct: "He'd be the best president. Every day in his heart and mind, John lives the code of conduct—duty, honor, country—which I admire. I always told the kids: 'Daddy's on a mission, serving his country. We have to be supportive.' And he's never been neglectful of our family. Naturally, there were times I wish, like every wife, he'd been home more . . . that he'd sit down, hold my hand, say, 'I'm sorry, honey,' but I respect his dedication. John's a real patriot."

Cindy McCain has pursued her own campaign of sorts; she has been deeply involved with children's rights, devoting time and resources to such organizations as CARE, Operation Smile, and HALO. She has served on their boards and traveled on missions to India, Sri Lanka, Vietnam, and Angola. She also is chair of the family liquor distribution business.

John McCain's seven children offer a jolly range of ages and professional pursuits. McCain's three children from his first marriage to Carol McCain, are Doug (born in 1959), a pilot for American Airlines; Andy (born in 1962), who works for Hensley & Company; and Sidney (born in 1966), who is a music publicist. From his second marriage, his eldest daughter, Meghan (born in 1984), is a graduate of Columbia; and his youngest daughter, Bridget (born in 1991), is in high school. His sons John Sidney "Jack" McCain IV (born in 1986) and James (born in 1988) are both pursuing careers in the military; Jack is a midshipman at the Naval Academy, and Jimmy has joined the marines. That his sons are serving adds an additional layer of authenticity to McCain's expressions of compassion for military families and their sacrifices.

The Maverick

Almost immediately after George W. Bush was inaugurated for his second term in 2005, political insiders began looking down the road to 2008. John McCain was singled out as the most likely Republican successor to Bush and the most likely forty-fourth president of the United States. The Bush White House assumed that McCain would be the Republican nominee and a strong general election candidate, and showed little displeasure about such an outcome. McCain had handled the ugliness of the 2000 nomination battle with dignity, had been loyal during the 2004 reelection campaign, was a reliable proponent of continued funding for the Iraq War, and would offer the Republican Party a good chance of holding on to the White House—not such an easy feat given Bush's increasingly dismal poll numbers. Democrats, too, assumed McCain would be the nominee, and worried that he would be difficult, perhaps impossible, to beat.

But by mid-2007, McCain was scrambling to stay in the running. He had alienated the left and the right with his support for a continued military presence in Iraq and comprehensive immigration reform. In his early campaign efforts to win over the Republican establishment and grass roots, McCain initially appeared to stray from his maverick style and embarked on a more conventional-candidate approach. Then, in a bid to regain his mojo, he began to defend even his most unpopular positions, while also highlighting his conservative credentials on government spending and national security and his more centrist views on issues such as the environment. Rapprochement attempts with leading figures on the political right and some new positions were branded as phony and hypocritical by commentators and voters across the spectrum.

To capture the Republican nomination, it is important to have strong ties to some of the major base constituencies. McCain has neglected this at his own peril. Many leaders and members of the key interest groups in the conservative movement—including the National Rifle Association and the National Right to Life Committee—strenuously objected to the McCain-Feingold legislation and have never forgiven McCain for spearheading the bill. His twisty sanctimony has turned off other party players, who no longer trust his motives. Nevertheless, McCain remains one of the more reliably conservative Republican candidates in the race, and this, paired with his impressive résumé, and charisma could keep him from being buried during the nomination season.

As far back as 2005, some of McCain's friends said that his determination to succeed George W. Bush in the White House had made him "far more serious and focused than he has ever been," and that "the McCain they knew—irrepressible, occasionally outrageous, impolitic" had all but disappeared. McCain had stopped being McCain. There were still flashes of his former sardonic humor on the campaign trail, but that public image did not animate his campaign's political strategy. After shedding the first incarnation of his campaign team and strategy in the summer of 2007, he seemed unburdened and refreshed, more in touch with the qualities that once attracted voters, imbued him with edgy self-confidence, and fueled his maverick spirit.

Areas of Potential Controversy

– His age. If he falls off one stage (à la Bob Dole 1996), he could be in trouble.

– His health. There are days when he looks youthful and chipper, and days when he looks "older than dirt."

– His temperament. McCain's enemies in Washington and Arizona want America to know they think he is nuts and not mentally fit to control nuclear weapons. One major public outburst

from McCain will provide them with an opening to spread that
message.

– His family business dealings. His wife's family got rich in the
liquor business, with a post–World War II history involving
allegations of bootlegging.

– His relationship with donors who had business before the
Senate Commerce Committee when he was the chairman.
Reformers have to be purer than Caesar's wife.

Why McCain Can Win a General Election

- If McCain survives the Republican nomination process, his
  comeback will be a remarkable story, reviving the tales of
  his Vietnam heroism, his nonconformist sensibilities in the
  Senate, and his unflagging fortitude. The momentum of
  a come-from-behind nomination victory could carry him
  forward in the general election.

- He has long attracted independents and populists, who
  feel comfortable with his brand of intellectual conservatism and his emphasis on issues such as the environment.
  In 2008, getting the independent vote will be crucial. In
  addition, McCain might be able to draw significant Democratic votes, with a crossover appeal that could put several
  Blue states in play. From his Senate races, he also has had
  more experience wooing and winning Hispanic votes than
  have other leading presidential candidates.

- Veterans and their families can be a meaningful voting bloc
  all across the country.

- For years he enjoyed the cushy position as the media's
  favorite Republican. While the relationship has cooled of
  late, the love affair might reignite. Loathed and mistrusted
  though the press may be, they are an irreplaceable asset in
  a national political race.

- Experience, experience, experience. He was elected to two terms in the House and four terms in the Senate, and has volumes of real-life and extracurricular knowledge on which to draw. He has traveled the world extensively as a member of Congress and personally knows numerous world leaders, politicians, and diplomats. If the dominant issue in the election is national security—because of another terrorist attack and/or conditions on the ground in Iraq—McCain's résumé might trump all other considerations.

- He has been among the strongest Internet fund-raisers in the Republican Party. As the nominee, money would flow in from traditional sources as well, even from those who thus far have not supported him.

- He has run for president before, and has been active on the campaign trail and as a high-profile Republican spokesman for many years. No one else in the race can match that.

- He is terrific one-on-one. McCain might have a caustic nature and a blazing temper, but he is an empathetic and solicitous person, and, although aware of his celebrity and his status, he is unfailingly an officer and a gentleman. When meeting voters, he listens, reacts, and seems genuinely enthused by the human interaction on the campaign—not just the end result of snagging a vote.

- He may be old as the hills, but he is sharp as a tack.

Why McCain Can't Win a General Election

- If elected, McCain would be the oldest president to be elected to a first term in the country's history. (He would be seventy-two; Reagan was sixty-nine when he was first sworn in.) In polls, most voters express little enthusiasm for a seventy-something president. While McCain's mind is as keen as ever, his physical appearance might work against him. Although he has a naturally youthful energy and mien, his Vietnam injuries give a rigidity to his limbs and movements. The scars on the side of his face from skin cancer, from certain angles, can be disquieting.

- McCain has a volatile temper. This is not a consequence of his POW ordeal, nor is it a product of his strict military training. It is an inherent trait. In his memoir *Faith of My Fathers*, he writes of his unruly toddler years, "When I got angry I held my breath until I blacked out." He has shouted at his Senate colleagues during heated negotiations, and he famously lashed out at George W. Bush during the 2000 campaign. Occasionally McCain's touchy disposition has become evident in public. Behind the scenes, those who know him report his rage is even more explosive and frightening. Should voters get an inkling of this, more could blow up than just his temper—imagine the endless replays of a McCain meltdown.

- His support of some of the Bush administration's Iraq War policies, including the 2007 troop build up, or surge, could become a major obstacle. If the chaos of the Iraq War is hung around McCain's neck, his chances at the presidency could be negligible. No candidate is as identified with the war as is McCain, and he spent months presenting himself as the person most likely to carry on the policies of the Bush administration.

- He has alienated many in the Republican Party over the years, and his long-standing, aggressive espousal of comprehensive immigration reform offends still more Republicans, who might refuse to turn out to vote, or look elsewhere for a candidate.

- His jokes occasionally veer away from funny or appropriate, and into the territory of rude or even indefensible. While most will not be repeated here, stunts such as singing "Bomb Iran" to the tune of the Beach Boys' "Barbara Ann" have few laughing. His humor could get away from him in the general election, if heightened by competitive stress.

The Best Case for a McCain Presidency

- Smart, savvy, and motivated, he might solve some of the thorniest problems facing the country, such as preserving the fiscal solvency of Social Security, Medicare, and Medicaid. This might be made easier if McCain decides he is unlikely to seek reelection, and could put together deals unburdened by electoral concerns.
- He could use his skills at compromise to enact legislation addressing such complicated problems as global warming and immigration.
- Leveraging his appeal to Republicans, Democrats, and independents, he could unite the country, rendering Red-Blue America a shade of purple.
- He might use his military background to be the first hands-on commander in chief in decades, leading the country to an acceptable outcome in Iraq.
- McCain would not be daunted by the job of president, and he could skip the "first hundred days" learning curve. As he said back in 1999, "I'm obviously aware of the enormous responsibilities. But I don't find it intimidating."

The Worst Case for a McCain Presidency

- After two tumultuous decades in the Senate, he has alienated a lot of people. Payback could result in gridlock.
- He might carry over the Bush administration's Iraq War strategy, thus continuing an unpopular war that could effectively cripple his presidency before it starts.
- His lack of executive experience and a failure to pay attention to detail could leave a McCain administration floundering. The fractiousness and grim financial straits of his current presidential effort are not good signs—the early days were plagued with competing centers of power, carelessness, and questionable hiring and firing choices, practices that would be disastrous in the White House.
- His many years in Washington and his own strident confidence could cause him to underestimate the numerous challenges of the presidency.
- His age could have people focused on ousting (or replacing) him in 2012, rendering him prematurely inconsequential.
- That whole "McCain is crazy" theory might turn out to have some merit.

What to Expect If McCain Is President

- The Iraq War would be priority number one. The war against terrorism would be number two. Having sold himself as the supreme foreign policy expert, and having spoken openly and often about his views on military action, expectations would be high for him to acquit himself well as commander in chief. If one or more of his sons were serving in Iraq or Afghanistan, their personal situation, and the impact on McCain's decision making, would be widely discussed. He would take steps to outlaw interrogation practices that could be considered torture—after his own POW experience, he views torture as not only immoral but ineffective.

- A presidential crackdown on excessive government spending would far exceed anything tried by Ronald Reagan or George W. Bush. Legislators would have to decide whether to fight for their traditional ability to spend taxpayers' money or accept a fundamental change to the process. Those who chose to fight would face McCain's wrath and his attempts to call them out publicly.

- His cabinet would likely be a mix of conservative Republicans and moderate Democrats, with a few possibly selected from his cadre of Senate friends. Some corporate CEOs would be considered as well.

- McCain has always had a healthy ego, and he would relish the top job. The White House would be a merry place, for the media as well. Rose Garden events and East Room press conferences would be peppered with cutting humor and good-natured insults.

- McCain would take office in 2009 as a 72½-year-old man. There would be quite a lot of interest in his health—every skin cancer screening, every medical exam, every bad cold would be studied and debated. His participation in the 2012 race would be an issue of constant speculation, even if McCain used his typical relaxed and self-deprecating humor to poke fun at his dotage and reassure the American people of his political and biological longevity. Either way, his vice president would undergo a lot of scrutiny, and, regardless of whether McCain sought a second term, there could be a bigger field of Republican candidates in

2012 than is usual with a sitting president from the same party.

- McCain's temper would probably result in at least one irritable tantrum while in office.
- On the other hand, America would have a president who would more eagerly anticipate delivering his comedy routine at the annual White House Correspondents' Dinner than giving his State of the Union address.
- Cindy McCain would bring her firm but delicate touch to the East Wing, and would likely engage in foreign travel on behalf of children in need. The McCains' teenage daughter Bridget would finish her high school years in the White House, and the older children would bring some cute grandkids around on holidays.

McCain's Own Words

"I believe in evolution. But I also believe, when I hike the Grand Canyon and see it at sunset, that the hand of God is there also."

—Republican presidential debate, May 2007

"We must win in Iraq. If we withdraw, there will be chaos; there will be genocide; and they will follow us home."

—on staying the course in Iraq, May 2007

"We must, whatever our disagreements, stick together in this great challenge of our time. My friends in the Democratic Party, and I'm fortunate to call many of them my friends, assure us they share the conviction that winning the war against terrorism is our government's most important obligation."

—speech at the 2004 Republican National Convention, New York, August 20, 2004

"I like her. I know you're not supposed to say that, but I do."

—about Hillary Clinton

"I am fully prepared to be commander in chief, I need no on-the-job training, I am fully prepared to assume those duties tomorrow, and I am the most fully prepared to do that."

—on his presidential qualifications, February 29, 2000

What His Supporters Say

"I don't think John McCain had even been associated with Hispanics or any minorities, given where he lived and the school he went to, but yet he picked me, a Mexican American, to be his roommate [at the Naval Academy] . . . I've heard the comment that he has always done well with minorities. He's the most color-blind person I've ever met in my life. He treats me like a brother."

—Frank Gamboa, Annapolis roommate
and first-generation Mexican American

"He stood out because he was just one of those people that you liked and you got a chuckle out of. He was somebody who was always moving at top speed in one direction or another. He was never one to hang back."

—Ron Thunman, who commanded
McCain's plebe, or first-year, class

"Everybody in town, from the makeup artist at the local news station to the producers and directors, every reporter and every editor, loves working with John McCain because he does not stand on ceremony, he has no airs."

—former press secretary Torie Clarke

"The cancer put him in a hurry, and made his zest for life even more robust."

> —longtime political aide John Weaver, who encouraged McCain to run for president in 2000 and 2008

"John is seventy going on thirty. Last summer he and our son Jack hiked the Grand Canyon rim to rim. Just try keeping up with him."
> —wife Cindy McCain

What His Critics Say

"When I hear McCain using liberal rhetoric to bust up the conservative coalition, I think, what the hell is this? This guy's a Republican. . . . I'm just an honest-to-God thoroughbred conservative, and I don't see McCain as that." —Rush Limbaugh

McCain is "yesterday's news" and "the nut-job from Arizona."
> —Grover Norquist, prominent conservative activist and the head of Americans for Tax Reform

McCain Facts and Stories

– He has two siblings, sister Sandy and brother Joe.
– As a child, he was a newspaper delivery boy.
– In high school, five feet nine inches and agile, he was a talented and tough lightweight wrestler.
– He has a curious mind, and can chat knowledgeably about history, pop culture, current events, classic literature, and modern fiction.
– His military honors include the Silver Star, the Bronze Star, the Legion of Merit, the Purple Heart, and the Distinguished Flying Cross.
– His nicknames are an indication of his colorful and challenging

life. He has been called Punk and McNasty (as an assertive
lad and high school wrestler), John Wayne McCain (as a naval
student—dynamic, popular, and suave with the ladies), Crip
(good-natured teasing from his fellow POWs, due to his limp),
the White Tornado (as a spirited congressman), and a host of
media-selected monikers, including Senator Hothead.

– He was thrice considered as a presidential running mate:
by George H. W. Bush in 1988, by Bob Dole in 1996, and by
Democrat John Kerry in 2004.

– He is a member of the Council on Foreign Relations, and serves
on a variety of boards, including several affiliated with the military.

– He reportedly engaged in a vodka drinking contest with Senator
Hillary Clinton during an official trip to Estonia in 2004.

– He has hosted *Saturday Night Live*, and appeared on programs
such as *The Late Show with David Letterman*; *The Tonight Show
with Jay Leno*; and *The Daily Show with Jon Stewart*, where he is a
particularly welcome guest. He had a brief cameo appearance (for
which he received some flack) in the raunchy hit film *The Wedding
Crashers*, and another on the television program *24*, of which he is
a fan.

– McCain family pets include two dogs (Sam, an English springer
spaniel; Coco, a mutt); one cat (Oreo, coloring self-explanatory);
two turtles (Cuff and Link); a ferret; three parakeets; and a dozen
or so saltwater fish.

– His first car was a 1958 Corvette. He currently drives a Cadillac
sedan.

– John and Cindy McCain own a large ranch near Sedona,
Arizona, and a home in Coronado Shores, California. He also
keeps a residence in Washington, D.C.

Quirks, Habits, and Hobbies

– He has said his favorite word is "principle."

– He enjoys baby back ribs, ice cream (particularly blackberry and chocolate), doughnuts and Raisin Bran. He often cites his love for coffee as a vice.

– His musical tastes include rock 'n' roll from the 1950s and the 1960s. He likes the Beach Boys and Frank Sinatra, and has said his favorite song is "Smoke Gets in Your Eyes." He owns an iPod, a gift from the U.S. Merchant Marine Academy, Class of '07, as thanks for his commencement speech (they loaded it with patriotic songs).

– He is an avid hiker. His war injuries have made certain forms of exercise impossible, but he has tackled all the famous mountains and trails of Arizona, and often hikes on vacation with his family.

– McCain loves to gamble, at times playing craps in Las Vegas for fourteen hours straight.

– He likes watching boxing and baseball, and roots for his home baseball team, the Arizona Diamondbacks.

– He has cited Theodore Roosevelt as a personal hero, because of Roosevelt's conservative philosophies and efforts at reform. McCain keeps a Roosevelt figure holding a teddy bear in his office.

The Undecided Voter's Guide Questionnaire

For what unhealthy food do you have the biggest weakness?

Sugared doughnuts.

In what way would you hope America would most fundamentally change by the end of your time in the White House?

Regain confidence and trust in the government.

What is your most memorable childhood activity?

Going to camp in San Diego.

What is the biggest single difference between men and women, besides physiology?

Women are more sentimental.

What is your most strongly held superstition?

If you see a penny on the ground heads up, pick it up; if it is tails up, that is not good luck.

Name someone you would like to see in your cabinet, or at least tell us what would be most distinctive about your cabinet.

Fred Smith (FedEx founder), John Chambers (chairman and chief executive of Cisco Systems, Inc.), and Carly Fiorina (former Hewlett-Packard CEO and business executive).

What is the worst thing you did as a teenager?

Started smoking. [He quit decades ago.]

How are you most different as a person than your parents?

They were endowed with many more fine and good qualities.

What is your favorite way to relax (besides spending time with your family)?

Barbecue on the grill, hiking in Sedona.

Where is your favorite place to vacation?

Sedona, Arizona.

Presidential Announcement

John McCain launched his 2008 bid in Portsmouth, New Hampshire, on April 25, 2007. Several months earlier, in late February, McCain was a guest on *The Late Show with David Letterman*, and he gamely told the host, "I am announcing that I will be a candidate for president of the United States," although he emphasized his entry would not be official until he made a formal pronouncement in April. So on a damp and chilly day in Portsmouth, McCain appeared in Prescott Park, with the water behind him, to try one more time for the presidency. He was dressed neatly but casually in a dark sweater over an oxford shirt, and seemed stern and determined, gripping the podium and staring out into the crowd. Cindy McCain, in a bright pink suit and pearls, smiled and applauded nearby. McCain did not mention President Bush by name, and gave a grim assessment of the state of the country. When discussing problems with care for veterans, rising fuel costs, Social Security and Medicare, taxes, and foreign oil, he repeated the phrase: "That's not good enough for America. And when I'm president, it won't be good enough for me." He touched on the issue of his age, but gave his standard reminder: "I'm not the youngest candidate. But I am the most experienced." He continued his New Hampshire trip with a stop in Manchester, then traveled to other early-voting states, South Carolina, Iowa, and Nevada. Excerpts from his statement:

April 25, 2007
Portsmouth, New Hampshire

Today, I announce my candidacy for president of the United States. I do so grateful for the privileges this country has already given me; mindful that I must seek this responsibility for reasons greater than my self-interest; and determined to use every lesson I've learned through hard experience and the history I've witnessed, every inspiration I've drawn from the patriots I've known and the faith that guides me to meet the challenges of our time, and strengthen this great and good nation upon whom all mankind depends . . .

We are fighting a war in two countries, and we're in a global struggle with violent extremists who despise us, our values, and modernity itself. If we are to succeed, we must rethink and rebuild the structure and mission of our military; the capabilities of our intelligence and law enforcement agencies; the purposes of our alliances; the reach and scope of our diplomacy; the capacity of all branches of government to defend us. We need to marshal all elements of American power: our military, economy, investment, trade, and technology. We need to strengthen our alliances and build support in other nations. We must preserve our moral credibility, and remember that our security and the global progress of our ideals are inextricably linked . . .

Government spends more money today than ever before. Wasteful spending on things that are not the business of government indebts us to other nations; deprives you of the fruits of your labor; fuels inflation; raises interest rates; and encourages irresponsibility.

That's not good enough for America. And when I'm president, it won't be good enough for me.

We face formidable challenges, but I'm not afraid of them. I'm prepared for them. I'm not the youngest candidate. But I am the most experienced. I know how the military works, what it can do, what it can do better, and what it should not do. I know how Congress works, and how to make it work for the country and not just the reelection of its members. I know how the world works. I know the good and the evil in it. I know how to work with leaders who share our dreams of a freer, safer, and more prosperous world, and how to stand up to those who don't. I know how to fight and how to make peace. I know who I am and what I want to do.

Read More About McCain

John McCain with Mark Salter, *Faith of My Fathers: A Family Memoir* (New York: HarperCollins, 2000). McCain's uplifting (if at times harrowing) memoir describing the military careers of his father and grandfather, his early life, and his ordeal as a POW during the Vietnam War.

John McCain with Mark Salter, *Worth the Fighting For: A Memoir* (New York: Random House, 2002). McCain's second memoir, covering his political career.

Robert Timberg, *The Nightingale's Song* (New York: Simon & Schuster, 1995). An examination of the lives of five Naval Academy graduates, including John McCain.

http://www.johnmccain.com/

MITT ROMNEY

The Basics

Name: Willard Mitt Romney

Born: March 12, 1947,
Detroit, Michigan

Political party: Republican

Spouse: Ann Davies Romney,
married March 21, 1969

Children: Taggart, Matthew, Joshua,
Benjamin, Craig

Religion: The Church of Jesus Christ of
Latter-Day Saints (Mormon)

Education: Brigham Young University,
B.A., 1971
Harvard Law School, J.D., 1975
Harvard Business School, M.B.A., 1975

Career: Management consultant, Boston
Consulting Group, 1975–1977
Management consultant, Bain &
Company, 1977–1984
Private equity investor, Bain Capital,
1984–2001
Senate candidate, Massachusetts,
1994 (unsuccessful)
CEO, 2002 Olympic Winter Games,
1999–2002
Governor, Massachusetts, 2003–2007
Presidential candidate, 2007–present

IRAQ WAR

High Priority? ☑ *Yes* ☐ *No* ☐ *Maybe*

Record/Position: Consistently supported the Bush administration's goals and strategy, and only rarely criticized the execution of the war before the 2007 introduction of more American forces into Iraq. Implicitly contrasts himself with George W. Bush by saying he would listen to diverse expert opinions before making decisions about war policy.

Quote: "The road ahead will be difficult but success is still possible in Iraq. I believe it is in America's national security interest to achieve it."

WAR ON TERROR

High Priority? ☑ *Yes* ☐ *No* ☐ *Maybe*

Record/Position: Says defeating Islamic terrorists is essential for America's future. Supports a new type of Marshall plan to spread liberty around the world, a reshaped and larger military, and a reorganized diplomatic corps to match the threat.

Quote: "The jihadists are waging a global war against the United States and Western governments generally with the ambition of replacing legitimate governments with a caliphate, with a theocracy."

GOVERNMENT SPENDING/DEFICITS

High Priority? ☑ *Yes* ☐ *No* ☐ *Maybe*

Record/Position: Advocates a full audit of government spending to look for waste and areas of consolidation and a cap on nondefense discretionary spending of inflation minus one percent, which he says would save $300 billion over ten years. Working with a Democratic legislature in Massachusetts, he supported some spending increases but tried to cut an inherited deficit. Wants a bipartisan consensus on finding solutions to the Social Security funding crisis.

Quote: "Every legislator and politician knows this spending can't be justified, so why do they do it? Because it gets politicians praised— and reelected. There's no courage involved in spending more money."

ENERGY/ENVIRONMENT

High Priority? ☐ *Yes* ☐ *No* ☑ *Maybe*

Record/Position: Opposes government and international mandates because of concerns over jobs and the economy. As Massachusetts governor, he withdrew from a multistate agreement to cut power plant emissions. Supports development of alternative sources of energy, and energy efficiency measures.

Quote: "We're using too much oil. We have an answer. We can use alternative sources of energy—biodiesel, ethanol, nuclear power—and we can drill for more oil here. We can be more energy-independent and we can be far more efficient in the use of that energy."

HEALTH CARE

High Priority? ☑ *Yes* ☐ *No* ☐ *Maybe*

Record/Position: Signed into law a plan in Massachusetts intended to provide health coverage for nearly every resident, based on an individual mandate and contributions from businesses that don't offer coverage to their employees. Is concerned about the cost strains on businesses and states from the status quo, and would encourage state experimentation with different plans spurred by federal encouragement and assistance. Does not support a federal individual mandate to obtain insurance. Has proposed medical malpractice reform, expanded health savings accounts, and full deductability of all premiums, deductibles, and co-pays for individuals who buy their own insurance.

Quote: "We can't have as a nation of forty million people—or, in my state, half a million—saying, 'I don't have insurance, and if I get sick, I want someone else to pay.' "

TAXES

High Priority? ☐ *Yes* ☐ *No* ☑ *Maybe*

Record/Position: Supported some increase in fees in Massachusetts, but opposed any broad-based tax increases. Has not championed a national sales tax or flat tax, or major tax cuts, but opposes any increases. Proposes some rate cuts on interest, dividends, and capital gains to spur middle-class savings.

Quote: "Raising taxes hurts working people and scares away jobs."

JOBS/ECONOMY/TRADE/AGRICULTURE

High Priority? ☑ *Yes* ☐ *No* ☐ *Maybe*

Record/Position: Has emphasized the importance of preparing America to compete in the global economy, particularly against the rising powers in Asia. Wants to increase the annual number of high-skilled legal immigrants allowed into the U.S.

Quote: "We have to keep our markets open or we go the way of Russia and the Soviet Union, which is a collapse. . . . What you have to do in order to compete on a global basis long-term is invest in education, invest in technology, reform our immigration laws to bring in more of the brains from around the world, eliminate the waste in our government."

ABORTION

High Priority? ☐ *Yes* ☑ *No* ☐ *Maybe*

Record/Position: Recently declared that he has changed from prochoice to "firmly" prolife (with rape, incest, and life of the mother as exceptions) as a matter of public policy, although he says he has always been personally opposed to abortion. Pledged to protect a woman's right to choose as a candidate in Massachusetts. Says there should be a human life amendment when the country is ready for it.

Quote: "I changed my mind on abortion when I was governor and a bill came in that was life and death. Ronald Reagan did the same thing. So did George H. W. Bush. If changing your mind is a problem in this country, we're in trouble. I won't apologize for changing to prolife."

EDUCATION

High Priority? ☐ *Yes* ☑ *No* ☐ *Maybe*

Record/Position: Claims to believe in a very limited federal role, although speaks favorably about the standards introduced by No Child

Left Behind. Rhetorically supports testing that measures results—along with school choice, means-tested vouchers, English-language immersion, and higher teacher pay. As Massachusetts governor, supported abstinence education programs in public schools.

Quote: "If we are going to compete in the global economy, we have to set our education goals higher."

STEM CELL RESEARCH

High Priority? ☐ *Yes* ☑ *No* ☐ *Maybe*

Record/Position: Prior to 2005, broadly supported research on embryonic stem cells, but changed his position after meetings with stem cell researchers. Opposes research that uses cloned human embryos, but supports research using human embryos from fertility treatments. Opposes embryonic stem cell research funded by the government.

Quote: "I became persuaded that the stem cell debate was grounded in a false premise, and that the way through it was around it: by the use of scientific techniques that could produce the equivalent of embryonic stem cells but without cloning, creating, harming, or destroying developing human lives."

GAY RIGHTS

High Priority? ☐ *Yes* ☑ *No* ☐ *Maybe*

Record/Position: Has become one of the country's most outspoken critics of gay marriage and a leading supporter of a federal constitutional amendment banning the practice. Is not supportive of civil unions except as a device to head off gay marriage. Earlier in his political career, favored domestic partner benefits for gays and put several prominent openly gay officials in his government in Massachusetts. Claimed in his 1994 Senate campaign that as a Republican he could fight more effectively for gay rights than incumbent Edward Kennedy.

Quote: "We as a society don't discriminate against people based on their sexual orientation. If people are looking for people who are antigay, they aren't going to find that with me. But I am going to fight to protect traditional marriage."

GUN RIGHTS

High Priority? ☐ *Yes* ☑ *No* ☐ *Maybe*

Record/Position: Said he didn't "line up with the NRA," as a Senate candidate in 1994, supporting the Brady law and an assault weapons ban. Supported more restrictive gun laws but also gun owners' rights as governor. Recently joined the NRA and has emphasized his support for the Second Amendment as a presidential candidate.

Quote: "I have a gun of my own. I go hunting myself. I'm a member of the NRA and believe firmly in the right to bear arms."

WELFARE/POVERTY

High Priority? ☐ *Yes* ☑ *No* ☐ *Maybe*

Record/Position: Proposed a plan in Massachusetts requiring that some welfare recipients work in order to receive welfare benefits. Has a mixed record on when and how to increase the minimum wage, expressing concerns about its impact on businesses.

Quote: "People want a chance to work so they can build self-sustaining lives, instead of relying on a welfare check that will keep them trapped in poverty. By providing support services and incentives where necessary, we want to give welfare recipients the opportunity to achieve independent and fulfilling lives."

IMMIGRATION

High Priority? ☐ *Yes* ☐ *No* ☑ *Maybe*

Record/Position: Opposed 2007 congressional legislative efforts for undocumented workers, which he considered amnesty. Supports a fence on the Mexican border and an employment verification system using identification cards. As governor, opposed in-state tuition rates for the children of undocumented immigrants, and supported giving state troopers the power to arrest illegal immigrants.

Quote: "We need to make America more attractive for legal immigrants—for citizens—and less attractive for illegal immigrants. I want
to see more immigration in our country, but more legal immigration
and less illegal immigration."

For all current issue positions, check out http://www.mittromney.com/
Issue-Watch/index.

Meet Mitt

Mitt Romney's biography looks a lot like that of George W. Bush.
Both men are vigorous, well-educated sons of politicians. Both
watched their fathers seek the presidency. Both earned Harvard
M.B.A.s and then worked in the business world before assuming
elected office. Both served as the Republican governor of a prominent state. Both have been married only once, and have put their
personal faith front and center in their lives. Both have tapped various national networks to become prodigious fund-raisers for their
campaigns and for the Republican Party.

But for Romney, the differences between him and Bush are far
more important than the similarities, particularly if the nation follows the historical trend of choosing a fresh brand of leader after
a two-term administration. Indeed, given President Bush's flail-
ing poll numbers and questionable foreign policy choices, it is in
Romney's interest to stress the contrasts.

Most notably, Romney's private sector business record is far superior to Bush's. The nation's forty-third president was somewhat
of a disappointment as an oilman, although he succeeded as the
managing owner of the Texas Rangers. Eventually Bush made a
fortune selling the baseball team, after which he entered politics
full-time. Romney, meanwhile, was one of the most successful venture capitalists of his era, earning many tens of millions of dollars as

the head of Boston-based Bain Capital. His reputation as a skilled and ethical CEO led to his illustrious assignment as president and savior of the scandal-ridden 2002 Olympic Winter Games in Salt Lake City, a role that burnished his celebrity and facilitated his run for Massachusetts governor. Romney has spoken eagerly of translating the hard work that salvaged the Olympics and the challenges of being a Republican governor in a Democratic state into cleaning up what he calls the "mess" of Washington.

Even though Romney has already appeared on *60 Minutes*, *The Tonight Show*, and the cover of *Time* magazine, the country is still just getting to know him. He seems anxious for them to do so. Coming from the competitive worlds of Harvard Business School and Harvard Law School (which he attended simultaneously), management consulting, venture capital, the Olympics, and Massachusetts politics, Romney has developed an impressively vast number of people willing to testify enthusiastically about his character and his competence, and there is an equally impressive absence of those who wish to offer negative comments. It has become a cliché to say Romney looks like a president and to point out the storybook aspects of his life: his Matinee Mitt handsomeness; his gleaming, winsome large family; and his impeccable record of professional success. But there are some big problems in this picture-perfect bio, and the biggest happens to be his birthright.

> *"There's nothing like hard work and time to heal the pain and sorrow of a tragic loss. What we do with our time is not for frivolity, but for meaning."*

A Candidate Who Happens to Be a Mormon

Threatening Romney's chances at the White House, according to many analysts, is his membership in the Church of Jesus Christ of Latter-Day Saints, better known as the Mormon religion. Romney's faith is going to be a real test for the Republican electorate and, if he is nominated, the American people. Nothing in Romney's record suggests that his religion would play a major or insidious role in the governance of the White House. But for whatever reasons, voters seem particularly wary of having a Mormon president. According to polls, about one in three Americans say they would be reluctant to vote for a Mormon as president, and some voters openly rule it out.

As Amy Sullivan wrote in the *Washington Monthly*, "Some of this anti-Mormonism is a fairly fuzzy sort of bias, based mostly on rumors and unfamiliarity and the vague feeling that Mormons are kind of weird. It's a wobbly opposition that can be overcome by

"There are no stick figures in politics, you have human beings, who have families, who have lived careers, who have political positions, whom you have watched debate. You know them as human beings, and their religious affiliation actually becomes only one small part of the person."

good public relations that defuses concerns about the religion and shifts focus to the personality of the candidate . . . [But Romney's] obstacle is the evangelical base . . . For them it's a doctrinal thing, based on very specific theological disputes that can't be overcome by personality or charm or even shared positions on social issues . . . To evangelicals, Mormonism isn't just another religion. It's a cult."

There are about six million Mormons in the United States and a comparable number overseas. Romney has raised a great deal of money from this community, and its legendary organizational abilities are expected to turn out votes in Mormon neighborhoods around the country. But such support is a double-edged sword, because it inflames suspicions that Romney would owe his election to the church. The Mormon Church, in which Romney has served as a local officer, formally stays out of electoral politics more than many other American religious institutions, but polls indicate that its members vote overwhelmingly for Republican candidates.

Although Romney might find a way to defuse any negative effects of his religion, and although Mormon support supplies a solid base of votes and fund-raising, his religious affiliation is probably a net negative for his presidential chances. Imagine if Romney brought his résumé and strengths to the 2008 race, but was, say, a Methodist. He likely would have been hailed as the GOP frontrunner from the start of his campaign in 2007.

Romney's problem is exacerbated by the so-called mainstream media's lack of interest in the prospect of a first Mormon president. Contrast the series of dubious press profiles ("Will It Be Mormon in America?" "Can a Mormon Be President?" "Latter-Day Lifer") with the media's rapturous anticipation of the first woman president or the first black president, as Hillary Clinton and Barack Obama navigate the race.

Romney once told the conservative writer Terry Eastland, "This is a nation that will always welcome people of faith, and my party, in particular, will welcome people of faith. I think if you said,

'Look, we have a candidate for you, and you can know nothing about this person, except [his] religion, that's the only thing that you can know, this person is a Mormon, but that's all you can know. Do you want [him] as president?' Well, my guess is with all of the misunderstanding and lack of understanding and differences between one religion and another, that I think a lot of people would say, 'Gosh, I am not sure that that makes me feel real comfortable.' But if you said, 'Here's a human being that has done this and this and this, and here's [his] family, and here [are his] political views,' and so forth, then [the person is] going to get defined by those other things far more than by [his] religion alone and [his] religion would be seen as the basis of values that would either be consistent with the voters' or inconsistent."

Romney is familiar with his ancestors' struggles to fit into the mainstream world. His grandfather left a polygamous Mexican colony (founded by Mitt Romney's great-grandfather) to try to assimilate into conventional America, and experienced financial hardship. His father, George W. Romney, never graduated from college, but, while courting the lovely and privileged Lenore LaFount, who was also from a Mormon family, moved with her to Washington, D.C., when President Coolidge appointed her father to the Federal Radio Commission. George Romney worked as a lobbyist, and later made a real splash in the auto industry as the president and chairman of American Motors, where he introduced the Rambler, one

Mitt's mother, Lenore LaFount Romney, was the Republican nominee for U.S. Senate in Michigan in 1970, although she lost the general election. (As a young woman, she aspired to be an actress, and reportedly appeared in some films before her marriage.)

of the iconic cars of the 1950s. In Mitt Romney's presidential announcement speech, he proudly announced: "The Rambler automobile that [my father] championed . . . was the first American car designed and marketed exclusively for the purpose of economy and mileage. He dubbed it a compact car, and a car that would slay the gas-guzzling dinosaurs. And it transformed the industry."

George Romney saved American Motors from bankruptcy, made a personal fortune, and became a national figure. He ran for governor of Michigan and served three terms, from 1963 to 1969, and then launched a bid for president in 1968, a campaign derailed by an offhand comment suggesting that his early support for the Vietnam War was based on his having been "brainwashed" by military officials during a visit to the country. He was secretary of housing and urban development during the Nixon administration, and afterward retired from public service. Throughout his prominent career, George Romney maintained a leading role in the Mormon Church. He headed a Detroit chapter and served as a patriarch until his death.

Mitt Romney avoids responding to detailed questions about the tenets of Mormonism. Facing questions about his own faith, John F. Kennedy gave a famous September 1960 address to the Greater Houston Ministerial Association proclaiming his respect as a Catholic for the separation of church and state. Romney's three-part strategy has been to declare his fidelity to the nation's Judeo-Christian tradition, to express his own belief in the separation of church and state, and to put his wholesome wife, children, and grandchildren front and center. Therein lies his effort to contextualize his religion and substitute "family man of values" for "curious cult member."

A Principled Man or a Flip-Flopper?

Romney's greatest strengths as a candidate are his extraordinary organizational abilities; his capacity to hire strong people and leverage their assets; his great personal wealth, a portion of which he is willing to expend on his political future; and his preternaturally consistent performance on the campaign trail. In every speech, pitch to potential campaign donors, or media interview, Romney exhibits the same positive tone, the same unshakable on-message rhetoric, the same dapper bearing, the same unflappable demeanor. While other candidates have their good days and bad, and can be uneven from one event to the next, Romney is unfailingly upbeat at each public and private appearance, as if it is his unique pleasure to be there—which, in fact, it seems to be. As Rich Lowry of *National Review* wrote, "It is impossible to be around Romney and not be impressed—by his obvious intelligence, by his fluid speaking style, by his accomplishments in business and government, by his appearance."

But Romney's reliability as a campaign trail performer highlights the other nagging controversy, besides his religion, that has plagued his candidacy: his consistent inconsistency on a wide range of crucial issues. Every politician flip-flops at times, often with good reason, but Romney's conversions have been remarkable in at least two respects. First, there is the sheer range of issues—abortion, gun control, immigration, funding for stem cell research, and gay rights among them—on which, say his critics, he has taken starkly different positions, often absolute 180-degree turnarounds. Second, while other politicians tend to adjust their positions gradually and over time, Romney evidently altered many of his stances after switching from Massachusetts governor to presidential candidate, moving from a more liberal or centrist posture to a harder-line conservative view in keeping with the preferences of whichever the electorate he was appealing to: in this case the core Republican base, which is instrumental in choosing the party nominee.

How much do these wholesale shifts reveal what kind of person Romney is and what kind of president he would be? In some cases, Romney downplays the discrepancies. In others, he says they signify his maturity and a refreshing willingness to change, which, for some voters, might provide a pleasing contrast with George W. Bush's intractable resolution. Critics and skeptics, including Romney's rivals for the GOP nomination, believe his reversals are political opportunism at its most craven.

Some consider Romney the biggest flip-flopper in the history of presidential politics—no small achievement that. When he ran for the Senate in 1994, he promised to be a better advocate for gay rights than Ted Kennedy; in recent years he has become one of the country's leading critics of gay marriage. After being a vocal supporter of gun control as governor, he revealed that he had purchased a "lifetime" membership in the National Rifle Association, conveniently, in 2006. He was forced to admit that his claim "I've been a hunter pretty much all my life" was true only if one counted the shots he took at "small varmints" as a teen, plus a single 2006 hunting trip with donors from the Republican Governors' Association.

As governor, he spoke favorably of centrist proposals on immigration and campaign finance reform, before adopting a sharply conservative position on those issues as a presidential candidate. In Massachusetts, Romney has acknowledged that he was "effectively prochoice," but in line with his Mormon faith, he insists that he has always personally been prolife. In November 2004, after a discussion with a Harvard scientist about stem cell research, Romney says he decided that his public policy view of abortion should reflect his personal beliefs. But what he casts as an awakening has been widely derided as an opportunistic maneuver to curry favor with the prolife activists who influence the Republican nomination process.

These audacious metamorphoses have convinced some political insiders that Romney cannot win the Republican nomination or survive a long general election fight. After all, American voters prefer a president who knows his or her own mind and expresses authentic views, and the current politico-media environment doesn't forgive those who waver, waffle, and wobble. (Think of how the George W. Bush campaigns eviscerated Al Gore and John Kerry for their stumbles and inconsistencies.)

Potential Romney voters should ask a simple question: if you agree with his current philosophies, do you buy his explanation for changing his views? If you don't believe him, you might conclude that he is too scheming to be a trustworthy president. Perhaps you might allow that politics can be an opportunistic business, and no real harm has been done. Or maybe Romney just changed his mind.

The unease triggered by Romney's acrobatics is reinforced by the perception that he is too robotic, too slick, too self-consciously polished. Devoted observers worry that his meticulous planning and careful study can translate into a somewhat mechanical vibe; others call him a flat-out android. Whether brought on by latent anti-Mormonism or not, to put a fine point on it, some people find Mitt Romney unnerving, and Americans usually don't go looking for such a quality in their presidents.

A History of Problem-Solving

Despite candidate Romney's emphasis on principles and values, a President Romney likely would focus more on compromise and problem-solving than on pushing an ideological or partisan agenda. This conclusion comes from examining Romney's professional path

"I pray that this graduating class will choose a different kind of life, that we may develop an attitude of restlessness and discomfort, not self-satisfaction. Our education should spark us to challenge ignorance and prepare to receive new truths from God."
—to his graduating class at Brigham Young University, where he was the valedictorian in 1971

up until now, and on the avid manner in which, when delivering his stump speech, he anticipates tackling the many challenges of the White House.

Think of Romney's career in three parts. First, from 1977 to 1984, he worked as a vice president of Bain & Company, a Boston management consulting firm, where he proved to be mature and focused beyond his years. Then he helped found a spin-off private equity investment firm called Bain Capital, which he ran for a total of fourteen years. During his tenure, the firm prospered by investing in companies such as the office supply store Staples, Domino's Pizza, and the Sports Authority. His acumen, judgment, frugality, and dedication made Romney and his investors rich. Romney's experience at Bain is an essential component of his persona. It proved his competence, risk-taking capacity, management skills, and ability to handle pressure (apparently he perspired a lot, but got the job done). It allowed him to make national connections in the business world, and to understand different aspects of the American economy. It positioned him to run for president by giving him fund-raising contacts and immense personal wealth. It also made him part of a management consultant and investment culture that some have said has callously turned the American economy from one of manufacturing, which creates middle-class jobs with high wages and strong benefits, to one of investments, which enriches aggressive investors with short-term profits, at the expense of communities that lose jobs as local operations are shuttered.

Phase two of Romney's career was in Salt Lake City, where he served as president and CEO of the 2002 Winter Olympics. Fiscal mismanagement and charges of alleged bribery had left the games in crisis, and in early 1999, Romney was brought on board to rescue the effort, even though he had never even attended an Olympic event. His strict management was widely credited with preserving the integrity of the enterprise. He streamlined the budget, despite the challenge of the unprecedented security require-

"We went home and asked each other, what will ever compare to this again? We're hosting the world and helping create something that costs over a billion dollars. What an extraordinary experience, and what phenomenal people we've met. I don't see how you top this."

ments for the first post–September 11 Olympics, and enabled the organization to make a profit. The title of Romney's book about his experience—*Turnaround: Crisis, Leadership, and the Olympic Games*—neatly sums up a period of his life that might well be a political consultant's dream, combining sports, patriotism, public visibility, determination, hypercompetence, and ultimate success.

The third major phase of Romney's career occurred in 2002 when he ran for governor of his adopted home state of Massachusetts. He had unsuccessfully tried to unseat Senator Edward Kennedy in 1994, his only high-profile professional failure (although challenging a Kennedy in Massachusetts was quite a long shot—and, as Romney now jokes, at least he came in second). But he used the heroic sheen of his Olympic triumph as a springboard to the governor's office.

On the one hand, his eventual election as Massachusetts governor seemed easy. Although the state was heavily Democratic, it had elected Republican governors for several cycles, and Romney was willing to spend some of his own fortune (more than $6 million) on the race. On the other hand, several obstacles were in his way. First, acting Republican governor Jane Swift had already announced her intention to run and keep the office to which she had been elevated after the resignation of her predecessor. Second, the Democrats chose popular state treasurer Shannon O'Brien, who came from a prominent politically connected family, as their nominee. Finally, Romney had all of the same baggage and drawbacks that Kennedy exploited in the 1994 Senate race (his religion, his corporate background, his robotic precision). Romney nudged the unpopular Swift from the race, painted O'Brien as a status quo insider candidate, paid for an effective negative ad campaign (after running some ill-received family-centric spots), and presented himself as an agent of efficient reform. He won by 5 percentage points, and took over a state government dominated by Democrats.

Overall, Romney's gubernatorial record was mixed, with critics claiming he fell short of his goals and supporters insisting he was as successful as a Republican could be with a legislature and a constituency monopolized by the opposing party. He worked at controlling spending and keeping taxes low (while raising some fees and shifting costs to local governments), but he received national attention when the state's Supreme Judicial Court made Massachusetts the center of the debate over gay marriage, legalizing the practice in February 2004. Romney became a national spokesman against gay marriage, and used that platform to reach out to social conservatives around the country. He was similarly outspoken on stem cell research, which also attracted a spotlight to the state and to Romney's conservative line in the sand.

He made a concerted effort to uproot some of the state's infamous patronage positions, and surrounded himself with a mix of loyalists and outsiders with a history of accomplishment. His senior advisers and cabinet officials included some Democrats and independents. He took steps to fulfill his promise to function as a CEO governor, but he did not fundamentally reshape the state's political culture.

Romney's most important substantive achievement as governor came late in his term, when he made a deal with the legislature and his old rival Ted Kennedy to pass a law extending health insurance to nearly all of the state's residents. The plan mandated that individuals must purchase health insurance, just as drivers must insure their automobiles. Some conservatives embraced the plan,

> Mitt Romney was fifty-five when elected governor of Massachusetts; his father, George Romney, was fifty-five when elected governor of Michigan.

while others argued it represented an excessive big-government intrusion into the private sector. Romney touted the law, which has yet to be fully implemented, as evidence of his problem-solving abilities and his capacity to strike bipartisan deals, rather than as a model for how he would extend health coverage nationally.

Romney chose not to run for a second term as governor, but before formally entering the presidential race, he used his political committees to funnel money to Republican candidates in key states. When he did announce his 2008 candidacy, on February 13, 2007, his high-profile forays in business, sports, and politics enabled Romney, a first-time presidential candidate, to assemble a nationally potent political fund-raising network.

A Commitment to Family and Public Service

Mitt Romney's father, George Romney, served as a governor and as a cabinet secretary for Richard Nixon, and his commitment to public service and charitable giving reinforced the teachings of the Mormon Church. Mitt Romney's family has, over the years, given millions of dollars in donations to groups around the country, particularly in Massachusetts and Utah. When Mitt performed his traditional missionary service, expected of all young Mormon men, he spent two and a half years in France. He has said that the experience exposed him to foreign cultures but also made him "love America more."

Although both Mitt and his wife, Ann Romney, grew up in wealthy families, there were times in young adulthood when they roughed it, comparatively speaking. During his mission in France, Romney says he lived in Spartan apartments and had little spending money. Romney says he converted fewer than twenty people in the heavily Catholic country, and mostly fielded complaints about the Vietnam War. After returning home, he reunited with

Ann, and the couple recalls living in inexpensive and cheaply furnished student apartments at both Brigham Young and Harvard.

Put Mitt Romney in a time machine and send him back to the 1950s, and one could argue that in the era of rock 'n' roll and *The Catcher in the Rye*, he still would seem a bit like a fuddy-duddy. In the racy, overwrought current era, those who know him are not surprised when he appears on television and unself-consciously says things like, "When I was a little kid, there used to be the ditty that went around: first comes love, then comes marriage, then comes the baby in the baby carriage. Today that idea is foreign to some kids." The strongest expletive he typically will use is "golly." As Ann Romney attests, her husband never swears. It helps that he rarely loses his cool, in business or in politics. As a rule, he tries to avoid confrontation, but when challenged, he is tough, resolute, and, on occasion, indignant. During the overstuffed early Republican debates, he appeared visibly frustrated by the constraints and vagaries of the format, and chafed when he was unable to make a point or answer a question. Nevertheless, he retained his good manners, albeit with a grimace.

Romney's family-friendly image is buttressed by his exceedingly media-friendly clan. The public face of the Romneys is as blemish-free as their complexions. Mitt and Ann, their five adult sons, along with assorted daughters-in-law and grandchildren, present themselves as smart, attractive, tightly knit, like-minded, and utterly unified in the hope of seeing Mitt elected president. As Ann told Fox News, "We're totally with him, the whole family. The five boys, the five daughters-in-law, the . . . grandkids . . . [his candidacy] was a family decision. And I'm convinced he's going to be an awesome president." Mitt's three older siblings (attorney G. Scott Romney of Michigan, writer Jane Romney Robinson of Beverly Hills, and Lynn Romney Keenan of Michigan) speak about their brother with warmth and pride. His sons are active in the campaign, with their Five Brothers blog bursting with campaign updates and scattered with photos of dogs, children, and friendly supporters. In keeping with Mormon tradition, the Romneys have always made scheduling family time a priority. In part because of this regular contact, they are all exceptionally close—it is not a surprise that the five sons are so deeply committed to and involved in the campaign. The homey videos they produce, showing glowing domestic get-togethers, meals, and chat sessions, loping dogs and laughing kids, are a picture of wholesome morality that will certainly appeal to voters who hold religious and family values dear.

Ann Romney

Ann Romney was born Ann Davies in Bloomfield Hills, Michigan, in 1949. She and Mitt met at a party in 1965 when she was fifteen and he eighteen, and they both remember an instant romantic connection; they call each other "sweetheart" to this day. Raised Episcopalian, Ann converted to Mormonism under the tutelage of her future father-in-law while Mitt was serving as a missionary in France. Interestingly, her brothers Jim and Rod converted as well, although her father, Edward Davies, a prominent businessman and mayor of Bloomfield Hills, was against the conversion. Her mother, however, eventually converted, too, shortly before her death in 1993. After graduating from high school, Ann enrolled at Brigham Young University; upon Mitt's return from France, he transferred to BYU from Stanford, and they were married. Son Tagg was born a year later, with four more boys to follow. When Mitt went on to Harvard for law and business school, the family moved to Massachusetts, and Ann completed her college degree through Harvard's extension program. Ann Romney did not pursue a career, but instead chose to raise their five sons, and was by all accounts an enthusiastic, dynamic parent.

In the late 1990s, she was diagnosed with multiple sclerosis, an illness that exhausted and depressed her, particularly given her athletic nature. Her disease has been in remission since 2001, which she credits to holistic treatments including reflexology, acupressure, acupuncture, deep-breathing ex-

> Although his great-great-grandfather Miles Park Romney was a polygamist with five (!) wives, Romney has declared that he "can't imagine anything more awful than polygamy."

ercises, yoga, and riding horses. (She has ridden competitively and owns several horses.) Ann Romney has been involved in such charities as the United Way, and now is a highly visible presence on the campaign trail. She appears in her husband's television advertisements and Internet campaign videos. Looking stylish and radiant, she chats, cooks, teases, and serves as family raconteur and devoted spouse. Mitt Romney, uxorious to the extreme, says he relies on his wife for advice across a range of issues, but regularly praises her ability to evaluate loyalty and trustworthiness. Their sons call her "the great Mitt stabilizer."

Areas of Potential Controversy

– While serving as CEO of Bain Capital, Romney took the lead in restructuring a number of companies, which often resulted in lost jobs for employees (and added revenue for shareholders). The issue was used against Romney in his 1994 Senate race.

– A chronology of quotes documenting his flip-flops on major issues could raise eyebrows, generate lots of unfavorable press, and launch a slew of negative ads. YouTube will supply the

visuals—there is no longer a way to backpedal or hedge in this age of ubiquitous video.
– Questions about the cost and effectiveness of the Massachusetts health care plan Romney signed into law could distract from his message.
– Some of the more unusual aspects of Mormonism are sure to be discussed.

Why Romney Can Win a General Election

- Romney is a strong debater and an even stronger fund-raiser, two skills that will be vital in determining who will become the next president.
- His family roots in Michigan could put that state's electoral votes (which in 2000 and 2004 went to Al Gore and John Kerry) in play.
- Romney's emphasis on values and change could make him a strong candidate in the suburbs and exurbs that have become major Republican electoral battlegrounds.
- His rhetorical focus on the "three-legged stool" of economics, national security, and family values could reinvigorate the center-right coalition that has won five of the last seven presidential elections for the Republican Party.
- Romney loves data, thrives on hard work, and insists on being prepared.
- He is mostly unflustered by negative campaigning and complex or trenchant questions.
- If he has any personal skeletons in his closet, they are likely the size of baby gnats; more likely, the closet is scrubbed, polished, and ventilated by a fresh breeze.
- As the wealthiest Republican candidate in the race, Romney could tap into his personal fortune—estimated

at more than $200 million—to help fund his campaign
throughout the summer and fall of 2008.

- He has put together a talented campaign team made up of
longtime loyalists and operatives with substantial experience in presidential politics. To date he has extracted from
them a high level of collegiality and competence, conduct
he has always demanded from his staff. His campaign has
excelled in using new technologies to reach voters and to
perform other tasks efficiently.

- Five sons, fifty states: do the math. Those hardworking,
handsome boys (even Bill and Hillary Clinton have remarked on their good looks) can cover a lot of ground.

- Romney has great discipline, in life and on the stump.
Like George W. Bush and Bill Clinton before him, he is
able to give speech after speech and always stay on message, always hitting the essential arguments. Political
reporters and regular C-SPAN viewers may find the
repetition tedious, but this kind of diligence is important
when connecting with potential new voters around the
country.

Why Romney Can't Win a General Election

- That whole Mormon thing (see above).
- That whole flip-flop thing (see above).
- He has not proven he can take a major-league political
punch.

The Best Case for a Romney Presidency

- Romney is masterful at gathering experts around him,
listening to their ideas, formulating a plan, allowing the
plan's implementers to do their jobs, demanding results,

and overseeing the plan to victory. Throughout his professional life, Romney has achieved executive success while empowering subordinates and avoiding even a hint of personal scandal or rule-breaking.

- Making progress on many of the major problems facing America—the war in Iraq, terrorism, health care, energy, the environment, international competition, education— will require the kind of strong executive leadership Romney has exhibited. In addition, with the likelihood that the Democrats will continue to control Congress at least at the start of the next presidential administration, Romney would be well served by his experience in Massachusetts working with a legislature overwhelmingly controlled by the opposition party.

- No candidate running against Mitt Romney will ever outwork him, outorganize him, or outplan him. He relishes the process of fixing things. He could probably spew a detailed summary of his 2009 first-hundred-days plan right now.

- With roots in three states from different regions— Massachusetts, Michigan, and Utah—and extensive business and personal travel throughout the country, Romney can lay claim to a national perspective. His fluency in French and affinity for the country, a trait so unattractive in 2004 when John Kerry was mocked for his purported effete European sensibilities, now could come in handy when mending international fences, as could his expressed tolerance of cultural differences.

The Worst Case for a Romney Presidency

- Although voters often find candidates from outside of Washington, D.C., enticing, Romney's lack of direct experience dealing with Congress, the national security community, and world leaders could leave him unprepared to forge compromise, handle a crisis, or remake America's alliances.

- Is Romney tough enough to be president during a time of crisis? In this age of terror and unrest, a CEO president might lack the requisite mettle of a commander in chief.

What to Expect If Romney Is President

- A Romney presidency would, in style, evoke a fictional golden era of America. The West Wing would hum with diligent productivity, good manners, conservative dress, mature propriety, and a consistent message. He would look for skill, loyalty, and competence in his staff rather than rigid ideology.

- Romney would take a CEO's approach to ending the war in Iraq, and would likely consult a range of military, Middle East, and safety experts to address the arduous aftermath. He also would likely cut federal spending and make all parts of government more efficient, including at the Pentagon; seek to reduce health care costs; rely more on market-driven changes than tax increases; review America's intelligence-gathering methods; and push for free-trade agreements while aiming to increase America's competitiveness around the world.

- Romney would take steps to streamline the executive branch. In all of his jobs, he has made a point of instilling frugality in the workplace and running a frill-free, efficient office, whether it was cutting back on office supply waste, expensive travel, or complementary food. A Romney administration would run a tight White House ship.

- Romney would keep a steady eye on reelection—he would

probably govern as a centrist but would minimize the chance of alienating the Republican base.

- Romney's cabinet would likely include a mix of close friends from the business world, experienced political hands from the Republican Party, moderate Democrats, and scholarly experts.

- Ann Romney might continue making the videos she did during the campaign to impart information about goings-on at the White House. Christmas and other traditional holidays would be emphasized (and customs unique to Mormonism would be downplayed, albeit not entirely—the Romneys have made a point of saying they are proud of their religion). The five Romney sons would play prominent roles, perhaps with official White House assignments or other government jobs. They certainly would visit frequently, families in tow.

What His Supporters Say

"You got the feeling you were dealing with a guy with a very strong moral fiber who is very devoted to church and family. You're not going to hear from Mitt a joke at anyone's expense, and you're not going to hear any swear words. You know when you meet him and when you're with him that you're dealing with a very serious-minded guy."

—Harvard Business School classmate and Boston Consulting Group colleague Howard B. Brownstein

"He was always someone you would say, 'Why can't we have someone like that in politics?' He comes across as too good to be true, and it's true."

—Chip Baird, a former partner, friend, and business competitor

"If Mitt was wearing the same suit for two days, it would just never get wrinkled. That's just Mitt. If I get nervous, I eat. If Mitt gets nervous, he loses weight, that's just Mitt."

—former sister-in-law Ronna Romney,
who was married to G. Scott Romney

"He loves emergencies and catastrophes. He would never have considered doing it if it wasn't a big mess."

—Ann Romney, on her husband's
decision to take over the troubled
2002 Salt Lake City Winter Olympics

"He's gone through all the usual Mitt stages. First it's Mr. Worry-wart: 'This will never happen; it's going to be a disaster.' Then it's: 'Let's take it all apart, then put it back together.' Now it's: 'Let's make this the greatest success we can.' "

—political adviser Charles Manning on
Romney's Olympics experience

"If you pay sufficient attention to detail you have less risk. And with him, nothing is left to chance unless it has to be. He is running his campaign that way—marvelous planning at all levels"

—William Weld, Republican former
governor of Massachusetts

What His Critics Say

"I think Mitt's accustomed to getting his way. If he didn't, he got upset."

—Ken Bullock, executive director, Utah League of Cities,
on dealing with Romney at the Olympics

"Mitt Romney is a politician who is devoid of any real principles, devoid of any real moral compass. I don't think he believes in anything but the advancement of his own political career."

—Phil Johnston, former chairman
of the Massachusetts Democratic Party

Romney Facts and Stories

– The fit and vigorous Romney has expressed a love for outdoor activities such as water-skiing and boating, which he enjoyed as a child with his brother Scott, and as an adult with his equally sporty wife and children. One of the chief charms of his vacation home in Wolfeboro, New Hampshire (along with its plum location in the first-primary-in-the-nation Granite State), is its proximity to Lake Winnipesaukee, the largest lake in the state. Not only has the locale been used for politically productive parties, such as a well-received September 2005 fund-raiser for the New Hampshire Republican Party, but it also has served as the venue for some good press. In July 2003, Romney and sons Josh and Craig, hearing screams from across the water and seeing people floundering four hundred yards from shore, leapt upon their Jet-Skis and retrieved three men, three women, and a dog, whose boat was sinking on the lake. The Romneys, along with other rescuers, got the family back onshore without injury; the nineteen-foot boat was later recovered from the bottom of the lake. Josh Romney told Boston's WCVB-TV, "My dad pulled two of them onto his boat and ferried them back and forth to shore while Craig and I waited with the others in the water." Mitt Romney added that after the group was on dry land, "they gathered their things and we gave them some towels. We put them on our regular boat and took them to their home. They have a boathouse and a house on the lake. At that point, I introduced myself to

them and they said, 'Yeah, we know who you are.' " Romney
noted he was unaware of their politics; "I don't know their party
affiliation. I didn't ask. We rescue all parties here." And this was
not Romney's first save—he previously had assisted kayakers
caught in the lake's currents.
– In June 1981, on a family outing at Boston-area Lake
Cochituate, Romney was arrested and charged with disorderly
conduct after launching his motorboat on the water despite a
park police officer's warning of a fifty-dollar fine because the
boat's license was partly obscured by paint. Romney decided to go
aboard anyway, aware of the fine, because, as he told the *Boston
Globe* in May 1994, when the juicy tale surfaced during his Senate
campaign, "I figured I was at the state park with my kids. My
five kids were in the car wondering why we weren't going out in
the boat, so I said I'd launch and pay the fine . . . I was willing
to pay the fine. But if he had said don't launch the boat and not
mentioned the fine, I would not have done it." The irate guard
handcuffed Romney, brought him to the local police station, and
had him booked, although Romney was released without bail.
"There I was, dripping wet in a bathing suit," he recalled. Romney
told the *Globe* that the park guard "did not have the right to arrest
me because I was not a disorderly person. This was an obvious
case of false arrest . . . The officer obviously agreed because he
agreed to drop the case." Indeed, the charges were dropped
within days, when Romney threatened to sue over false arrest, and
subsequently dismissed in February 1982, with the records sealed
upon Romney's request.
– Lenore Romney referred to son Mitt as her "miracle baby"
because doctors believed she could not have another child
(Romney has two older sisters and an older brother).
– He was named for hotel magnate J. Willard Marriott, a family

friend and fellow Mormon, and for his great-uncle Milton Romney, a Chicago Bears football player.

– Two other great-uncles (the brothers of namesake great-uncle Mitt Romney) went by the names Ott Romney and Att Romney. Seriously.

– He spent his early years in Detroit, until the family moved to Bloomfield Hills.

– He was an Eagle Scout.

– He attended the prestigious Cranbrook School for boys. Ann Romney attended its sister school, Kingswood in Michigan.

– He and Ann Romney met when they were eighteen and fifteen, respectively, nearly the same ages as his parents when they were first introduced. On their first date, they went to see *The Sound of Music*.

– He received a draft deferment from Vietnam as a Mormon "minister of religion" during his missionary term.

– His Stanford resident assistant was prominent anti–Vietnam War protestor David Harris, who later married singer Joan Baez.

– He survived a serious car accident as a missionary in France, when the Citroën he was driving was hit by another car (all accounts say he was not at fault, and was driving carefully and below the speed limit). One of Romney's passengers was killed, the rest were injured, and a policeman on the scene mistakenly declared Romney dead ("*Il est mort*" was written in his passport).

– Future president Gerald Ford attended his wedding. Then-president Richard Nixon telegrammed his best wishes.

– In school and in his career, he carried his father's briefcase, embossed with his father's initials.

– He received dual degrees from Harvard Business School and

Harvard Law School, graduating with honors in law and in the top 5 percent in business.
– Both he and George W. Bush received their M.B.A.s from Harvard Business School in 1975.
– He was in Washington, D.C., at a meeting about Olympic security on September 11, 2001, when the Pentagon was struck.
– He was named one of *People* magazine's "50 Most Beautiful People" in 2002.
– He is said to possess a great singing voice (he himself has acknowledged it as a hidden talent).
– He is fluent in French (and has quite a good accent), from his mission work in France.
– He likes to make light of one of the more notorious perceptions of the Mormon religion by joking, "Marriage should be between a man and a woman and a woman and a woman."
– He has served on the boards of City Year and the Boy Scouts.
– Prominent supporters include eBay president and CEO Meg Whitman.
– His car of choice is a 2005 Ford Mustang convertible.
– The Romneys have always had dogs, including one Irish setter, Seamus, who, as the *Boston Globe* revealed, rode in a rooftop car carrier en route to family vacations. Romney said when the canine scandal broke and animal rights groups protested the setter's transportation mode, "[Seamus] scrambled up there every time we went on trips, got in all by himself, and enjoyed it."
– Well-known Mormons include U.S. Senate Majority Leader Harry Reid (D-NV), actor John Heder (*Napoleon Dynamite*), actress Katherine Heigl (*Grey's Anatomy*), actor Billy Barty, actor Wilfred Brimley, TV and radio host Glenn Beck, *Jeopardy* champion Ken Jenkins, actor Aaron Eckhart, singer Gladys Knight, singers Donnie and Marie Osmond and the Osmond

family, NFL quarterback Steve Young, the Marriott hotel family, former national security adviser Brent Scowcroft, and U.S. senator Orrin Hatch (R-Utah).

– Romney told the Associated Press that his choice for an alternate career would be "auto company chief executive." As a youth, he thought he would follow his father into the car business.

– Both Mitt Romney and George Romney appeared on the cover of *Time* magazine.

– His favorite presidents are the Roosevelts, John Adams, Dwight Eisenhower, Ronald Reagan, and George Washington.

– He and Ann Romney have eleven grandchildren (and counting).

– He owns homes in Massachusetts, Utah, and New Hampshire.

Quirks, Habits, and Hobbies

– Romney doesn't drink alcohol, coffee, or tea, in keeping with Mormon canon (which also forbids smoking and premarital sex), but he does like his Diet Coke (not to mention Vanilla Diet Coke). He does not object to non-Mormons drinking alcoholic beverages, including wine or beer, and will go so far as to serve them to guests in his own house.

– For years, he has eaten what he calls a "Jethro bowl" (that's a *Beverly Hillbillies* reference) of sugary cereal before bedtime.

– Despite his fit appearance, Romney was never much of a natural athlete. Nevertheless, he enjoys many sports, including tennis, basketball, soccer, football, and water-skiing, and goes on regular morning jogs to keep in shape.

– His grandchildren call him "Papa," or sometimes "Ike" (as in Eisenhower, a favorite president), as he prefers. Ann, naturally, is "Mamie."

– He is known to be frugal, despite his wealth, and has popped his own popcorn to bring to the movies.

– He claims to be a fan of *American Idol*, and likes the music of Roy Orbison, Johnny Cash, and the Beatles. He told *People*, "I've got an oldies file [on my iPod], of course, because I am one. But also Clint Black, Toby Keith and Paul Simon."
– When nervous, he has a tendency to flap his tie.
– He told the Associated Press that his worst habit is "fidgeting."

The Undecided Voter's Guide Questionnaire
For what unhealthy food do you have the biggest weakness?

My favorite is pie. I love pies. And there's almost no pie I don't like. I love rhubarb pie. I love coconut cream and banana cream pie. I love good apple pie, cherry pie, blueberry pie. I just like pies. And so if there's a really good pie, I have a hard time saying no. Of course, I always joke about liking Hostess Twinkies, and that kind of junk food. I now and then will have a Hostess Twinkie, that's pretty rare. But a piece of pie, that I'm going to get occasionally to have on a pretty regular basis.

In what way would you hope America would most fundamentally change by the end of your time in the White House?

I'd like to see America become a stronger nation by virtue of its goodness and the strength of its military, the strength and vitality of our economy, and the strength of the values of American families and citizens.

What is your most memorable childhood activity?

As a child and young person I got to spend a good portion of my summer on Lake Huron, which is one of the Great Lakes, where my family and I had barbecues, went swimming and boating. And established close friendships with a number of folks nearby.

What is the biggest single difference between men and women, besides physiology?

Women like horses and men like cars.

What is your most strongly held superstition?

I'm afraid I really don't have any superstitions that guide my life in any way. So I have walked under ladders with impunity. I step on cracks. I don't worry if a black cat crosses my path. I don't knock on wood, other than to make a point.

Name someone you would like to see in your cabinet, or, at least, tell us what would be most distinctive about your cabinet.

I'd like to have people of extraordinary excellence and capability whose background included nongovernment service. So people from the private sector, from science, from the widest array or careers who had established a measure of excellence in their career. I'd also like to have people who are outspoken, willing to express their views openly, comfortable with debate, and who make their points using data and rigorous analysis rather than conjecture and opinion.

What is the worst thing you did as a teenager?

I'm not telling.

How are you most different as a person than your parents?

First and foremost, I was raised in a home with a terrific family and also with great advantages. I got education and opportunity that my dad would have never dreamed of having in his life. His family went bankrupt more than once, he lived in a very poor setting for many of his early years and so I got to see things that he did not and have experience that he did not. Perhaps the greatest difference was that I got to watch my dad and my mom in settings where their skills as leaders and managers and as people of capability were evident and that gave me perspective—which they developed on their own and I developed by watching them.

What is your favorite way to relax (besides spending time with your family)?

But you know my favorite thing is to be with my family. And particularly where we can turn all the lights off in the room and just talk with each other about our concerns, our ambitions, our hopes, and our innermost feelings. I love being at the beach with them, I love going boating with them, I love going out to dinner with them. I mean family is the whole center of my life. I also like to read, and at the end of a day on the campaign trail, I like to get out a book and read for an hour or so and that can be a book that expands my mind or a book of escape. And I like movies. I don't see as many movies as I might otherwise like because of my responsibilities, but Ann and I go on "date night" to a movie.

Where is your favorite place to vacation?

Lake Winnipesaukee in New Hampshire.

Presidential Announcement

Mitt Romney formally entered the presidential race on February 13, 2007, in Michigan, the state of his birth (and a key general election swing state, free of the liberal overtones of his adopted

Massachusetts; a world away from Mormon-centric Utah, home of his ancestors; and firmly removed from the precarious taint of ever-unpopular Washington, D.C.). Romney delivered his address at the Henry Ford Museum in Dearborn, with a vintage Rambler and a modern hybrid beside him onstage, his wife, Ann ("my sweetheart"), to introduce him, and his whole family in attendance (grandchildren as well as sons, daughters-in-law, and siblings). Within the cozy Americana setting, he comfortably invoked his own CEO style of leadership, his straight-arrow family values, and George Romney's American Dream biography as three-term Michigan governor and chairman of American Motors. Romney mentioned neither President Bush nor the Mormon religion, although he offered the denominationally neutral sentiment: "I believe in God and I believe that every person in this great country, and every person on this great planet, is a child of God. I believe that we are all sisters and brothers." Looking pristine and spruce in his blue suit and tie and crisp white shirt, he was calm and upbeat as he talked cars, country, innovation, family, and freedom, and stern as he talked Washington, taxes, national security, health care, and Iraq. Nevertheless, his choice of venue was not controversy-free: Henry Ford's notorious anti-Semitism raised the hackles of Jewish groups, and Massachusetts papers such as the *Boston Globe* sulked over Romney's perceived neglect of his longtime home state. Excerpts from his statement:

February 13, 2007
Dearborn, Michigan
Throughout my life, I have pursued innovation and transformation. It has taught me the vital lessons that come only from experience, from failures and from successes, from public, private, and voluntary sectors, from small and large enterprises, from leading

a state, from actually being in the arena, not just talking about it. Talk is easy, talk is cheap. It's the doing that's hard. And it's only in the doing that hopes and dreams can come to life . . .

I love America and I believe in the people of America. I believe in God and I believe that every person in this great country, and every person on this great planet, is a child of God. I believe that we are all sisters and brothers. I believe that the family is the foundation of America—and that it needs to be protected and strengthened. I believe in the sanctity of human life. I believe that people and their elected representatives should make the laws, not unelected judges. I believe that we are overtaxed and government is overfed. Washington is spending too much money. I believe that homeland security begins with securing our borders. I believe that our best days are before us, because I believe in America! . . .

America must also regain our standing in the world. Our influence must once again match our generosity. Over the twentieth century, no nation gave more, shed more precious lives, and took less for itself than America. Our sacrifice for freedom and human dignity continues unabated today. But this is not the way it is seen by others. America's goodness and leadership in the world must be as bright and bold as our military might!

Let me turn to the home front. America can also overcome the challenges and seize our abundant opportunities here at home, but only if we follow the right course. There are some who believe that America's strength comes from government—that challenges call for bigger government, for more regulation in our lives and our livelihoods, and for more protection and isolation from competition that comes from open markets . . . America faces unprecedented challenges. We are under attack from jihadists, we face new competition from Asia unlike anything we have known before. We are spending too much money here, our schools are failing too many of our kids, forty-five million people don't have health insurance, we are using too much oil. And what does Washington do? It talks and debates and talks and kicks the ball down the field. It is time for less talk and more action in government.

Read More About Romney

Mitt Romney, *Turnaround: Crisis, Leadership, and the Olympic Games* (Washington, D.C.: Regnery, 2004). Romney's personal account of his time in Salt Lake City, offering insight into his philosophy of managing.

Hugh Hewitt, *A Mormon in the White House? 10 Things Every American Should Know about Mitt Romney* (Washington, D.C.: Regnery, 2007). The conservative commentator's highly favorable take on Romney, and a preemptive attack on critics of Mormonism.

The *Boston Globe's* multipart series "The Making of Mitt Romney," http://www.boston.com/news/politics/2008/specials/romney/.

http://www.mittromney.com/

FRED THOMPSON

The Basics

Name: Fred Dalton Thompson

Born: August 19, 1942,
Sheffield, Alabama

Political party: Republican

Spouse: Jeri Kehn Thompson,
married June 29, 2002

Children: Tony, Daniel, Elizabeth
(deceased) (with Sarah Lindsey)
Hayden and Samuel (with Jeri
Kehn)

Religion: Protestant

Education: Memphis State University,
B.A., 1964
Vanderbilt University Law School,
J.D., 1967

Career (Law/Politics): Lawyer,
private practice, Lawrenceburg,
Tennessee, 1967–1969
Assistant U.S. Attorney, Tennessee,
1969–1972
Partner, law firm, Nashville,
Tennessee, 1973–1974
Minority counsel, Watergate
Committee, 1973
Lawyer, private practice, Nashville
and Washington, D.C., 1974–1994
Special counsel to Governor Lamar
Alexander, Tennessee, 1980

Career (Law/Politics) (*cont*.): Special counsel, Senate Foreign
Relations Committee, 1980–1982

Special counsel, Senate Intelligence Committee, 1982

Member, Tennessee Appellate Court Nominating Commission,
1985–1987

Partner, Arent, Fox, Kinter, Plotkin, & Kahn, Washington,
D.C., 1991–1994

U.S. senator, Tennessee, 1994–2003

Presidential candidate, 2007–present

Career (Actor/Highlights): *Marie*, 1985

No Way Out, 1987

The Hunt for Red October, 1990

Die Hard 2, 1990

In the Line of Fire, 1993

Law & Order, 2002–2007

IRAQ WAR

High Priority? ☐ *Yes* ☐ *No* ☒ *Maybe*

Record/Position: Supported the Bush administration's decision to
remove Saddam Hussein and the 2007 military strategy and policy.

Quote: "We're the leader of the free world whether we like it or not.
People are looking to us to test our resolve and see what we're willing
to do in resolving the situation that we have there . . . If Saddam
Hussein was still around today with his sons looking at Iran developing a nuclear capability, he undoubtedly would have reconstituted
his nuclear capability. Things would be worse than what they are
today."

WAR ON TERROR

High Priority? ☒ *Yes* ☐ *No* ☐ *Maybe*

Record/Position: Supportive of the Bush administrations's emphasis on
the issue, and of the characterization of the threat as grave.

Quote: "We've seen our country attacked time and time again over the last decades. Now you see it, whether it's Madrid, whether it's London, whether it's places that most people have never heard of, they're methodically going around trying to undermine our allies and attack people in conventional ways. Meanwhile they try to develop nonconventional ways, and get their hands on a nuclear capability, and ultimately to see a mushroom cloud over an American city."

GOVERNMENT SPENDING/DEFICITS

High Priority? ☑ *Yes* ☐ *No* ☐ *Maybe*

Record/Position: Has made reducing the size and reach of the federal government one of his signature issues. Emphasizes reforming the three major entitlement programs, Social Security, Medicare, and Medicaid to make them fiscally solvent and avoid passing a burden on to future generations—but has not offered detailed plans on how to make the necessary changes.

Quote: "Audits have shown we've lost control of the waste and mismanagement in our most important agencies. It's getting so bad it's affecting our national security."

ENERGY/ENVIRONMENT

High Priority? ☐ *Yes* ☑ *No* ☐ *Maybe*

Record/Position: Has questioned the idea of global warming on earth by noting evidence of warming on other planets. Voted against an amendment to increase federal funding for solar and renewable energy programs and against the study of tougher fuel efficiency standards.

Quote: "Some people think that our planet is suffering from a fever. Now scientists are telling us that Mars is experiencing its own planetary warming: Martian warming. It seems scientists have noticed recently that quite a few planets in our solar system seem to be heating up a bit, including Pluto . . . This has led some people, not necessarily scientists, to wonder if Mars and Jupiter, nonsignatories to the Kyoto Treaty, are actually inhabited by alien SUV-driving industrialists who run their air conditioning at sixty degrees and refuse to recycle."

HEALTH CARE

High Priority? ☐ *Yes* ☑ *No* ☐ *Maybe*

Record/Position: Has criticized "socialized medicine" and European national health care systems as impractical. Favors improved electronic medical records.

Quote: "Out-of-control medical malpractice lawsuits have been a problem in many parts of the country for a long time. Malpractice insurance costs can be driven so high, that doctors and insurance companies flee to more reasonable business climates. With too few doctors, it's the patients who suffer the most."

TAXES

High Priority? ☑ *Yes* ☐ *No* ☐ *Maybe*

Record/Position: Believes in the power of supply-side economics tax cuts to expand the economy. Generally has opposed tax increases.

Quote: "Reagan showed what can be done if you have the will to push for tough choices and the ability to ask the people to accept them . . . Lower marginal tax rates have proven to be a key to prosperity now by Kennedy, Reagan, and Bush. It's time millionaires serving in the Senate learned not to overly tax other people trying to get wealthy."

JOBS/ECONOMY/TRADE/AGRICULTURE

High Priority? ☐ *Yes* ☐ *No* ☑ *Maybe*

Record/Position: Has standard laissez-faire Republican views holding that if the federal government stays out of the way, the private sector economy will grow.

Quote: "Someone who is eighteen today may well have ten employers in their career. That's completely different from how their parents lived. I would address that insecurity and help people adapt without shooting ourselves in the foot with protectionism and income redistribution."

ABORTION

High Priority? ☐ *Yes* ☑ *No* ☐ *Maybe*

Record/Position: Voted consistently prolife as a senator, although some of his statements and actions before his election suggested a mixed position. Says he has become more prolife in recent years with the birth of his two youngest children. Supports the overturning of *Roe v. Wade*, which he says was based on "bad law and bad medical science." Indicated in 1994 that he agreed with the statement "abortions should be legal in all circumstances as long as the procedure is completed within the first trimester of the pregnancy." Answered a survey in 1996 with, "I do not believe abortion should be criminalized. This battle will be won in the hearts and souls of the American people."

Quote: "In 1994, I made my first run for the U.S. Senate. I was proud to receive the National Right to Life endorsement . . . On abortion-related votes I've been one hundred percent."

EDUCATION

High Priority? ☐ *Yes* ☑ *No* ☐ *Maybe*

Record/Position: In the Senate, voted against increasing tax credits for college tuition and student loan payments, and for tax-free savings accounts for educational expenses, vouchers, and federally funded high school abstinence education.

Quote: "Perhaps the clearest example of federal overinvolvement in state and local responsibilities is public education. It's the classic case of how the federal government buys authority over state and local matters with taxpayer money and ends up squandering both the authority and the money while imposing additional burdens on states . . . A little more federalist confidence in the wisdom of state and local governments might go a long way toward improving America's public schools."

137

STEM CELL RESEARCH

High Priority? ☐ *Yes* ☑ *No* ☐ *Maybe*

Record/Position: Supports adult stem cell research, but not stem cell research when embryos are destroyed.

Quote: "It looks to me like there is a lot of promising developments as far as adult stem cell research is concerned anyway."

GAY RIGHTS

High Priority? ☐ *Yes* ☑ *No* ☐ *Maybe*

Record/Position: Says Americans should be "a tolerant people" but opposes "special rights" for anyone. In line with his federalist views, believes states should decide for themselves whether to allow civil unions. In the Senate voted against expanding federal hate crime protections to include sexual orientation.

Quote: "Marriage is between a man and a woman, and I don't believe judges ought to come along and change that."

GUN RIGHTS

High Priority? ☑ *Yes* ☐ *No* ☐ *Maybe*

Record/Position: Strong supporter of Second Amendment rights, including the right to carry concealed weapons to deter crimes, as in the case of the shootings at Virginia Tech.

Quote: "The statistics are clear. Communities that recognize and grant Second Amendment rights to responsible adults have a significantly lower incidence of violent crime than those that do not."

WELFARE/POVERTY

High Priority? ☐ *Yes* ☑ *No* ☐ *Maybe*

Record/Position: Has opposed economic redistributionist policies as "defeatist." Has voted against minimum-wage boosts and in favor of tax reductions for married couples.

Quote: "In the end, we may be hurting the very people we should be concerned about—the inner-city poor, those who already have to live with many risks in their daily lives, those who do not have clout here in Washington."

IMMIGRATION

High Priority? ☐ *Yes* ☐ *No* ☑ *Maybe*

Record/Position: Highly critical of the Bush administration efforts at comprehensive reform. Emphasizes border enforcement before other remedies. Has criticized Mexican government policies for contributing to illegal immigration. In the Senate, voted to limit welfare benefits for legal immigrants.

Quote: "If you have the right kind of policies, and you're not encouraging people to come here and encouraging them to stay once they're here, they'll go back, many of them, of their own volition, instead of having to, you know, load up moving vans and rounding people up. That's not going to happen."

For all current issue positions, check out http://www.fred08.com.

Last Best Chance

Fred Thompson may be a star, but he is not a mystery. Unlike some candidates (and presidents), one need not plop him on an imaginary psychiatrist's couch to dissect his psyche or call forth his inner child. Fred Thompson is pretty easy to figure out. First of all, he is an intelligent man. He is clever and vigorous, with a sophisticated mind. He is also a sanguine man. He is upbeat and down-to-earth, with a healthy ambition to enjoy an interesting, fulfilling life. He does not seem to be plagued by insecurity, self-doubt, or self-loathing. He likes himself, and that is part of his charm.

Such confidence, rare and irresistible, has made possible his unusual career, juggling some of the most desirable jobs in America—senator, film actor, and perhaps even president. "I have never taken on a major challenge that I have not come out of" on top, Thompson has said.

In the movies, of course, whether playing a good guy or a bad guy, a maverick or a bureaucrat, he generally puts forth a version of his own persona. He has presence, believability, and appeal, but few talk Oscar after they see him perform. When he was elected to the Senate in 1994, he was immediately greeted as a major player, despite his junior status. Usually, a freshman senator needs to struggle and maneuver for years to stand out and intrigue the media. But within a few weeks of his win, he was tapped to deliver the Republican response to President Clinton's first postmidterm election address—a major assignment, and an explicit acknowledgment of the expectations he carried with him. His presentation was praised by his party and the press. Nevertheless, other than participating in a few high-profile votes and projects, he did not shine as a legislator during his tenure, and after eight years, he quietly took his leave.

For most of the past decade, Thompson has intimated that his interest in the presidency does not burn brightly, but has admitted that he would be prepared to run if he felt his skills and experience were required. What some see as vagueness in Fred Thompson, others call a clear-eyed adherence to the simple virtues of American conservatism—strong defense, smaller government, reform of corrupt and bloated institutions. While detractors believe his celebrity and lavish lifestyle suggest a man out of touch with his roots and the less fortunate, supporters hail a consistent populist sensibility that elevates the wisdom of the people over the Washington elite.

Now, despite his rather slim record in the Senate and a reputation for being lazy, he is in a curious position as the personified hope of many in the Republican Party. Before even forming an exploratory committee, without any state or national infrastructure, campaign treasury, significant fund-raising base, or a specific issues platform, Thompson was discussed as a possible candidate—

and potential front-runner—in magazines, on television and talk radio, in newspaper headlines. He jumped ahead of announced contenders in national polls while remaining enigmatic about his intentions, finally joining the race in September 2007. With his commanding presence and a résumé

> Thompson established the Young Republicans group in Lawrence County, Tennessee, in the late 1960s.

that echoes Ronald Reagan's, it seemed not to matter that Thompson was a little light in political accomplishments and policy specifics. In 2008, with the Republican Party in disarray and White House control in peril, Reagan-Lite might be weighty enough.

Born Yesterday

Frederick Dalton Thompson reveals his heritage most directly in his rolling, gravelly southern baritone. There have been innumerable attempts to describe his deep, distinctive voice: sonorous, booming, reverberating, mellifluous, rich, resonant, unmistakable, comforting, commanding, slow and sticky as molasses. As Senator John McCain has joked, "I've often said if I had his voice I'd be president of the United States today." And from that voice, which is ever so pleasant to listen to (a great asset on the stump), pours the strains of the South.

He was born in Sheffield, Alabama, and as a baby, moved to Lawrenceburg (founded by Davy Crockett), over the state line in Tennessee. During his childhood, his father, Fletcher, was a used-car dealer; as Thompson has pointed out, "There's nobody who has to be more honest than the used-car dealer, because sooner or later he's going to have dealings with everyone in town." Thompson recalls a near-idyllic small-town existence, living a few blocks from the town square, where his grandparents ran a diner. He attended the local church and reveled in the friendly southern setting. As a teenager, Thompson was popular and affable, with a lively sense of humor, a taste for mischief, an affinity for sports, and a craze for girls; he once laughed, "I barely got out of high school. I was interested in two things—and sports was one of them." His friends and teachers remember him as very bright but academically indifferent, a combination of intellect and indolence that continued long into adulthood.

His unfettered immaturity came to an abrupt halt, however. He and his high school sweetheart, Sarah Elizabeth Lindsey, married in September 1959, when he was seventeen, with their first child on the way. Then, after finishing high school in 1960, he attended Florence College on a partial basketball scholarship and graduated from Memphis State University with a B.A. in philosophy and political science. It could not have been easy for the couple, raising a young family while they both went through college. At one point, Thompson, who held a variety of jobs to support his family and fund his education, took a

> *"I had the best kind of background. Dad wasn't a leading lawyer I had to try to measure up to. On the other hand, because they had little education, they were totally proud of me. When I got my high school diploma they were proud of me."*
> **—on his happy youth**

semester off to make some more money. By the time he earned his law degree at Vanderbilt, he and his wife were the parents of three. After passing the bar in 1967, he worked in his wife's uncle's law firm until he was named an assistant U.S. attorney in Nashville, where he had a good record of convictions. He puttered about in local politics, and in 1972 resigned his prosecutor's job to help manage Republican Tennessee senator Howard Baker's successful reelection campaign. Baker considered him both trustworthy and a rising star, and within a year Thompson was headed to Washington, D.C., to assist Baker in investigating the biggest political scandal of a generation.

Necessary Roughness

When Howard Baker appointed Thompson as the minority counsel for the Watergate hearings, Thompson was, in his own words, "a very young thirty," but as a lawyer and a father of three, he was not naïve. "Watergate was not a monumental shock to my system," he later said. "Once you have practiced law and been involved in politics, you are not disabled by the discovery that people—even good people—do bad things." In the glare of Watergate, the spotlight shone brightly on Thompson. He got credit for composing Senator Baker's signature query "What did the president know and when did he know it?" and for pressing, in his own line of questioning, White House aide Alexander Butterfield to reveal the existence of Nixon's secret Oval Office taping system, which led to the president's resignation.

Thompson became nationally celebrated for his role during the affair, and has since endeavored to frame his Watergate participation as a nonpartisan battle against government corruption. In fact, as Republican counsel, he was in frequent contact with the Nixon White House, and discussed the committee's awareness of the Oval

Office tapes with Nixon's lawyers before Butterfield testified. In July 2007, Scott Armstrong, a Democrat on the Watergate committee, asserted that "Thompson was a mole for the White House. Fred was working hammer and tong to defeat the investigation of finding out what happened to authorize Watergate and find out what the role of the president was." Thompson, who had written about his role in his 1975 memoir, responded to Armstrong with typical insouciance and indirection: "I'm glad all of this has finally caused someone to read my Watergate book, even though it's taken them over thirty years." In the book, *At That Point in Time: The Inside Story of the Senate Watergate Committee*, Thompson identified himself as a Nixon supporter, and expressed his hope that the tapes would exonerate the president: "I was looking for a reason to believe that Richard M. Nixon, President of the United States, was not a crook." President Nixon, meanwhile, did not have a particularly high opinion of Thompson; on those infamous tapes, Nixon judged him "dumb as hell" and referred to him as "that kid."

After eighteen months, the hearings ended, Nixon resigned, the nation—wiser, angrier, and more cynical—tried to repair itself, and Thompson returned to Nashville to practice law. Despite having been a prominent and daily fixture on national broadcast television (in the pre-cable-television universe, when such a presence had a greater significance), Thompson's fifteen minutes of fame appeared to be over. He claimed not to be bothered by the dwindling attention. "It wasn't that hard to adjust because I knew it was going to happen," he said. From then on, though, he kept one foot on home soil in Tennessee and the other in the nation's capital.

Days of Thunder

With his Watergate luster and Washington connections, particularly to the powerful Howard Baker, who would become his party's leader in the Senate, Fred Thompson was able to establish a lucrative career as a lobbyist and lawyer. He opened a practice in Nashville with two law school classmates, where he was eventually joined by his son Tony Thompson. He worked in Washington, D.C., as a lawyer and lobbyist on his own and with the powerhouse firm Arent, Fox, Kintner, Plotkin, & Kahn. Clients included General Electric, Toyota

> Thompson has a varied palate, enjoying bourbon and wine, southern home cooking, and fine dining. He also likes to mix sleek business suits with worn cowboy boots.

Motor Corporation, Westinghouse (the focus was on pronuclear legislation), and the Tennessee Savings and Loan League. He also represented the Teamsters' Central State Pension Fund; in 1985, Thompson acknowledged, "They were allegedly the bankroll for the Mob, to put it in delicate terms. But it has been cleaned up." For several years in the early 1990s he was registered as a foreign agent serving on behalf of Jean-Bertrand Aristide, the exiled president of Haiti, who was attempting to regain power with American help. Thompson made hundreds of thousands of dollars from his lobbying, although his main focus was on legal work. His specialty was providing his clients with access to Republicans on Capitol Hill and in the White House. In recent years, his adult sons also worked as lobbyists.

Lobbying can be dicey business for those with political aspirations, and in Thompson's presidential bid, some awkward facts have emerged about his past clientele, which has reportedly included a prochoice organization. Thompson has tried to head this off with a legalistic, blanket response separating himself from his clients' positions while defending his right as an American citizen to make a living. As he wrote in a July 2007 column, "[I]f a client has a legal and ethical right to take a position, then you may appropriately represent him as long as he does not lie or otherwise conduct himself improperly while you are representing him. In almost thirty years of practicing law I must have had hundreds of clients and thousands of conversations about legal matters. Like any good lawyer, I would always try to give my best, objective, and professional opinion on any legal question presented to me."

He also offered the preemptive warning: "As we get further into this political season we will undoubtedly see the further intersection of law, politics and the mainstream media . . . I intend to keep in mind the appropriate distinction and separation between law and politics, and I do not intend to get sucked in to doing a disservice to either of them or to myself."

The financial lures of lobbying and, later, moviemaking, did not distract Thompson from his interest in politics. Staying involved in government, Thompson occasionally served as a special legal adviser in congressional investigative efforts. When he ran for the Senate in 1994, to fill the remaining two years of the Tennessee seat vacated by then vice president Al Gore (Democrat Harlan Mathews had been appointed as a caretaker for the job in 1993), it was a bit of a surprise. Although Thompson had been active in Republican politics as a speaker and strategist, he had developed a jaundiced view of the Senate over time, saying in 1985, "I thought that standing on the Senate floor, engaging in a great debate and making a difference was the pinnacle of political activity. The more I've seen it, the less interested I am."

Still he jumped into the Senate race with gusto. Initially, Thomson was duly pegged as a D.C. lawyer (he owned a nice house and a fancy car in the District) and struggled until he changed his game plan and revved up his campaign. He began to rally when he started to tour the state in a red 1990 Chevrolet pickup truck, which got nearly as much attention as he did, for both its flash and its symbolism. That the truck was leased was equally symbolic, at least for Thompson's foes, who attempted to paint him as a rich, artificial Washington insider. Still, he emphasized his southern authenticity, dressing in jeans and plaid work shirts and tossing about the vernacular of his youth. One observer said he looked "more like a man who would stuff and mount a largemouth bass than like the lawyer, lobbyist, and big-time Hollywood character actor that he is."

Thompson used his celebrity to charm voters, reciting lines of movie dialogue, joking about his Hollywood experiences. He ran on a platform of fiscal conservatism; supported gun owners' rights, welfare reform, and term limits for members of Congress; suggested that abortion was a state issue, or should be left to individual choice; and made a series of homey ads with a theme of common sense: "To get elected today, politicians will say just about anything. And then they get to Washington and we find out what they really believe. I'm Fred Thompson and I want to tell you what I believe right now. I believe you can't spend more

> *"Regardless of whether you agreed with his politics, you knew [Ronald] Reagan was sincere in what he said. To appear believable, you have to really believe."*

than you got coming in. And we can't tax ourselves into prosperity. I believe you can't pay people more not to work than to work. And criminals can't hurt anybody if they're behind bars. Common sense? Maybe. But it sure isn't common in Washington right now." Thompson and his shiny red truck, which he called "this ol' baby" and "this rascal," were hits with the voters and the media, and his poll numbers rose accordingly.

His opponent was the impressive, Clintonesque, six-term Democratic congressman Jim Cooper, forty, the son of a former governor, a Rhodes scholar, a Harvard Law School graduate, and an experienced career politician (in his first race for Congress, he beat Howard Baker's daughter). The Cooper campaign took issue with Thompson's folksy presentation; an ad described Thompson as a "lobbyist and actor who talks about lower taxes, talks about change, while he drives a rented stage prop and plays the role of senator." For the most part, Thompson focused on his own image and qualifications, and avoided initiating negative ads, until he aired one that showed Cooper jogging with Bill Clinton, whose unpopularity that year was the Republican Party's trump card in races around the nation.

Clinton's first two years in the White House were bumpy, beset by blunders large and small. Like many in his party running that year, Thompson was able to take advantage of the backlash, which resulted in the famous Republican 1994 midterm sweep into majority control in both the Senate and the House. Thompson imparted a warning back during his 1994 race, a version of which he currently is using in his presidential run: "I think we're probably at a crossroads right now. I think a case can be made that we're where every great power in history was before they started their decline . . . People sense that. It's a dangerous time." To be sure, the line perhaps has more resonance now, in a terror-plagued post-9/11 world, but it hit home then, too. Thompson won the race by 60 percent to 39 percent.

No sooner had Thompson been sworn in to the Senate than

he found himself presenting the televised Republican response to President Clinton's postmidterm election address. Thompson spoke for fewer than five minutes, but Senate minority leader Bob Dole, who picked him for the job, called him a good spokesman for the Republican Party and said he expected Thompson to serve in that capacity for years to come. Pundits and television reviewers alike were impressed; Frank Rich's *New York Times* column announced "a star is born," while *Washington Post* television critic Tom Shales called him "a first-class communicator, one whose actor's training serves him well but who didn't give the appearance that he was acting. In this he bears a resemblance to Ronald Reagan, the Great Communicator himself, and that can only work to his advantage."

> *"I am, in many respects, an average Tennessean. I worked in a factory. I drive a truck. I practice law. I was a federal prosecutor. I've worked without health insurance. I've worked for minimum wage."*

After that auspicious beginning, Thompson scaled back both his media presence and his senatorial exploits. Even so, he was often mentioned as a presidential candidate. Talk of a White House bid came early and often, with ABC News's Sam Donaldson and others asking him if he planned to participate in the 1996 White House race. Thompson demurred, and instead helped Bob Dole in his 1996 presidential campaign by portraying Bill Clinton in debate preparations.

He also ran that year for his first full term in the Senate. He put his mother, Ruth, in his ads ("I want you to meet my No. 1 adviser on Social Security and Medicare") and had an easy reelection, trouncing Democrat Houston Gordon. At Thompson's campaign rallies some people held "Fred for President" signs.

Thompson continued to follow the conservative line, supporting tax cuts, gun owners' rights, curbs on environmental regulations, welfare reform, social spending cuts, and drilling for oil in the Arctic. He did, however, oppose tort reform and was an early proponent of the McCain-Feingold campaign finance reform bill. (He later said, "I have always looked at this process as a citizen and as an outsider, not as a politician. It never made sense to me to have a system where huge amounts of money were allowed to be given to politicians and then to have those very same donors come up and lobby politicians on issues.") He also was willing to follow his own path, occasionally casting the only negative vote in the Senate when voting in favor of the rights of states or individuals against the power of the federal government, or in support of trial lawyers.

Thompson opposed abortion, and voted for the ban on late-term abortion. Any concern that he was ambivalent about the abortion issue was alleviated by his consistently prolife voting record, although in 2007 he admitted the issue meant "more" since the conception of his two young children: "I have seen the sonograms of my babies." Nevertheless, as a senator he rarely used his rhetorical skills or standing to promote an antiabortion message, preferring to emphasize government reforms. Religious conservative leader Richard Land said of Thompson's abortion record, "He voted the right way, but I wouldn't say he was an activist."

In 1997, Thompson was presented with another high-profile assignment, as chairman of the Committee on Governmental Affairs. That year he held investigative hearings into alleged Clinton-Gore campaign fund-raising violations growing out of charges about the influence of 1996 election donations from foreign sources. Many Republicans hoped the hearings would finally expose the corruption they believed to be at the heart of the Democratic administration. But Thompson caused controversy on both sides of the aisle with his large $6.5 million budget request (eventually reduced to $4.35 million), and angered members of his party by extending the scope of the hearings to include GOP activity as well. Republicans felt this was an unnecessary concession, given their party's majority status, and a troublesome distraction from the Clinton administration's perceived offenses.

Thompson's committee consequently explored several acts of alleged Republican wrongdoing, including a probe into Republican National Committee chair Haley Barbour. Thompson found himself feuding with the Senate majority leader Trent Lott, who had campaigned for him during his reelection bid but who now believed Thompson was promoting his own reputation as a government watchdog and was squandering an opportunity to strengthen the Republican power base. Members of the party witnessed the Senate squabble, and some questioned Thompson's competence, disposition, motivation, and political acumen. One Senate Republican aide told the conservative *Weekly Standard*, "This is easily the worst congressional investigation in recent memory. He doesn't understand how to run a Senate hearing, and he never bothered to learn because Fred Thompson's agenda has always been Fred Thompson. He's trying to look bipartisan because he thinks that will win him the favorable media coverage he needs for his presidential campaign."

Thompson's bipartisan investigation received a great deal of attention in the national media, taking the focus off the Clinton administration, and resulting in an "everybody does it" headline on the hearings overall. Republicans were both embarrassed and chagrined. They believed Thompson had squandered their long-awaited opportunity to get Bill Clinton. (The president's perjury scandal and subsequent impeachment were, at this point, still a year away.) Thompson stuck to his message throughout, even as his allies worried about his long-term standing in the party—he was, after all, a relative novice whose celebrity was starting to flag. Thompson said as the hearings were getting under way, "You know how it is in this country, and especially in this town. There are tremendous quick buildups and tremendous quick takedowns. There are going to be good days and bad days. There are going to be missteps and mistakes and misquotes. There's nothing you can do about it, so you might as well relax and not enjoy it."

The Republicans may have been disappointed with Thompson's chairmanship (although the hearings revealed some misconduct from both parties), but White House talk did not abate, and Thompson held meetings with strategists to discuss his options for 2000. Instead, Thompson supported the candidacy of his fellow Tennessean Lamar Alexander. When Alexander withdrew from the race in 1999, Thompson quickly switched his allegiance to the long-shot bid of one of his closest friends in the Senate, Arizona's John McCain, with whom he shared a commitment to a reform agenda. Although Thompson regularly traveled the country, giving political and fund-raising speeches on behalf of the Republican Party and its candidates, his support for McCain (who was unpopular with most of his Senate colleagues) and his unwillingness to defer to his party's leadership rubbed some people the wrong way. He still had a following, but many insiders had stopped thinking of him as a potential luminary.

In late September 2001, with George W. Bush in the White House, and the 9/11 terrorist attacks resonating, Thompson declared his intention to seek reelection, asserting that public service was more essential than ever. In the wake of that cataclysmic event, Thompson set aside his normal opposition to government expansion, determining that America could only be defended effectively with the establishment of a mammoth entity designated for domestic safety. So in what was arguably his most central role as a legislator, Thompson helped broker a series of compromises that led to the creation of the Department of Homeland Security.

Six months after stating he would run again for the Senate, however, he changed his mind, and announced his retirement in March 2002. He was disenchanted by the endless partisan struggles and intraparty bickering, but seemed most affected by the sudden death of his daughter, Betsey Thompson Panici, in January 2002 from complications related to taking prescription drugs. As he told a fellow Tennessee politician at her funeral, "I've just lost my heart for [public] service. I've lost my heart." In a public statement, he said, "We just have some other priorities right now we need to take care of . . . I simply do not have the heart for another six-year term." He left politics and returned to acting full-time with his role on *Law & Order* as D.A. Arthur Branch.

Thompson's tenure in the Senate was for some a happy surprise, for others a disappointment. For Republican loyalists, Thompson ended up with a strong conservative voting record, quelling fears that he was a Hollywood moderate camouflaged by beat-up boots and folksy rhetoric. But his lackluster record as a leader and abrupt departure frustrated those who expected him to emerge as a lasting political player.

Thunderhearts

In 1977, Fred Thompson made headlines when he successfully represented Marie Ragghianti, the former chair of Tennessee's parole board, who was fired after she blew the whistle on corruption and pardon-selling in the Tennessee prison system and sued for reinstatement. Ragghianti said she hired Thompson in part because of his Watergate reputation. When producers were casting the 1985 film *Marie*, based on a book about the trial, starring Oscar winner Sissy Spacek as the title character, they ended up hiring Thompson to portray himself; he recited dialogue based on his actual courtroom argument, and wore his own clothes. How exactly this happened is a matter of some confusion. Thompson has alternately said he was invited to appear and that he lobbied for the role. In any case, Thompson's first acting venture turned out to be a critical success even if he was playing to type; the *New York Times* film critic wrote, "Fred Thompson gives one of the film's better performances playing himself," while the *Washington Post*'s review called Thompson "the real discovery of *Marie*," with his "booming voice and noble rock of a forehead."

> *"As an idealistic teenager I could think of nothing more inspiring than the notion of representing a just cause against the most powerful forces in the country, including the government."*

Thompson enjoyed the experience, got himself an agent, and soon was cast in a slew of big-budget films, with costars such as Kevin Costner, Tom Cruise, Nicole Kidman, Paul Newman, Robert De Niro, Bruce Willis, Sean Connery, and Clint Eastwood. Thompson also acted alongside James Belushi and Roseanne Barr.

Although Washington politicians and journalists regularly refer to Thompson as a "movie star," technically he is a character actor, a midlevel supporting player. And he almost always plays some version of himself. As his friend Fred Grandy (a former congressman from Iowa and, more famously, Gopher on *The Love Boat*) said, "Fred Thompson is a very convincing Fred Thompson; no one's going to ask him to play Lear."

Nonetheless, Thompson's film and television roles have only served to bolster his political aspirations. He often has portrayed a person in power: a military official, the head of the CIA, the White House chief of staff, a senator, and even the president of the United States, allowing the moviegoing public to consider him a real-life leader by osmosis. Being part of the super-successful *Law & Order* franchise on NBC and in syndication on cable television, with its millions of weekly viewers and iconic cultural status, has made Thompson an even more familiar presence in American households. Movies make actors seem larger than life; television makes them seem like old friends.

Major players in Washington, D.C., with their interchangeable conservative blue suits and haggard features, are inevitably fascinated with Hollywood and its alluring world of sunshine, sports cars, and entertainment pursuits. Hollywood types, meanwhile, can be a bit sensitive about the perceived superficiality of their profession, and are often impressed and intimidated by the authoritative gravity of Washington leaders. Thompson, who has conquered these two worlds, easily makes fun of both, playing them off each other and absorbing into his persona their particular positive aspects: the substance and command of Washington and the style and excitement of Los Angeles. Thompson's favorite campaign trail joke is to tell listeners with a deadpan delivery that his time in Washington makes him "long for the sincerity and honesty of Hollywood." He has made an effort to underrate the showbiz fascination, but explained, "If you talk about it, people think you're trying to capitalize on it, and if you don't talk about it, people think you're trying to hide it."

Some in the media welcome Thompson's double life because it gives political reporters the opportunity to inject glamour into typically mundane coverage, while entertainment correspondents enjoy the novelty of chatting about politics and world affairs rather than box office numbers and celebrity feuds. Thompson eagerly pokes fun at his glowering, imposing image, suggesting Tab Thompson as a stage name because "No one is named Fred except uncles and dogs," and laughing, "when they need an old, beat-up, middle-aged guy who'll work cheap, they call me." These days, he is content to repeat his standard line: "When I acted, I was only playing myself."

Jeri Kehn Thompson

Fred Thompson may not be a classically handsome man, but is often praised for his pleasantly craggy features, personal magnetism, and macho allure. After his marriage to Sarah Lindsey (now remarried and known as Sarah Knestrick) ended in 1985, after a long separation, he spent more than a decade and a half as a dedicated ladies' man, squiring a parade of women from coast to coast, including country singer Lorrie Morgan and Republican fund-raiser and activist Georgette Mosbacher. Former senator and mentor Howard Baker once observed, "He has an active social life. He's usually fully occupied. He turns up at parties, receptions, and fund-raisers with some of the most beautiful women you ever saw." Socially active, surely, but never a rake; Knestrick and Thompson's various other exes and paramours seem to have only fond things to say about him, and enthusiastically encourage him in his presidential ambitions. Thompson, for his part, has been entirely unapologetic about his roving bachelor days, telling a group of early supporters for his presidential candidacy, "I was single for a long time, and yep, I chased a lot of women. And a lot of women chased me. And those who chased me tended to catch me." People dubbed him "The Tennessee Stud" with doting smiles rather than with disapproving sighs.

> *"I think I'm a pretty good guy—with certain bad-guy characteristics. Like failing to keep in mind what's important and not important."*

In 2002, Thompson at last settled down again, marrying Jeri Kehn, a DePauw University graduate, Republican operative, and media consultant twenty-four years his junior. Their courtship was not initially smooth, and, after meeting in Nashville on July 4, 1996, they dated on and off for several years. In 2000, Kehn complained to the *New York Post* that Thompson was too attractive to other women: "They just won't leave him alone. I can't get up to get a cocktail at a party without coming back and finding some girl sitting in my chair." The couple eventually married in a small family ceremony in her hometown of Naperville, Illinois, and had daughter Hayden Victoria in October 2003 and son Samuel in 2006. Kehn Thompson, attractive and blond, has garnered some negative attention from the press. The *New York Times* suggested she was a "trophy wife," adding that her "youthfulness, permanent tan, and bleached blond hair present a contrast to the sixty-four-year-old man who hopes to win the hearts of the conservative core of the Republican Party." The *New York Post* identified her as a "babe wife," and *CNN* called her a "pretty face . . . with a pretty impressive résumé." It has been speculated that her glamorous appearance and the couple's vast age difference may raise eyebrows and turn off both conservative voters and older women.

Mrs. Thompson is her husband's closest adviser on his presidential campaign. Some early campaign staffers left the fold in reaction to the internal power Jeri Thompson wields. In addition, the media have scrutinized her past, including her former relationships and several claims court suits over unpaid debts. Nevertheless, she is an eye-catching, astute, media-savvy presence, and a couple of adorable little kids on the campaign trail are always bonuses.

In the Line of Fire

When Thompson announced in March 2002 his decision not to seek another term in the Senate, Vanderbilt political scientist John Geer remarked, "If he had the drive, he could have become a player on the national stage at the biggest level if he really wanted it. But you gotta be willing to work very hard for a very long period of time that it will all come to naught. Obviously, that is not where his values are."

> *"The lazier a man is, the more he plans to do tomorrow."*
> —Thompson's high school yearbook quote

This reputation—of not working too hard—has followed Thompson his entire life, from his youth as a joking cutup to his senatorial years. His high school coach told the *Nashville Tennessean*, "He was smart, but he was lazy. He probably could have been a straight-A student if he'd applied himself." He has had his defenders; Republican U.S. senator from Maine, Susan Collins, who along with Thompson and McCain supported the McCain-Feingold campaign finance bill, insisted the lazy label is a "misread" and that "[Thompson] is not a person who lets others see the amount of work he puts into something. He projects this relaxed, easygoing, down-home demeanor." A former aide, Tom Ingram, explained, "Fred is a big man who moves literally and figuratively at his own pace, he has the appearance of kind of ambling. It is part of his charm. But people who worked closely with him will tell you he spends hours in his office looking at issues from 360 degrees." And Thompson's former wife, Sarah Knestrick, said in 1997, "It's difficult to see the real drive he has, because his style doesn't seem to be one of great ambition. But it's there. It's always been there."

More common, however, is the view put forth by another former adviser: "While the Senate is filled with ambitious men who aren't in a rush to get home at night, Senator Thompson kept a lean formal schedule, did the bare minimum to get by, and then high-tailed to the Prime Rib or the Capitol Grille."

Until spring of 2007, Thompson used especially self-deprecating language to downplay presidential expectations, common in D.C., where coy evasion is the norm. In 1994 he said in a television interview, "There's one thing, I think, for certain that I've observed around here over the period of time that I've been here, and watching all this for years, and that is when people come to town, somewhere along the line, if they do anything at all, if they're shown to be able to put one foot in front of the other, they're mentioned for the national ticket. So now you've mentioned me, and I appreciate it, so we can move on to more serious topics." Thompson's own description of his enduring, high-powered career has been low-key: "Yeah, I go to

> In 2005, Thompson shepherded through the Senate the nomination of John Roberts to the Supreme Court, including coaching Roberts for the confirmation hearings, and introducing him to senators.

Hollywood and make a movie once in a while, and, yeah, I go to Washington and practice law." Thompson has plenty of critics who agree with such dismissive analysis.

But despite the energetic attacks on Thompson's alleged laziness, beginning in the spring of 2007, there was a very vigorous effort to drag him into the race. In March 2007, the Internet blogging community launched an intense, well-publicized Draft Fred campaign, partly as a response to the perceived flaws in the top three Republican candidates already officially running, all of whom had questions raised about their conservative credentials and none of whom was from the party's base region of the South. His supporters liked Thompson's personal appeal and name recognition, his Reaganesque charisma and résumé, his camera-ready presence and smooth oratory skills, and his conservative Senate voting record and history with the party. His stance on the intensely polarizing I. Lewis "Scooter" Libby perjury trial—Thompson served on the Libby Legal Defense Trust Advisory Committee for the former Bush White House aide, despite no previous acquaintance—proved his conservative bona fides, with his outspoken devotion to a cause activists held dear. He emerged as a serious candidate almost overnight, before even forming an exploratory committee. Big-money donors announced they would hold off on contributions to other hopefuls until Thompson declared his intentions, a number of well-known Republicans asserted their support and excitement, and conservative columnists begged for his candidacy, with Robert Novak calling him "cool, careful, and conservative."

Areas of Potential Controversy

– His lobbying and legal career.
– His evolving position on abortion, and his alleged lobbying work for a prochoice group in the 1980s.

– His reputation for being lazy.
– His slight senatorial record.
– His bout with lymphoma.
– His much younger wife.

Why Thompson Can Win a General Election

- Fred Thompson is very tall. At nearly six feet six inches, he'll definitely be the tallest player in the race, historically a symbolic advantage in most presidential elections. Thompson's emphasis on national security and the dangers that America faces around the world—along with his Papa Bear stature—are well-suited for the Republican Party's determination to maintain its traditional edge with voters on what could well be the biggest issue in the 2008 election. Americans psychologically may feel most comfortable with a hulking physical presence and a soothing baritone to protect them against the terrorist threat.

- Many people seem to like him, even if grudgingly, on both sides of the aisle. Former political opponents as well as ex-girlfriends have positive things to say about him. The one-on-one likability factor extends to his public personality; he is naturally a disarming fellow. His movie and television career has given him some fame and name recognition, and potential voters may already feel comfortable with him.

- Thompson is skilled at using all types of media— including writing his own essays on the Internet, reaching out to conservative bloggers, unfurling his melodious voice on the radio, and, of course, appearing on camera. Excelling at that kind of targeted media has been a hallmark of successful Republican campaigns in the last few years. He would likely be a strong performer in the presidential debates, which can be critical in determining the outcome of the race.

- He's not shy about talking plainly. In spring 2007, before announcing his candidacy, he explained, "It has to do with electability. I don't want to turn the keys of this country over to Hillary Clinton . . . I think with me, we wouldn't have to do that." Given the divisions in this country, such simple—and tough—talk is a solid strategy.

- In Tennessee, he secured his share of Democratic and female votes, which indicates he might be able to challenge the Democratic nominee in some Blue states. As a southerner and a reliable conservative, he would be in a strong position to hold the Red states in the South and near-West that President Bush won in 2000 and 2004.

Why Thompson Can't Win a General Election

- For a man known for a wan work ethic and who prefers to follow his own whims and schedule, a grueling months-long campaign could be too much to endure.

- He has received relatively little attention in past campaigns for various aspects of his personal and professional lives. In the 2008 campaign there have already been new questions about his early stand on abortion, and there may be more charges of flip-flopping headed his way. Often when Thompson's record or statements have been challenged in the past, he has gotten away with a nonresponsive, colorful quip, distracting the press with casual charm or brittle flippancy. That cannot work in a long presidential campaign. Said his friend, former Republican Senate leader Bill Frist, "He will develop enemies very quickly [when] he gets in the race. He has never been put on the defense. This is going to be a challenge."

- Decades of lobbying—which he continued even in recent years while appearing on *Law & Order*—can expel near-limitless potential controversy related to social issues, international relations, corporate irresponsibility, and governmental improprieties.

- Thompson was diagnosed and treated for non-Hodgkin's lymphoma in 2004. While his cancer is currently in remission, and while his particular form was low-grade, there may be some concerns about his health. In spring of 2007, he stated, "I have had no illness from it, or even any symptoms. My life expectancy should not be affected. I am in remission, and it is very treatable with drugs if treatment is needed in the future—and with no debilitating side effects."

- He accomplished little in the Senate, by general standards of legislative responsibility and achievement. Members of his own party (and some of his friends) have questioned his discipline and aptitude. This will not play well in an election in which competence and capability will be major priorities. Thompson might be too openly ambivalent to fight for the job. As he told an interviewer in 2007 about running for president, "one advantage you have in not having this as lifelong ambition is that if it turns out that your calculation is wrong, it's not the end of the world."

- He may have an insufficient command of policy areas outside his experience, and be unable to answer detailed questions in a debate or interview.

- Thompson has at times been criticized for not relishing the kind of schmoozing with voters and local elected officials that is normally expected on the path to the White House, even if he excels at it.

- He would be ill-positioned to continue the Republican Party's success in attacking Democrats for their ties to the alleged out-of-touch cultural liberalism of Hollywood, which was a big advantage for George W. Bush in his two presidential victories.

The Best Case for a Thompson Presidency

- Even Thompson must recognize he'll have to work hard, very hard, every day, if he wins. And if he applies himself, he could be a strong leader. In addition, his engaging personality would come in handy when dealing with Congress, foreign leaders, and the general public.
- Solving some of the country's most intractable problems—Social Security, Medicare, Medicaid, health care, education—will require a president who is not afraid of taking on special-interest groups and risking reelection. Thompson's political career suggests he has the right mind-set for those challenges.
- Although he is ambitious, he is not markedly power-hungry, and he would likely appoint a strong, sensible staff who could give him solid advice.
- His two youngest children are toddlers, extra incentive for leading the country to a stronger future. As he has said, "We need to think about what kind of world they're going to grow up into. That's why I'm doing it."

The Worst Case for a Thompson Presidency

- Perhaps he will be all talk and no action after all. Perhaps his rumored laxity and relative inexperience will be regrettably exposed in the face of national and global crises. Perhaps he won't know how to handle the power of the office; perhaps he'll have no real ideas to enact; perhaps he will realize he is incapable of the strenuous, incessant labor required of leadership. He might count down the days of his first and only term, becoming obsolete early on and throwing both parties into disarray, as politicians jockey for power to fill the void (and, in 2012, the job), distracting from government business at all levels. He has never been a manager or a governmental leader under pressure, nor has he tackled many of the substantive problems facing the United States.

What to Expect If Thompson Is President

- Thompson would bring his southern charm and urban sophistication to the White House, in a manner that would enliven Washington, D.C. He would likely put an emphasis on protecting America's security at home and abroad, including in the Middle East. His support for President Bush's Iraq policy suggests he would subscribe to many of the same principles that have guided the current administration. Thompson has always talked like a hawk on foreign policy, and he likely would be one as president.

- On domestic policy, Thompson would look to cut the size of government whenever he could. He would try to reform the big entitlement programs such as Medicare, Medicaid, and Social Security by crafting bipartisan deals. He might do the same on issues such as the environment, energy, and health care.

- His cabinet and staff would likely consist of old-timers with gravitas and newcomers with energy, mostly Republicans with conservative sensibilities. Three Tennessee Republicans—former senators Baker and Frist, and current senator Alexander—would serve as influential advisers.

- State dinners and events such as the White House Correspondents' Dinner would be inundated with Hollywood and New York celebrities, in a flood of razzle-dazzle not seen since Bill Clinton was president.

- Jeri Kehn Thompson, as a certified Generation X woman, would have to find a balance between the traditional First Lady role and her instincts as a former Republican operative. She would place her focus on her husband's image, White House personnel, and strengthening the Republican Party. But her primary occupation likely would be raising her young children. The press would churn out style articles galore examining her attire and appearance, and dissecting her wardrobe choices for every occasion.

Thompson's Own Words

"I was particularly interested in the intellectual battle between Burke and Rousseau about whether man was prone to do the wrong thing or was naturally good and corrupted by society. I think I come down on the side of Burke—I think that people are prone to error, that more often than not it's a hell of a lot harder to do the right thing than it is to do the wrong thing, and I think that's what makes the right thing so admirable sometimes, because it's so tough."   —on studying philosophy as an undergraduate

"Up here, it's a town on the make. Everybody is here for a purpose. And I'm a part of that. But I need the distance and variety. I need to go down to General Sessions Court in Lawrence County once in a while and sit around and whittle and chew a little tobacco with the ones who knew me when I was a kid."

—on Washington versus Tennessee

"It has to do with lawyers and politicians and the mine fields a young lawyer encounters. A personal thing as to the choices one makes and the dichotomy so many of us have to live by in balancing our ideals. Not running over the other guy on one hand and on the other, the pressure that society brings on us where we're measured in terms of our income, of who we're able to do in, and the pressures of a big law firm. And how the good guys turn out not to be so good and the bad guys turn out not to be so bad."   —on a novel he once drafted

"Every public official has to understand that he or she is a public official and that's the price you pay. For the most part, that's appropriate. That's the price your whole family pays. There are lines to be drawn."   —on intrusive media coverage

What His Supporters Say

"I am delighted he ran for public office. He's not just a partisan. He has an overall view of what is good for America. I have a lot of confidence in his candor and integrity."

—the late Sam Dash, the Watergate committee's top
Democratic lawyer, who worked with Thompson

"Sometimes you feel he is not working hard enough. But when he is working, he can go longer than anybody I've ever seen . . . He is a 'tell-it-like-it-is' guy. He is not part of a clique and speaks his own mind."   —Ron McMahan, Thompson campaign
strategist in 1994 and 1996

"Fred is a perfect example of chivalry. He's the kind of man little girls dream about marrying, who opens doors for you, lights your cigarettes, helps you on with your coat, buys wonderful gifts. It's every woman's fantasy . . . I think he has a great chance of capturing the women's vote. He's majestic . . . He has such charisma. He can go to a down-home southern-fried chicken dinner and later that evening eat the best caviar and drink wine with an ambassador."   —former girlfriend, singer Lorrie Morgan

"Everybody makes their own luck to some extent, but Fred's been lucky beyond that. It's like a charmed life."

—Sarah Knestrick, Thompson's ex-wife
and current supporter

"He's not new at this game. He just wiggled his nose like that lady on *Bewitched*, and people swooned. They're still swooning."

—Rich Galen, Thompson adviser and
veteran Republican strategist

"Everybody's got a Fred Thompson story that went to school with him. He majored in 'people' in school, not necessarily the curriculum."   —Anne Morrow, a cousin who knew him when

"I have the greatest affection and respect for Fred Thompson. I think he would make an outstanding president of the United States."   —Arizona senator John McCain, in 1998

"He has a conservative bearing and a conservative presence, but he's independent in his thinking and his voting record . . . He has a commanding television presence that makes every other politician in America jealous."

—fellow Tennessean and friend Senator Lamar Alexander

What His Critics Say

"[He's] a Gucci-wearing, Lincoln-driving, Perrier-drinking, Grey Poupon–spreading millionaire Washington special-interest lobbyist."
—Jim Cooper, his Democratic opponent in the 1994 Senate race

"I just felt like that the work hadn't been done."
—a "disappointed" Republican Senate leader Trent Lott at the close of the 1997 Governmental Affairs Committee hearings into Clinton administration wrongdoing

Thompson Facts and Stories

– Thompson is the son of Fletcher Thompson (who died in 1990), a used-car dealer and state park inspector who once ran for county sheriff, and Ruth Thompson, a homemaker. He has a brother, Ken, eight years his junior.

– During his youth, the Thompson family lived in a one-story house near the town square and attended the local First Street Church of Christ.

– In high school, Thompson and his friend misbehaved so often the principal set up a special study hall for the two of them. Despite the mischief, Thompson was known for his sense of humor, high spirits, and good nature.

– At six feet five inches tall by his junior year in high school, Thompson was a valued member of the high school basketball and football teams; he might have considered a sports career, but suffered a shoulder injury during his senior year.

– Thompson's first wife's grandfather was a lawyer who gave him advice about the legal profession.

– When Thompson graduated from Lawrence County High School in 1960, he was already married and the father of Fred

Dalton "Tony" Thompson Jr. Friends from his youth recall that he matured quickly in the face of adult responsibility. He and his wife, who had graduated the previous spring and was considered an impressive and gifted young woman, lived with her parents that first year.

– Thompson worked a number of jobs to put himself through college, including in a bicycle factory, at the post office delivering packages, in a shoe store, in a clothing store, as a truck driver, as a bouncer at his uncle's drag strip, and at a drive-in movie theater. His wife's parents also hired him to work at their church-pew factory.

– Thompson served on the Libby Legal Defense Trust Advisory Committee, and expressed relief when President Bush commuted I. Lewis "Scooter" Libby's prison sentence: "This will allow a good American, who has done a lot for his country, to resume his life."

– Thompson has, in recent years, been a regular contributor to conservative sites on the Internet, and a frequent guest on the Fox News Channel. He also has worked as a substitute host for renowned radio personality Paul Harvey.

– Prominent supporters include former Tennessee senators Howard Baker and Bill Frist, and Indianapolis Colts quarterback Peyton Manning.

– Nicknames during his life have included Moose, Hollywood Fred, and the Tennessee Stud.

– Thompson lives with his wife and two youngest children in a well-appointed home in upscale McLean, Virginia.

Presidential Announcement

Fred Thompson officially entered the race on September 6, 2007, with a video message posted on his campaign Web site. The previous evening, Thompson was a guest on *The Tonight Show with*

Jay Leno, where he announced "I'm running for president of the United States," and talked about his goals for the country. Thompson skipped a Republican debate in New Hampshire to appear on the program, and his absence was noted on the stage by his rivals and in the media by journalists and pundits. But as Thompson joked to Leno, "It's a lot more difficult to get on *The Tonight Show* than it is to get into a presidential debate." After leaving Leno's couch, Thompson followed a more traditional route, and went to Iowa with his family to begin his campaign.

Excerpts from his video statement:

> Just within the next few years, some very serious challenges are moving toward us that will present a difficult and dangerous time in the life of our nation. There are grave issues affecting the safety and security of the American people and our economic well being. I'm going to do my level best in this campaign to address these problems. I'm going to give this campaign all that I have to give, and I hope that you will join me.

Read More About Thompson

Fred Thompson, *At That Point in Time: The Inside Story of the Senate Watergate Committee* (New York: Quadrangle, 1975). Thompson's memoir of the Senate Watergate Committee.

http://www.fred08.com/

MORE REPUBLICANS

SAM BROWNBACK

The Basics

Name: Sam Dale Brownback

Born: September 12, 1956,
Garnett, Kansas

Political party: Republican

Spouse: Mary Stauffer Brownback,
married August 1, 1982

Children: Abby, Andy, Elizabeth,
Mark, Jenna

Religion: Catholic

Education: Kansas State University,
B.S., 1979
University of Kansas, J.D., 1982

Career: Farm broadcaster, KKSU, 1978
Lawyer, Ogden & Leonardville, Kansas,
1982–1986
Secretary of Agriculture, Kansas,
1986–1993
White House fellow, 1990–1991
U.S. congressman, Kansas, 1995–1997
U.S. senator, Kansas, 1997–present
Presidential candidate, 2007–present

Over the Rainbow

Sam Brownback is a farmer by birth and a politician by nature. He was raised on an eight-hundred-acre farm in tiny Parker, Kansas, where his parents still live. His ancestors were Pennsylvania farmers of German descent who moved to Kansas after the Civil War. In college, he majored in agricultural economics. His first job as an adult was as a farm broadcaster, hosting a weekday radio show. He later said, "I'd grown up listening to farm broadcasters. Conversation stopped around our table when the broadcaster read the markets . . . It stirred my interest in international affairs, since what was going on in the Soviet Union or Brazil or Australia affected our markets for wheat and soybeans."

Brownback showed leadership qualities early on. He was the state president of Future Farmers of America in high school, student body president at Kansas State University, and president of his class at the University of Kansas Law School. He volunteered for Ronald Reagan's presidential campaign in 1980, became Kansas's secretary of agriculture in 1986 at the record age of thirty, and spent a year in Washington from 1990 to 1991 as a White House fellow working on trade issues. In 1994 he ran for Congress and was part of the famous Republican midterm sweep, defeating two Republican opponents in the primary and a Democratic former Kansas governor in the general election. As part of his goal to eliminate the specter of a big federal government altogether, he and his fellow "New Federalists" advocated doing away with the departments of Housing, Energy, Education, and Commerce; he learned to scale back his grander expectations over time. Two years later, he won his Senate seat in a special election after Bob Dole left the job to run for president in 1996.

In the Senate, Brownback continued his emphasis on family values and reducing the size of government, casting consistently conservative Republican, values-friendly votes, and occasionally stepping forward as a leader. He voted against partial-birth abortion, and supported drilling in the Arctic National Wildlife Refuge, reducing income taxes, ending the estate and gift taxes, and launching the Iraq War (although he opposed the so-called "surge" of more American troops into the country). With farmers as his family and his constituents, he also has taken a lead in promoting the exportation of U.S. beef to Asia.

At the same time, following his own "compassionate conservative" sensibility, he has pursued bipartisan legislation involving human rights and some family issues. He has worked with liberal Democrats such as Ted Kennedy (on the subject of care for disabled children) and Barack Obama (on the AIDS crisis). Brownback has also been an active participant in the One campaign, founded by U2 singer and humanitarian Bono.

As a presidential candidate, Brownback has made a particular appeal to social conservatives. He is adamantly against stem cell research, and he often speaks for the rights of "fetal citizens." He opposes gay marriage and civil unions, and advocates education vouchers and school prayer.

His faith motivates his empathetic sensibilities—he describes himself as a "bleeding-heart conservative," leading him to champion some issues that are not part of every conservative's agenda. Brownback supports global human rights, speaking out against genocide and sex trafficking across the world. He opposes the death penalty. He supports a path for citizenship for illegal aliens because, as he has explained, the agricultural industry is so dependent on low-wage workers. He likes to refer to himself as "being prolife but being fully life—working on issues like human rights and children in Darfur—because I think we have to stand for life in the womb, but we also have to stand for the young woman that's in poverty or the guy that's trapped in his own bondage by what he has done in prison."

Brownback's life has been shaped by his religion, which itself has evolved over time. He was raised a Methodist, belonged to a nondenominational evangelical church, and, in 2002, converted to Catholicism, which he has characterized as a natural transition. Former Pennsylvania senator Rick Santorum, then his colleague and Capitol Hill roommate, sponsored Brownback's conversion and participated in the ceremony, which took place in a Washington, D.C., chapel run by Opus Dei. Brownback often cites God as his reason for pursuing the White House. He takes a scholarly approach to religion and has read the Torah, the Koran, and historical Christian works.

In 1995 he was treated for melanoma. Having cancer, he has said, inspired his spiritual transformation: "I did a lot of internal examination. My conclusion was that if this were to be terminal, at that point in time I would not be satisfied with how I had lived life. I had tried to be a Christian, but I had failed." Surviving melanoma also gave him a more intrepid attitude toward his earthly life and political ambitions, prompting his bold run for the Senate, and his bid for the presidency as well.

Why He Has a Chance

Brownback comes across as a stable, moral person, and he speaks in an unaffected, mellow fashion. He is a man of deep faith, and his passionate yet stately talk of his spiritual dedication has stirred some observers. Many evangelicals are drawn to him, and his embrace of nonpartisan compassion has the potential for wider appeal.

He has exuded a certain confidence throughout his political career. A competent man, he has taken a tortoise vs. hare approach to the race (he's the tortoise). His cool modesty and values-oriented composure contrast in his favor with some of his colorful, dramatic rivals.

He is well liked and respected by his Senate colleagues, of both parties.

If the Iraq War and the Republican Party's association with it is the unpopular centerpiece that animates the electorate in 2008, Brownback's break with White House policy—he has called for a plan to end the war more quickly by dividing Iraq into three sectarian states, with Baghdad as a shared capital—might help him win support.

Brownback Facts and Stories

– His hometown of Parker, Kansas, has fewer than three hundred citizens. His parents, Robert and Nancy Brownback, raised cattle, hogs, wheat, and corn. He has three siblings: Jim, Alan, and Mary. He played football, went to drive-ins, and was described as an All-American boy.

– His wife Mary Stauffer Brownback comes from a wealthy family that owned a Midwest media conglomerate; the company was sold for a hefty sum in 1995.

– He and Mary have three biological children—Abby, Andy, and Elizabeth—and two adopted children: Jenna, a girl from China, and Mark, a boy from Guatemala (both adoptions coincidentally came through at the same time in 1999; the children are the same age). Brownback talks and writes movingly about the joys of adoption and the struggles his children might have endured in the countries of their births.

– When at home in Topeka, he attends two Sunday church services—one with his family at a nondenominational church, and Catholic Mass by himself (his family has not converted to Catholicism).

– He has said an alternate career would be farming, the family business. He also is skilled as an auctioneer.

– He uses an elliptical trainer for exercise.

– He listens to Christian music and prefers to read Christian-themed literature as well as books of religious history.

– He drives a Ford Taurus in Washington, D.C., and a Honda Civic hybrid in Topeka.

– The Brownback family keeps cats, dogs, and fish in their Topeka home.

About Brownback

"He was just a wholesome, All-American, Kansas country boy. He had the country values; the family values; and, as far as my knowledge, still has that same value system."

—childhood friend Joe Atwood

"As a farmer, I know that Senator Brownback understands the economic issues and social values of the agricultural community."

—veteran Iowa state senator Nancy Boettger

Read More About Brownback

Sam Brownback, *From Power to Purpose: A Remarkable Journey of Faith and Compassion* (Nashville: Thomas Nelson, 2007).

http://www.brownback.com

NEWT GINGRICH

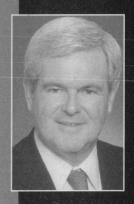

The Basics

Name: Newton Leroy McPherson
  Gingrich

Born: June 17, 1943,
  Harrisburg, Pennsylvania

Political party: Republican

Spouse: Callista Bisek, married
  August 18, 2000

Children: Linda Kathleen, Jacqueline
  Sue (with Jackie Battley)

Religion: Baptist

Education: Emory University, B.A.,
  1965
  Tulane University, M.A., 1968
  Tulane, University, Ph.D., 1971

Career: Assistant professor,
  West Georgia College, Carrollton,
  Georgia, 1970–1978
  U.S. congressman, Georgia, 1979–1999
  House minority whip, 1989–1995
  Speaker of the House, 1995–1999
  Chairman, The Gingrich Group,
  1999–present

The Not-So-Distant Past

There was a time not so long ago when Newt Gingrich was one of the most powerful people in the world. Gingrich, armed with his conservative "Contract with America" and promising major government reform, orchestrated the historic 1994 Republican takeover of the House of Representatives, the first time the Republicans had controlled that body since 1953. Gingrich was elected to the Congress in 1979 and as House minority whip in 1989. He became Speaker of the House after the takeover, where he began to rapidly and successfully implement some of the contract's major provisions in the first hundred days of the new Congress.

President Clinton, who was halfway through his first term, struggled to keep his administration afloat, and was forced to revamp his political and policy strategy (in his 1996 State of the Union speech, under pressure from Gingrich and other aggressive conservatives, Clinton acknowledged that "the era of big government is over"). Gingrich was able to set much of the political agenda for the country, and established himself as one of the most influential Speakers of the twentieth century. He forced Clinton to balance the budget, enact welfare reform, increase military spending, and cut taxes, and was a leader in pushing Clinton's impeachment for lying under oath about his relationship with Monica Lewinsky. But in pursuing those goals, Gingrich overreached. He gambled and lost to the Clinton White House after he helped force a government shutdown over the budget in 1995, excessively flogged the Starr report and details of the Clinton investigations, and engaged in tricky semantic exercises to distinguish his own moral and legal missteps from those of Clinton and the Democrats. Gingrich's foes closely scrutinized his every move to exploit potential financial, legal, or moral lapses.

Toward the end of Clinton's second term, Gingrich's star began to fall. With a weak Republican showing in the 1998 midterm elections, and his own ethics scandal brewing over the improper use of the political organization GOPAC, Gingrich was put on the defensive. He was pressured to return a multimillion-dollar book advance, which he did only grudgingly. After a lengthy congressional investigation, he was required to pay a $300,000 fine for ethics violations. In 1999, in the wake of various clandestine Republican attempts to dethrone him, Gingrich resigned his seat and abandoned public office, leaving President Bush and Karl Rove to define the Republican Party in his wake. Some conservatives had begun to worry that Gingrich was not a true believer in the morality of their cause, while others feared he had become too controversial to effectively lead the movement. It was a shocking turnaround, and even the most jaded in Washington shook their heads in wonder and bemusement over his dramatic implosion.

Gingrich's pollster, Frank Luntz, said, "He was the single smartest political figure of the last fifty years, and now no one seeks his advice. It's a Shakespearean tragedy." But close Gingrich observers, who respected his intellectual heft, imperious command, and virtuoso policy schemes, fully expected Gingrich to return one day to the political stage. The Republican Party's current disarray and imperfect presidential field may present him with his cue.

Gingrich was born in Harrisburg, Pennsylvania, to teenage Kathleen Daugherty and Newton C. McPherson Jr. McPherson soon disappeared from the scene. Three years later, Daugherty married army officer Robert Gingrich, who adopted the boy. The Gingrich family was based in Pennsylvania, lived for several years in Europe, and eventually settled in Georgia, where Newt graduated from high school, having been voted "most intellectual" in his class. Young Gingrich, always deeply curious and scholarly, loved reading and animals, and initially planned to be a zoologist or a paleontologist.

He enrolled at Emory University in 1961, and after his fresh-

man year, married his high school math teacher, with whom he had
been involved as a student. The couple had their first child in 1963
(the pair had another child and divorced in 1981; he remarried
later that year). He received his degree in history, got his Ph.D. at
Tulane, and embarked on a teaching career at West Georgia College
in Carrollton. In addition to administering his history courses, he
cofounded an environmental studies program.

In 1974 and 1976 he ran for Congress, and while unsuccessful,
made a strong showing both times, winning at last in 1978. He set
his sights on the Speakership, and positioned himself as a young
Republican leader, pushing conservative legislation and grassroots
political training, challenging senior members of both parties, fero-
ciously raising money for the party and championing Republican
candidates. He helped take down Democratic Speaker Jim Wright,
and won election as minority whip in 1989. He spent the next five
years plotting his ascendancy and that of the conservative Republican agenda, which culminated in his blazing, if ephemeral, 1994
triumph.

After Gingrich left Congress, he opened The Gingrich Group
consulting firm, joined the lucrative speaking circuit (making
$50,000 per speech his first year out, raking in more than $3 million), and became a consultant to Fox News. He joined think tanks
and participated in academic studies. He has always had something to contribute to the dialogue, although even his supporters
say that while he is fantastic at generating a steady stream of new
ideas—many of them good—some are impractical or downright
implausible.

In 2000, Gingrich divorced his second wife and married longtime paramour and Capitol Hill staffer Callista Bisek, with whom
he had been having an extramarital relationship. Gingrich had
been one of Bill Clinton's harshest critics during the Lewinsky affair

and impeachment scandal, and many considered his own conduct with Bisek decidedly hypocritical and shameful. Gingrich resisted the comparison to Clinton by saying he never lied under oath, that his indiscretion, while improper, was of a purely personal nature. In March 2007, Gingrich was a guest on the radio show of conservative Christian activist James Dobson, and expressed regret over his behavior. He admitted, "There were times when I was praying and when I felt I was doing things that were wrong. But I was still doing them. I look back on those as periods of weakness and periods that I'm . . . not proud of." He continued to reject a parallel with Clinton, asserting that "the president of the United States got in trouble for committing a felony in front of a sitting federal judge." Many speculated that Gingrich agreed to the interview in preparation for a presidential run, confronting the trouble of his adultery head-on with a stern yet irreproachable Christian arbiter.

Gingrich has also stepped up his crusade against the evils of partisanship, even as he has continued to push conservative ideas and acidly criticize the Democratic Party. He has decried the nonstop nature of American political campaigns, and called for less personal invective and more substantive debate in politics. These reversals and inconsistencies have sparked suspicion and curiosity, both from his old Democratic foes who harbor lingering rage over his divisive actions in the 1990s, and from his longtime allies, who count on him to lead the charge against their liberal enemies. He has even, for example, urged Republican audiences to set aside their disdain for Republican target number one, Hillary Clinton, and consider some of her ideas—for instance, on health care reform. Health care is one of the key issues Gingrich has focused on in the last few years, along with national security and terrorism. His efforts at rehabilitation have been thorough and purposeful—he seems to have learned important lessons from his downfall a decade ago.

Why He Has a Chance

Gingrich is an exceptional politician, capable of taking charge, enacting change, and rallying his followers. He applies his intellectual, academic strengths to formulating coherent and intensely detailed policy plans. In learning from his past mistakes, he has taken an active role in making amends and refining his image.

The country faces major problems, and Gingrich, known as a scholar, a communicator, and a showman, regularly offers up paradigm-altering solutions—he is not afraid to devise plans on a grand scale. Unlike most other candidates in the race, he has hands-on experience in literally every relevant policy area, from foreign affairs to the environment to health care to tax reform to national security. He also has had a long history in dealing with the press, and will be prepared to handle controversy or a media storm.

He could potentially reunite the conservative coalition that has won all but three presidential elections since 1968. Bush proved that a Republican can win Red states and the Electoral College by rousing conservative voters and getting them to the polls. While the political environment has changed radically during Bush's final years, Gingrich might have a chance to employ this strategy once again.

Americans are intrigued by celebrities, and Gingrich remains, for good or ill, one of the major political icons of recent decades.

Gingrich Facts and Stories

– Gingrich was named *Time* magazine's Man of the Year in 1995.
– He has written a number of public policy books, as well as some historical novels.
– He has remained a fixture on the policy scene since leaving Congress, as a fellow at the American Enterprise Institute and the

Hoover Institution, and as a member of the Council on Foreign Relations.
– He is fascinated by futurology and the use of technology to solve public policy problems.
– He is the grandfather of two.
– His younger half sister, Candace Gingrich, is a gay and lesbian rights activist.
– In 1995, he was bitten by a baby cougar at the Washington Zoo.
– He and Callista Gingrich live in Virginia.

About Gingrich

"I know it's a bit of an odd fellow, or odd woman, mix, but Speaker Gingrich and I have been talking about health care and national security for several years."   —Hillary Clinton

"I call Newt an experiential conservative, as opposed to a deeply philosophical conservative. Newt has a deep knowledge and so he is somewhat professorial in that respect. But he does not have a deeply held philosophy, say biblically based philosophy as some of us do. And therefore, he is much more negotiable on a lot of issues and, as the old railroad timetables would suggest, 'subject to change without notice.' "

—longtime conservative activist
and Gingrich associate Paul Weyrich

Read More About Gingrich

Newt Gingrich, *Winning the Future* (Washington, D.C.: Regnery, 2005).

http://www.newt.org/

MIKE HUCKABEE

The Basics

Name: Michael Dale Huckabee

Born: August 24, 1955, Hope, Arkansas

Political party: Republican

Spouse: Janet McCain Huckabee, married May 25, 1974

Children: John Mark, David, Sarah

Religion: Baptist

Education: Ouachita Baptist University, Arkadelphia, Arkansas, 1977
Southwestern Baptist Theological Seminary, Fort Worth, Texas, 1980

Career: Advertising director, Focus, 1976–1980
Pastor, Immanuel Baptist Church, Pine Bluff, Arkansas, 1980–1986
President, ACTS-TV, 1983–1986
President, Beech Street Communications, 1986–1992
Pastor, Beech Street First Baptist Church, Texarkana, Arkansas, 1986–1992
President, KBSC-TV, 1987–1992
President, Arkansas Baptist State Convention, 1989–1991
President, Cambridge Communications, 1992–1996
Candidate, U.S. Senate, 1992 (unsuccessful)

Career (*cont.*): Lieutenant governor, Arkansas, 1993–1996
 Governor, Arkansas, 1996–2007
 Chairman, National Governors Association, 2005–2006
 Presidential candidate, 2007–present

The Other Man from Hope

Mike Huckabee shares some fundamental similarities with Bill Clinton. They were both born in the small town of Hope, Arkansas, and participated in the Boys' State citizenship program as high school students. Both served for more than a decade as governor of Arkansas.

But Huckabee is utterly different from Clinton, both in temperament and in philosophy. Huckabee is calm and demure, a former pastor with an earnest, folksy manner and a humble, grounded approach to life. Politically, he is a socially conservative Republican, who is staunchly pro-gun rights and prolife. He is an outspoken opponent of stem cell research and gay marriage, and he dismisses evolutionary theory in favor of creationism.

Huckabee has said of President Clinton, "We're dramatically different, in lifestyle, etc. But I don't hate this man. Whether you liked him or not, give him credit for being a kid who came out of a dysfunctional family and an obscure town to become president. Don't take that away from him, because if you do, you take that away from every kid who grew up on the other side of the tracks. I want that kid to grow up, saying, 'By golly, I'm going to be president, I'm going to be a Ph.D., I'm going to be a nuclear physicist.' "

Huckabee served as lieutenant governor of Arkansas from 1993 to 1996, and replaced Bill Clinton's successor, Democratic governor Jim Guy Tucker, after Tucker was convicted for Whitewater-related offenses and resigned. Huckabee was elected to the job in 1998 and served two terms. While in office, he increased spending and raised taxes, including on gas and cigarettes, but also signed several tax cuts into law, eliminating the marriage tax, cutting the capital gains tax, and doubling the child care tax credit. He describes himself as a fiscal conservative, although some watchdog groups have challenged that characterization. He visited the Middle East in 2006, and went to Iraq during the war to observe the situation and speak to military officials firsthand. During his tenure he got a reputation for being rather thin-skinned, and was self-conscious about his modest means; he bristled at negative press, and was defensive when he was criticized for accepting allegedly improper gifts from friends and patrons.

As a presidential candidate, Huckabee has supported President Bush's policies in Iraq, including the influx of additional troops in 2007, and has made the war against Islamic fascism a high priority. He believes in energy independence; advocates replacing the Internal Revenue Service with a national sales tax system; and, like many in his party, supports strong border enforcement to stop illegal immigration, and free-market solutions to the health care crisis. He is a fan of charter schools and arts education. He also has a populist streak, and warns that Republicans risk ruination if they are seen as the "party of plutocrats."

Huckabee grew up in Hope with his parents and older sister; his father was a fireman and his mother an office manager. He married Louisiana-born, Hope-raised Janet McCain in 1974. She was diagnosed with spinal cancer shortly after they wed, but recovered fully, and they now have three grown children. She is an unaffected, energetic person with a daring streak who has nevertheless chosen to keep a low profile on the presidential campaign trail.

Huckabee spent his early career in radio and television production and in public relations, working at the same time with

Christian organizations and serving as a pastor. In 1983 he started a Christian television network, ACTS, in Arkansas, and in 1989 headed the Arkansas Baptist State Convention, a complicated enterprise that required him to use his political instincts to bring about cooperation and harmony. He decided to change course and embark on a career in politics, running unsuccessfully for the U.S. Senate in 1992 against Democrat incumbent and former Arkansas governor Dale Bumpers. The next year, a grassroots effort in a special election won him the lieutenant governor position, making him only the second Republican to hold the job since Reconstruction.

In 2003, Mike Huckabee, morbidly overweight, was diagnosed with adult-onset diabetes. He went on a diet and began to exercise so regularly and vigorously that he was able to compete in marathons. Eventually he lost more than one hundred pounds. He wrote about his weight loss and plan for sensible habits in his 2005 book *Quit Digging Your Grave with a Knife and Fork*, and has become one of politics' leading spokespersons on living a healthy life.

Why He Has a Chance

Huckabee has stood out in the Republican presidential debates of 2007 with his engaging demeanor, his quick humor, his softspoken pragmatism, and his unapologetic confidence in his views. He developed an interest in radio at age fourteen, studied speech, drama, and debate in college, and honed his oratorical skills working in radio and television and as a pastor. As a result, he has a smooth cadence, a way with a one-liner, an ability to entertain listeners and deliver his message, and a savvy understanding of the media. These are great assets for a presidential candidate. Also, he comes across as a nice, bright, likable man, and many political observers and members of the press have taken to rooting for him.

He had a strong showing in August 2007's Iowa Republican

Party straw poll without spending much campaign money on the effort, which demonstrated his gentle charisma and grassroots appeal. Even before that, people from both parties were impressed with his campaign appearances and growing popular support. In a field of Republicans with convoluted backgrounds and positions, Huckabee's solid conservative record and values could attract the party base and religious voters searching for a like-minded candidate. His advocacy for a national sales tax to replace much of the existing system inspires strong interest.

If nominated, he could rally the half of America who voted for George W. Bush in 2004, securing the Red states portion of the Electoral College, while winning over a few Blue states fans with his homey integrity and friendly disposition.

Governors and former governors have done well in presidential politics, as have southerners. Huckabee's ability to both compare and contrast himself to Bill Clinton intrigues Democrats and Republicans alike.

Huckabee Facts and Stories

– He was student body president at Hope High School.

– At Ouachita Baptist University he took a heavy course load and attended summer school classes, allowing him to graduate magna cum laude in just over two years.

– His children, John Mark, David, and Sarah, went to public schools.

– He enjoys music and plays bass in a rock 'n' roll band called Capitol Offense. His favorite artists include John Mellancamp, the Rolling Stones, the Beatles, Led Zeppelin, the Who, and R&B singer Eddie Floyd. He told *People* magazine that when jogging, "I need a hard-driving guitar with a heavy beat to keep me in rhythm and in step."

– He likes to tell jokes and puns, and do celebrity impressions.

– He is an early riser, often waking at 4:30 A.M.

– The Huckabees live with their three dogs Jet, Sonic, and Toby in their North Little Rock home.

About Huckabee

"Mike's not afraid. He can go up against the big boys, with all the pressure, good talent, and better funding the other team has, with all the pressure in the world, and he does a great job. You can't scare him off, you can't shake him up. He's a constant."

—friend and political aide Jonathan Barnett

"[Huckabee] had this dual interest in the broad field of public affairs, as well as taking his Christian faith very seriously . . . The image of Mike as a preacher in politics is too narrow. It does not do him justice." —Dr. Dan Grant, president emeritus of Ouachita Baptist University

Read More About Huckabee

Mike Huckabee, *From Hope to Higher Ground: 12 Stops to Restoring America's Greatness* (New York: Center Street, 2007). An analysis of the nation's problems and how to remain optimistic and productive.

http://www.mikehuckabee.com/

RON PAUL

The Basics

Name: Ronald Ernest Paul

Born: August 20, 1935,
Pittsburgh, Pennsylvania

Political party: Republican

Spouse: Carol Wells Paul,
married February 1, 1957

Children: Ronnie, Lori, Rand,
Robert, Joy

Religion: Baptist

Education: Gettysburg College, B.S.,
1957

Duke University School of Medicine,
M.D., 1961

University of Pittsburgh Medical
School, residency, 1961–1963

Career: Flight surgeon, U.S. Air Force,
1963–1965

Member, U.S. Air National Guard,
1965–1968

Obstetrician/gynecologist, Texas,
1968–1976

U.S. congressman, Texas 1976–1977

U.S. congressman, Texas 1979–1985

Candidate, U.S. Senate, 1984
(unsuccessful)

Obstetrician/gynecologist, Texas,
1985–1996

Presidential candidate, Libertarian
Party, 1988 (unsuccessful)

Career (*cont.*): United States Congressman, Texas, 1997–present
  Presidential candidate, 2007–present

The Doctor Is In

Ron Paul has been a milkman, served ten terms in Congress, delivered more than four thousand babies as an obstetrician, ran for president in 1988 as a member of the Libertarian Party, and launched his 2008 presidential campaign as an outspoken, antiwar, nonconformist Republican who believes in a strict reading of the Constitution and minimal federal government. He is one part Ross Perot, one part Marcus Welby, and one part Jimmy Stewart in *Mr. Smith Goes to Washington*.

Paul was raised and educated in Pennsylvania before attending medical school at Duke University; he returned to his home state for his residency. He was stationed in Brazoria County, Texas, while in the air force, and settled there in 1968 with his wife, Carol, after his service ended. He opened his own local practice as the resident obstetrician (refusing to accept Medicare or Medicaid from his patients), and studied economics in his spare time. He was particularly influenced by the Austrian economist Ludwig von Mises, a proponent of free markets and libertarian ideals. Paul made an unsuccessful try for Congress in 1974, but won a special election in April 1976; he lost the job that November but won it back in 1978. In 1984 he left the seat (later occupied by Tom DeLay) to run for the U.S. Senate, but was defeated by Phil Gramm and went back to medicine. In 1987 he joined the Libertarian Party, and in 1988 ran for president on their ticket, coming in third and winning more than 430,000 votes. After a decade more in private medical practice, he returned to the House, representing the 14th District in Texas as a Republican.

As a congressman, Paul has remained a staunchly independent thinker, dubbed "Dr. No" by his colleagues for often refusing to back legislation with near-unanimous Republican support. As he explained, "I interpret through the eyes of the Constitution. If we don't have direct authorization, I don't vote for it, even if there are good intentions." Although many of his Texas constituents often disagree with his politics and obdurate approach to legislation, they appreciate his personal commitment to the job and his diligent work on their behalf.

Paul's record is difficult to categorize. He has voted against the Patriot Act and NATO. He would like to do away with the Internal Revenue Service. His antiabortion stance dates back to the 1960s, when he saw a late-term abortion performed, and was solidified as an OB/GYN doctor delivering babies.

He has been an outspoken critic of the Iraq War and, alone among Republican presidential candidates, has called for an immediate withdrawal of American troops from the conflict. He blames the Bush administration's so-called neocons Dick Cheney, Paul Wolfowitz, and Richard Perle for the war's conception, and has risked censure for his controversial statements attributing 9/11 in part to U.S. military activity in the Middle East. Indeed, it was his comment during a May 2007 Republican debate—"Have you ever read the reasons they attacked us? They attack us because we've been over there; we've been bombing Iraq for ten years"—that put him squarely on the 2008 campaign map, raised his name recognition, and won him fans for his guts and frankness. Beyond his objection to the war in Iraq, he opposes most American military intervention worldwide.

Paul also follows the codes he hopes to apply to the federal government. His Web site boasts: "[Paul] does not participate in the lucrative congressional pension program," "he returns a portion of his annual congressional office budget to the U.S. Treasury every year," "he has never taken a government-paid junket," and "he has never voted to increase the power of the executive branch." If Paul wins the presidency, the office's existing powers will no doubt be sufficient for his needs.

Why He Has a Chance

He has an original platform, following his own beliefs rather than a formal Republican structure—or any structure at all, it sometimes seems. Beyond his vehement opposition to the war in Iraq, he is opposed to a constitutional amendment banning gay marriage, is prolife, and advocates tax cuts and a radical reduction in the size of the federal government. As a result, he sounds alternatively like a Republican, a Democrat, and a Libertarian. In a polarized nation, this could be seen as a refreshing change of pace. Many of his positions represent the views of tens of millions of Americans, and yet are not held by anyone else running for the presidency, opening up the prospect that Paul could pick up new adherents with his grab bag of positions, adding fresh supporters to his existing hard-core devotees.

During his current presidential campaign, he has enjoyed a grassroots groundswell, with Internet bloggers, C-SPAN viewers, and talk radio callers extolling his virtues and praising his forceful, idiosyncratic debate performances. He is intensely popular among young people and therefore has a huge Web presence—a Google search for Paul's name turns up thousands of MySpace pages, blogs, and fan sites, while searches for other presidential candidates result primarily in mainstream newspaper stories and government sites. Paul, in part due to his Internet power, has outpaced many of his rival candidates in raising campaign funds. As he sees his path to the nomination, "The bunching together of all the primaries is very antidemocratic. It is out to get the people that could build grass-roots support, like myself. You know, do well in New Hampshire, do well in the next one, and build some momentum. But you know the one way that might backfire? What if five of them split up the vote and there's no clear-cut winner? And then the minor states that come later on, maybe they will be up for grabs. And that would put us in a good position, because we can campaign in the small states."

Despite his intractable adherence to his own set of political viewpoints and personal values, he is admired by many of his congressional colleagues, who praise his devotion to principle and his equable, earthy style. If he gets the nomination, he could be hailed by Washington, by open-minded American citizens, and by the jaded press as a breath of fresh—if quirky—air.

Paul Facts and Stories

– Paul is the son of Pennsylvania dairy farmers Howard and Margaret Paul. The family lived in the town of Green Tree near Pittsburgh, and Paul was the third of five sons.

– Paul's parents were Lutheran, his children were baptized in the Episcopal Church, and he is a Baptist.

– As a youth, Paul delivered newspapers and milk, and played a variety of sports in school. He excelled at track in particular. He also headed the student council.

– He has been a distinguished counselor to the Ludwig von Mises Institute, a libertarian academic organization. He keeps a photograph of the Austrian economist on his office wall.

– He is a member of a group of conservative Republicans called the Liberty Caucus. He lunches weekly with his fellow Washington members to discuss ideas, such as ways to end the Iraq War.

– Ron and Carol Paul have at last count, three sons, two daughters, eighteen grandchildren, and a great-grandchild. He paid for the education of all five of his children, graduate school included.

– His personal finances are largely invested in silver and gold, and total between $1.5 million and $3.5 million.

– He and his wife reside in Lake Jackson, Texas. He lists his home address and phone number on his campaign Web site.

About Paul

"Ron Paul is a very charismatic person. He has charm. He does not alter his position ever. His ideals are high. If a little old man calls up from the farm and says, 'I need a wheelchair,' he'll get the damn wheelchair for him."

—Tim Delaney, editorial page editor of the *Victoria Advocate*, a Texas newspaper in Paul's district

Read More About Paul

Ron Paul, *A Foreign Policy of Freedom* (Lake Jackson, Texas: Foundtion for Rational Economics and Education, 2007).

http://www.ronpaul2008.com/

PART II: **THE DEMOCRATS**

HILLARY CLINTON

The Basics

Name: Hillary Diane Rodham Clinton

Born: October 26, 1947,
Chicago, Illinois

Political party: Democrat

Spouse: William Jefferson Clinton,
married October 11, 1975

Child: Chelsea Victoria

Religion: Methodist

Education: Wellesley College, B.A.,
1969
Yale Law School, J.D., 1973

Career: Staff lawyer, Children's Defense
Fund, Cambridge, Massachusetts,
and Washington, D.C., 1973–1974
Counsel, Nixon impeachment
inquiry staff, House Judiciary
Committee, Washington, D.C.,
1974
Director, Legal Aid clinic, University
of Arkansas School of Law, 1974–1977
Lawyer, Rose law firm, Little Rock,
Arkansas, 1977–1980
First Lady, Arkansas, 1978–1980
Assistant professor, University
of Arkansas School of Law,
1979–1980
Partner, Rose law firm, Little Rock,
Arkansas, 1980–1992

Career (cont.): First Lady, Arkansas, 1982–1992

First Lady, United States, 1993–2001

Head, presidential task force on health care reform, 1993

U.S. senator, New York, 2001–present

Presidential candidate, 2007–present

IRAQ WAR

High Priority? ☑ *Yes* ☐ *No* ☐ *Maybe*

Record/Position: Has said if the war in Iraq is still going on in January 2009, she would move to end it through the efficient withdrawal of U.S. troops over time. Says a small force of American troops must remain in Iraq to perform a more limited mission. Voted to authorize the war originally, but says President Bush misused the authority he was given.

Quote: "Since the election of 2006, the Democrats have tried repeatedly to win Republican support with a simple proposition that we need to set a timeline to begin bringing our troops home now . . . There is no military solution, and the Iraqis refuse to pursue the political solutions."

WAR ON TERROR

High Priority? ☑ *Yes* ☐ *No* ☐ *Maybe*

Record/Position: As a senator from New York, has been a champion of additional spending on homeland security and a supporter of aggressive efforts around the world to capture and kill terrorists.

Quote: "The current security policy—with its excessive reliance on unilateral force, its rejection of international agreements of all kinds, and its preference for policy-making based on ideology, not evidence—has to change."

GOVERNMENT SPENDING/DEFICITS

High Priority? ☐ *Yes* ☐ *No* ☑ *Maybe*

Record/Position: Has not made macro deficit reduction a major goal, but has called for various cost-cutting measures, including limiting no-bid government contracts, posting all contracts online, eliminating 500,000 government contractors, publishing budgets for all government agencies, limiting so-called corporate welfare, and making more rigorous efforts to track government inefficiencies.

Quote: "[During the Clinton administration,] we had a balanced budget and a surplus in America. All of that was squandered by the Bush administration. There's nothing conservative about squandering a budget that was in surplus."

ENERGY/ENVIRONMENT

High Priority? ☑ *Yes* ☐ *No* ☐ *Maybe*

Record/Position: Believes global warming is an urgent problem. Proposes a strategic energy fund paid for by oil-company profits to develop and deploy alternative energy sources. Suggests public and private investments in "green-collar jobs" to help the economy and reduce reliance on fossil fuels.

Quote: "The Bush administration has reversed decades of bipartisan consensus and progress on the environment by using executive action to weaken environmental safeguards in clean-air laws, clean-water laws, and laws protecting our public lands."

HEALTH CARE

High Priority? ☑ *Yes* ☐ *No* ☐ *Maybe*

Record/Position: Failed to advance a 1993 effort by her husband to pass universal health care, but says she deserves credit for the effort and as president would work for a coalition to overcome resistant vested interests—such as insurance companies, drug companies, hospitals, and doctors. Wants to phase in universal coverage by the end of a second term, which she believes requires a mandate that individuals obtain insurance.

Quote: "Few issues touch all of our lives more closely or cause us more anxiety than health care. While Americans receive some of the best care in the world, unfortunately our health care system has some serious flaws . . . Clearly, we must address these problems so that we can strengthen our health care system and prevent it from collapse."

TAXES

High Priority? ☐ *Yes* ☐ *No* ☑ *Maybe*

Record/Position: Proposes letting the Bush income tax cuts that benefit the wealthiest Americans making more than $250,000, expire in 2010 and raising taxes on private equity and hedge fund managers. Strong advocate of fixing the impact of the Alternative Minimum Tax. Has not been specific on her views of overall taxation levels.

Quote: "I'll tell you something that we are going to have to deal with, the Alternative Minimum Tax, which falls heavily on a lot of . . . families. For six years I've been saying, with all due respect, do the billionaires in America need more tax cuts? Don't you think we ought to cut the taxes of middle-income people?"

JOBS/ECONOMY/TRADE/AGRICULTURE

High Priority? ☑ *Yes* ☐ *No* ☐ *Maybe*

Record/Position: Supports an increase in minimum wage, loan programs for small business development, and some limits on trade agreements.

Quote: "The economic policies of the last six years have contributed to an erosion of U.S. economic sovereignty and have made us more dependent on the economic decisions of other nations . . . We need to take steps to restore fiscal responsibility and sound economic policies based on the facts, not ideology."

ABORTION

High Priority? ☑ *Yes* ☐ *No* ☐ *Maybe*

Record/Position: A staunch supporter of abortion rights. Would seek Supreme Court nominees who support *Roe v. Wade*. In favor of insurance coverage and government funding for abortions. Believes there is "an opportunity for people of good faith to find common ground in this debate." Advocates government efforts to minimize the number of abortions through better sex education and improved access to birth control. Has praised religious groups for promoting abstinence.

Quote: "I strongly believe that every child should be wanted, cherished, and loved. For more than a decade I have worked to reduce the number of unintended pregnancies, especially teen pregnancies."

EDUCATION

High Priority? ☑ *Yes* ☐ *No* ☐ *Maybe*

Record/Position: Supports an expansion of early childhood education, more charter and technical schools, extending the school year, and more widely available student loans.

Quote: "We are really depriving the majority of our kids who will never go to college from a chance to have the skills and the training that they need to get a job that will be competitive in the global economy."

STEM CELL RESEARCH

High Priority? ☑ *Yes* ☐ *No* ☐ *Maybe*

Record/Position: Strong supporter of stem cell research and a co-sponsor of the Stem Cell Research Enhancement Act of 2005, allowing federal financing of research on new embryonic stem cell lines derived from discarded human embryos originally created for fertility treatments. The legislation was vetoed by President Bush.

Quote: "Stem cell research holds the promise of new cures and treatments for countless diseases and millions of Americans with chronic and curable conditions . . . This is a delicate balancing act. I recognize that and acknowledge it. I respect my friends on the other side of the aisle who come to the floor with grave doubts and concerns."

GAY RIGHTS

High Priority? ☐ *Yes* ☐ *No* ☑ *Maybe*

Record/Position: Supports civil unions with full domestic partnership benefits. Wants don't-ask-don't-tell overturned so military eligibility is based on conduct, not sexual orientation. In favor of expanding the definition of "hate crime" to include acts against gays. Opposes gay marriage and a constitutional amendment to ban it, but supports the partial repeal of the Defense of Marriage Act.

Quote: "I believe in full equality of benefits, nothing left out. From my perspective there is a greater likelihood of us getting to that point in civil unions or domestic partnerships and that is my very considered assessment."

GUN RIGHTS

High Priority? ☐ *Yes* ☑ *No* ☐ *Maybe*

Record/Position: Has supported limits and regulations on handguns and assault weapons, as well as background checks.

Quote: "We need to stand firm on behalf of sensible gun control legislation. We have to enact laws that will keep guns out of the hands of children and criminals and mentally unbalanced persons . . . I realize the NRA is a formidable political group; but I believe the American people are ready to come together as a nation and do whatever it takes to keep guns away from people who shouldn't have them."

WELFARE/POVERTY

High Priority? ☑ *Yes* ☐ *No* ☐ *Maybe*

Record/Position: Has long championed programs in Arkansas and around the country to lift people out of poverty, with a focus on helping children. Supported her husband's efforts at welfare reform, including work requirements, in part because they came with increased funding for training, child care, and transportation spending. Supports increasing the minimum wage.

Quote: "It is unacceptable that Americans working full-time are living in poverty . . . We should tie the minimum wage to congressional pay raises."

IMMIGRATION

High Priority? ☐ *Yes* ☐ *No* ☑ *Maybe*

Record/Position: Favors comprehensive immigration reform, with a path to legal status for undocumented workers and increased border enforcement.

Quote: "I believe the Bush administration is failing to meet what should
be the basic requirements of immigration policy: continuing our
American tradition of welcoming immigrants who follow the rules
and are trying to build a better life for their families, while strengthening national security in a post-9/11 world."

For all current issue positions, check out http://www.hillaryclinton.com/
issues/.

All About Hillary

*Hillary Clinton. The Golden Girl. The cover girl, the girl next door, the
girl on the moon. Time has been good to her. Life goes where she goes—
she's been profiled, covered, revealed, reported, what she eats and what
she wears, and whom she knows and where she was, and when and
where she's going. Hillary. You all know all about Hillary . . . what can
there be to know that you don't know?*

With apologies to the classic film *All About Eve*, which inspired the
above passage, what can there be to know about Hillary Rodham
Clinton that you don't know? She is the most famous woman in
America (with competition on that front only from Oprah Winfrey). She is an icon, a heroine, a target, a villain, a punch line, a
symbol. She is the country's first truly credible female presidential
candidate, with a strong record of bipartisan cooperation and aggressive leadership since joining the Senate in January 2001. She
can also claim an exceptional decades-long career in public service,
most prominently her eight-year tenure as First Lady in the Clinton
White House. She has touted her experience as the chief selling
point of her candidacy.

Yet her solid résumé and abiding authority can be overshadowed by her capacity to inspire discord; she is perhaps the most
polarizing politician in America, after George W. Bush. Some in

the country—politicians, pundits, and the general public alike— despise her, no matter what she says or does, in government or out of it. Her Senate career has been punctuated by significant and sound bipartisan legislation. She has worked with Republican colleagues on the far right, including some who openly condemned her husband during his presidency. As a presidential candidate, she has chosen to incorporate more partisan invective into her rhetoric. Rather than regularly highlighting her record in the Senate and her efforts at compromise and competence, she has tried to connect with Democratic voters and to cater to the base by attacking the Bush administration, especially its policies on the Iraq War. These displays of partisanship have sowed more doubts about Clinton's ability to win a general election, or be a unifying figure in the White House. She also regularly reminisces about what she promotes as the zenith of recent presidencies, that of her husband.

Bill Clinton is her greatest strength and her greatest weakness. He also is her most important adviser, and he has helped craft and drive her campaign. But Senator Clinton cannot match one of her husband's chief advantages—his sheer skill as a politician. Additionally, she does not seem to enjoy the campaign process. She relishes the work once in office, but getting there is a chore. On the trail, she can appear tense, stressed, and defensive. Unlike Bill Clinton, who lights up in large Iowa crowds, beams in small New Hampshire diners, chats animatedly at private fund-raisers in New York and Hollywood, and captivates the cameras wherever he goes, Hillary Clinton has a rather hunted, deliberate air, stamped by forced humor and taut gravity. Policy is serious business, and the political game is the means to an end. To be sure, Clinton appreciates touring the country, meeting voters, gleaning ideas. But it tires her out, and she seems relaxed and cheerful only in the immediate wake of particularly strong poll numbers or a good debate performance. While politicians such as Bill Clinton find joy in the journey, Hillary Clinton merely anticipates—and battles for—the arrival.

Maybe Senator Clinton could benefit from a joke. Here is one that circulated during her husband's administration:

> Bill and Hillary Clinton are driving through Hillary's childhood town of Park Ridge, Illinois, when they stop for gas. The gas station attendant introduces himself as Hillary's high school boyfriend, whom she once considered marrying. As the Clintons drive away, Bill remarks, "If you had married him, you'd be the wife of a gas station attendant." Hillary replies, "If I had married him, he would be the president of the United States."

Not surprisingly, fans interpret that joke as an amusing reminder of her abundant natural ability and principled focus, while foes see it as creepy evidence of her power-hungry narcissism. You all know all about Hillary. You probably have heard that joke before, and have made your own assessment. But put aside the clichés and the caricatures, and instead analyze what a President Hillary Rodham Clinton might actually be like.

The Village

Hillary Clinton's life has been chronicled in dozens of books, hundreds of magazine cover stories, and thousands of newspaper articles. She uses her middle-class Americana background to buttress her campaign message. She was born in Chicago and lived there until she was three, when her father, Hugh Ellsworth Rodham, a drapery fabric businessman, moved his family to the cozy suburb of Park Ridge. Her mother, Dorothy, a homemaker, looked after Hillary and her younger brothers, Hugh and Tony.

Hillary Rodham was a jovial, hardworking student who took a diverse range of courses, was a Brownie, a Girl Scout, and a Goldwater Girl (the Rodhams were Republicans), and was a member of the debating team, the student council, and the National Honor Society. She also was active in programs at her church. Her mother was a Sunday school teacher, and Hillary was inspired by her youth minister, the Reverend Donald Jones, who focused on a "faith in action" philosophy and on the societal as well as the spiritual. He brought his white suburban charges into contact with minority teenagers and immigrant workers in Chicago, and, in 1962, when Hillary Rodham was fourteen, took her to hear Martin Luther King Jr. give a speech, which Clinton has described as one of the most significant experiences of her youth. Clinton's faith, established by her traditional upbringing and fostered by her community, remains an important part of her life today, and she credits it with helping her get through her very public marital woes and professional challenges.

> As a child, she hoped to be an astronaut (when she contacted NASA, she was told women were not eligible).

She went to Wellesley College in Massachusetts, one of the prestigious Seven Sisters women's colleges. As an undergraduate, she studied political science and psychology (both wise choices, considering her future), and was influenced by the turmoil of the 1960s as they swirled around her liberal arts school. She emerged as a natural leader and her politics changed from Republican (she headed the Young Republicans her freshman year) to Democrat. She protested the Vietnam War, campaigned for presidential hopeful Eugene McCarthy, was an active campus voice, and headed the

Wellesley College student government. As valedictorian, she was selected to be the school's first student commencement speaker. She told her fellow graduates, mixing 1960s idealism and her future worldview, "There's that mutuality of respect between people where you don't see people as percentage points. Where you don't manipulate people. Where you're not interested in social engineering for people . . . We're not in the positions yet of leadership and power, but we do have that indispensable task of criticizing and constructive protest."

Continuing her political path, she went to Yale Law School, and during her first year, met two people who greatly influenced her life—future husband Bill Clinton (Senator Clinton has recounted innumerable times her coy introduction in the campus library: "If you're going to keep staring at me and I'm going to keep staring back, we ought to at least know each other's name") and Children's Defense Fund founder Marian Wright Edelman. After hearing Edelman speak, Clinton realized "right away that I had to go to work for her," and interned at the organization the following summer, in 1970. Clinton frequently reminds the public of her long history working for the rights of children, which was spurred by her high school forays in public service and continued in earnest at Yale. She also interned at Yale–New Haven Hospital working on a legal system to report child abuse, and joined Edelman's group as a staff attorney when she graduated from law

> Clinton's senior thesis at Wellesley was about community organizer Saul Alinsky. She was featured in a 1969 issue of *Life* magazine after receiving kudos for her Wellesley commencement speech.

school. Over the years, Senator Clinton has served on innumerable panels and boards related to the issue of children's rights, written about the topic in her 1996 best seller *It Takes a Village*, and has made it a priority in her platform.

In 1974, the dean of Yale Law School, Burke Marshall, recommended her for the House Judiciary Committee's impeachment legal staff. She worked on the Nixon Watergate hearings and became close with Bernard Nussbaum, who was a top committee staff lawyer and another key influence for young Hillary Rodham. He has since recalled quibbling with Rodham after she insisted her then boyfriend Bill was "going to be president of the United States." Nussbaum would serve, with mixed results, as White House counsel in the Clinton administration. Hillary Clinton's experience during Watergate gave her a taste of heavyweight Washington politics. It imbued her with a sense of moral righteousness and a suspicion that the right was prone to the conspiratorial misuse of power.

Later in 1974, she moved with Bill Clinton to his home state of Arkansas, where they married in 1975 and set up house; she retained "Rodham" as her last name. They both taught at the University of Arkansas Law School in Fayetteville, where she helped establish the school's Legal Aid program. They relocated to Little Rock when Bill Clinton was elected attorney general in 1976 (he previously ran unsuccessfully for a congressional seat), and stayed on there when he became governor of Arkansas in 1978. He lost reelection two years later, but won back the job in 1982 and kept it until he became president. It was during the 1982 campaign that, bending to the wishes of voters, she gussied up her rather dowdy appearance and added "Clinton" to her name. Throughout the next decade, Bill Clinton was required to defend his job every two years, and Hillary Clinton actively campaigned for him, straining to learn the art of retail politics. As she once said of the constant campaign cycles, "We sort of feel like combat veterans."

As wife of the governor of Arkansas, Hillary Clinton had two functions. The first was to perform the customary duties of First Lady—dinners, galas, fairs, festivals, pageants, mansion tours—all while raising daughter Chelsea, who was born in February 1980. The second was earning a salary large enough to support the family—Bill Clinton received a paltry $35,000 annual wage from the state. Presumably because of this financial pressure, she left full-time advocacy work to join the Rose law firm in Little Rock (the oldest firm west of the Mississippi River), becoming its first female partner in 1980, and accepted lucrative board memberships at such Arkansas-based corporations as Wal-Mart and TCBY. Nevertheless, she continued to be a visible presence in the nonprofit community for children's rights, chairing the board of the Children's Defense Fund from 1986 through 1992, and working on local projects such as the Arkansas Educational Standards Committee.

When Bill Clinton ran for president in 1991, many observers commented that his wife was equally impressive. They pointed to her legal credentials and public policy

> *"I like having a role as a private citizen making a public contribution, and I'm really lucky my husband is the kind of man and governor who wants to involve me in his work, and I'm really pleased that I can help do what he's basically trying to do, and that's provide a better future for the state."*
> —on her years as first lady of Arkansas

215

participation, her academic accomplishments and professional prowess, and the Clintons' combined involvement in a national effort to remake the Democratic Party. Occasionally, in public, she would tip her hand and reveal just how deeply she was steeped in the details of politics and campaigns, but she mostly kept it a closely guarded secret that she could exhibit the soul, instincts, and ethos of a Chicago pol.

Early on in his presidential effort, Bill Clinton heralded his wife's two-for-the-price-of-one appeal. That fell very flat. Voters don't like to have a spouse shoved into their ballot box, no matter how accomplished she may be. Hillary Clinton spent the 1992 campaign defending her troubled marriage, her perceived uppity comments (she famously said during a flap over her legal work, "You know, I suppose I could have stayed home and baked cookies and had teas, but what I decided to do was fulfill my profession, which I entered before my husband was in public life"), and her hairstyle (blond, in a headband, but at one time mouse-brown and curly). She was the subject of apprehensive editorials, and she endured dismissive and even vicious comments from prominent Republicans. Political commentator and former presidential candidate Pat Buchanan directly assailed Hillary Clinton during his speech at the 1992 Republican National Convention, declaring, "Elect me and you get two for the price of one, Mr. Clinton says of his lawyer-spouse. And what does Hillary believe? Well, Hillary believes that twelve-year-olds should have the right to sue their parents, and Hillary has compared marriage and the family as institutions to slavery—and life on an Indian reservation. Well, speak for yourself, Hillary. This, my friends, this is radical feminism." And Richard Nixon told *Time* magazine, "Hillary pounds the piano so hard that Bill can't be heard. You want a wife who's intelligent, but not too intelligent."

Hillary Clinton took the blows, and stood by her man in the

face of allegations of adultery, effectively salvaging his up-and-down campaign. After the election, she was a key participant in the creation of the Clinton cabinet, along with her husband, Al Gore, and transition director Warren Christopher. By inauguration day, she already was planning her first major White House project—overseeing health care reform.

The East Wing

When Hillary and Bill Clinton moved into the White House in 1993, she chose an office in the West Wing, where presidential business gets done, rather than in the East Wing, where First Ladies traditionally set up shop, with social secretaries and assistants on hand to organize state dinners, welcome foreign dignitaries and domestic high school students, and pursue charitable tasks. Hillary Clinton's office (which notably would be inherited by George W. Bush's master strategist Karl Rove) instantly became the center of the effort for health care reform. On January 22, 1993, the day after the inauguration, the *Wall Street Journal* appraised her appointment by observing, "It may well be that the time has come to rethink the First Lady model that we've lived with for some 200 years . . . Deciphering the health care puzzle is a serious, complex job . . . If Mrs. Clinton is going to revise the way we think about First Ladies, better it should be in an assignment like this, as a public equal of her administration peers, than as a figure in the shadows."

Hillary Clinton's effort to spearhead health care reform was a complete disaster, collapsing in September 1994, and forcing her to concentrate on more traditional First Lady duties for the remainder of Bill Clinton's presidency. Beyond the health care fiasco, Hillary Clinton was intimately involved with many of the administration's early bad decisions, which led to the Democrats' loss of Congress in November 1994. After it was disclosed that she had played a part in several controversies, including the firing of the White House travel office staff, the administration's strategy for dealing with media, and the handling of congressional investigations into alleged wrongdoing, Hillary Clinton became a far different kind of First Lady than she had envisioned.

> *"When you work, work hard. When you play, play hard, and don't confuse the two. It's that sense of believing in something and committing yourself to something. That was one of the great bases of our relationship when we first met."*
> **—on her relationship with her husband**

Privately, she continued to be a highly influential presidential adviser, but publicly she was a more muted policy participant. She spent her time on international travel missions (she gave a well-received speech on women's rights in China and was a proponent of microloans, which enable women around the world to start small businesses), wrote books such as *It Takes a Village* and *Dear Socks, Dear Buddy: Kids' Letters to the First Pets*, appeared on family-friendly magazine covers, and did soft-focus interviews. Despite her retreat, she remained a target, and was constantly on the defensive. She was forced to contend with unrelenting enemies, concerns about her past actions (the Whitewater real estate deal, her involvement in a sweetheart cattle futures arrangement, missing billing records), and her husband's

infidelity and subsequent impeachment scandal. The most enduring images of First Lady Hillary Clinton remain the Pink Press
Conference, her appearance on the *Today* show in 1998 when she
blamed the fallout from the Lewinsky scandal on a "vast, right-wing
conspiracy," and her exit from the grand jury at which she gave testimony (unprecedented for a First Lady)—not to mention her suc-
cession of hairstyles. Her first major coiffure crop made headlines,
with the *New York Times* observing, "The paradox: The more Mrs.
Clinton simplifies her beauty rou-
tine to deflect attention from her
look, the more she draws attention
to it." Her appearance was always
scrutinized but rarely appreciated,
regardless of her undeniably good
looks.

But mingled with the snide cri-
tique was grudging respect for her
grit and a companionable familiarity with her persona, not to mention more than a little sympathy
for all she had endured. Warmer
feelings from the public and press
allowed her to take advantage of an
available Senate seat, with the retirement of New York's Democratic

> She was photographed
> for the December
> 1998 cover of *Vogue*
> magazine. Editor Anna
> Wintour observed,
> "As the year unfolded
> Hillary found this inner
> strength . . . I think she
> psyches herself into this
> battle mode and goes
> forward, not looking
> right or left."

icon Daniel Patrick Moynihan, just as the Clinton administration
was winding down. After careful planning and deliberation, with
dropped hints and a cautious testing of the waters, she went for it,
fully aware that she would have to seize control of her public image
once and for all. Starting in the early summer of 1999, she ran
a smart, prudent, aggressive, and New York–centric race, slough-

ing off the national and international media interest and focusing
on the local papers, the statewide concerns, the individual New
York voters. She cast her campaign as a "listening tour" in which
she was humbly getting to know her adopted homestate, to which
she had no previous ties. Bill Clinton, who carried with him the
cloud of Clinton fatigue after two dramatic terms in office, stayed
under the radar as much as a sitting president who loves a good
campaign could. When her Republican opponent, New York City
mayor Rudy Giuliani, dropped out due to health issues, Clinton's
path to the Senate was cleared. She savored her 55 percent to 43
percent win over Giuliani's replacement, Republican congressman
Rick Lazio, even as the Bush-Gore presidential race went into six
weeks of Florida overtime.

Once in the Senate, Clinton avoided situations that would highlight her celebrity, and behaved with the discreet graciousness of an
ordinary freshman. As she said with self-effacing charm shortly after
her 2000 election, "There are a lot of reasons why you, especially as
a beginning senator, have to sit back and learn. And there is a lot
I have to learn here . . . I'm on another 'listening tour.' " Installed
in her own powerful job, she ran her Senate office with the kind
of diligent care and solid staffing that her husband's White House
lacked. She hired people who were loyal, competent, leak-free, and
discreet, and her office was given high marks for constituent service, both for individuals and for New York State businesses and
organizations. She won over many New York Republicans, including former senator Alfonse D'Amato (who once led a Whitewater
investigation), and the highly partisan congressman Tom Reynolds
of Buffalo, who said, "I like Senator Clinton. I've found that when
she says she will take on a job with me, she does it." She also made
herself regularly accessible to the local New York media, and chose
to engage with the national press sparingly and gingerly, and on her

own terms. If a political opponent or journalist made an offensive move against her, Clinton's political advisers went instantly into "war room" mode to discredit the attackers and the attack. With the help of her team, she avoided controversy and earned a sound reputation as a member of the Senate.

To the Left, to the Right

Conservatives think Hillary Clinton is the scariest politician since Ted Kennedy (to misogynists, she's even scarier). Liberals decry her bipartisan activities and deplore her 2002 vote authorizing military action in Iraq. People on both extremes attack her as unprincipled, ruled by polls, and ruthlessly ambitious. Despite frantic rumors of her extreme radical leftism during the 1990s and a mostly liberal voting record in the Senate, she has often conducted herself as a centrist in philosophy and as bipartisan in practice. Her first years in Congress were diffused in a glow of the friendly remarks of new colleagues, who praised her competence, her professionalism, and her willingness to collaborate to achieve results. This approach mirrored the governing and campaign method of her husband, who regularly sought to realize political business through compromise and concession, even if he did not always succeed.

But as a presidential candidate, Hillary Clinton generally has, so far, abandoned this approach in favor of a political mode that closely resembles George W. Bush's campaign strategy of winning over the party base. She has largely eschewed discussions of potential bipartisan action, instead stirring crowds by attacking the Bush White House and condemning Republican sensibilities. On the stump and at Democratic events, she can be found making statements such as "If you are a hardworking single parent who can't afford health insurance or a small business owner who worries about energy costs or a student who can't afford to continue college, you are invisible to this administration . . . President Bush and the Washington Republicans have looked right through you."

Still, with most members of Congress voting almost uniformly in partisan lockstep with their party, Hillary Clinton is more distinctive for her work with conservative stalwarts such as Tom DeLay, Tom Coburn, John Sununu, Sam Brownback, Rick Santorum, and Trent Lott than for her voting record. The Iraq War, in particular, has forced candidate Clinton to the left in terms of style, and arguably, substance. This makes it difficult to evaluate (or even deduce) what kind of leader Hillary Clinton would be in the White House on the question of partisanship.

Regardless, the notion that Clinton is purely a reflexive liberal is misguided. In many ways she is a centrist in the New Democratic mold of the Democratic Leadership Council, the moderate group that helped her husband win in 1992 and with which she has long been affiliated. She shares her husband's position that abortion should be "safe, legal, and rare" and has taken pains both to emphasize the "rare," and to entreat the prochoice movement to tolerate those who are prolife. As a senator who represents Wall Street and who believes in the power of markets and the private sector, she has never been a champion of broad-based tax increases or (since her health care effort in 1994) a huge expansion of the government's role.

She is no liberal when it comes to foreign policy, either. Within her jurisdiction is the ever-targeted New York City, with its grave Ground Zero reminders, and Clinton is fully aware that the world is a dangerous place and that America has many enemies. She is an aggressive advocate of military, intelligence, and diplomatic efforts to protect the homeland and project strength abroad. Pentagon leaders, both civilian and uniformed, praise Clinton for her work on the Senate's Armed Services Committee, her knowledge of the numerous military facilities in New York state, her 9/11 conduct, and the hours she has logged with Defense Department personnel from the highest levels down to the troops in the field.

Clinton's centrism derives from her midwestern upbringing; her faith; her husband's struggles to be effective in rural, conservative Arkansas; and what she has called her "responsibility gene." Whether genetic or not, Clinton has occasionally ignored the polls and the advice of her political advisers in order to do what she thinks is right, often to the annoyance of the left. That may not be the popular analysis of how Bill and Hillary Clinton make political decisions, but in some instances, it is a practical reality.

Still, she does share her husband's belief that the federal government should take a progressive, activist role in improving the lives of the nation's citizens. In some areas, in fact, she has drifted to the left of the Clinton administration, including on gay rights and trade.

Regarding the chief domestic issue facing the country—health care—Clinton demonstrates both her liberal and moderate instincts. On the one hand, she still thinks the federal government should design, regulate, and pay for the health care of many Americans. On the other, she recognizes the importance of the free market and consumer choice in reform, and considers specifics for any plan less important than establishing a broad government coalition and consensus to address costs, quality, and the availability of insurance and treatment.

Her harshest critics insist she entered politics only because she is power-hungry. Clinton may be personally ambitious and driven, but she sees government work as a public service to better the lives of real people at home and abroad. One can disagree with her specific goals or how she chooses to achieve them, but it would be wrong to disparage her motives overall.

First in Her Class

What is there to know about Hillary Clinton that you don't know? Well, what does she really stand for? What does she fundamentally believe? What is her campaign message? It is a bit difficult to define, it seems, even for Clinton herself. In May 2006, she admitted unapologetically the absence of a thematic message such as her husband's "New Covenant" or George W. Bush's "Compassionate Conservative." As she justified, "I don't think like that. I approach each issue and problem from a perspective of combining my beliefs and ideals with a search for practical solutions. It doesn't perhaps fit in a preexisting box, but many of the problems we face as a nation don't, either." Talking at length about her undefined hopes for the future of America's children, or railing about the Bush administration's domestic misconduct and Iraq War blunders is all well and good, but it is not cohesive, uplifting, or consistently coherent. And in a troubled time, a leader offering a themeless pudding might not be satisfactory—Americans prefer it when presidential candidates have an overarching motif for their campaigns, a rationale for running, a philosophy for the job.

If she doesn't have a message, at least she has finally learned to understand the Freak Show environment of modern media and political culture. In Arkansas and in the White House, she lost control of her public image and allowed herself to be defined as shrewish, harsh, corrupt, and liberal. By 2000, when she ran for the Senate, she had absorbed that hard lesson, and defined herself on her own preferred terms: strong, smart, competent, respected. Her most consistent and ardent refrain on the campaign trail is that she is the candidate of experience, that she knows the rules, the game, the players, and the strategy to be president on January 21, 2009, a message she uses to diminish the candidacies of her chief rivals for the Democratic nomination. To those who say Americans are looking for change, she argues that it takes experience to bring about change as president. As for "liberal," during a July 2007 debate, she refused to apply that word to herself but suggested the term "progressive" instead.

Bill Clinton

William Jefferson Clinton was the forty-second president of the United States. He was also the only president to be impeached during the twentieth century. He is arguably the finest politician of his era, who can draw and inspire crowds; speak with fluid, comprehensive passion, and motivate his party. He also brings with him enough personal baggage to fill the cargo hold of *Air Force One*. But since his White House rollercoaster ride of economic highs and Lewinsky lows, he has redeemed himself to many with his international humanitarian efforts; his best-selling, if selective, autobiography; his sensible and scaled-back contributions to the political dialogue; and his visible restraint in handling his wife's political aspirations. He is currently the most popular figure in the Democratic Party, and polling suggests that he is now well liked and well thought of by more Americans than he was when he left office. His heart-related health scare of a few years ago also served to remind some in the country that, gee, perhaps it is nice to have the guy around, after all.

She received an $8 million book advance for her 2003 memoir *Living History*, and a Grammy for the book's audio version.

It is also nice for Hillary Clinton to have him around, as he is the best political strategist in the Democratic Party (in addition to strategy, he helps with her speeches; she has called him her "editor in chief"). Controversial though he may be, he is a godsend to any Democratic candidate running for office. He attracts audiences and holds them, raises heaps of money, and incites people to get to the polls. Wisely, however, Hillary Clinton chose to keep her distance from him when she ran for the Senate. Her signs ("Hillary!") and banners omitted her last name, and she conducted her "listening tour" alone.

Hillary Clinton's reelection campaign in 2006 was a low-key walk in the park, during which neither Clinton broke a sweat. But Bill Clinton, and the positives he represents, have been placed front and center in her presidential campaign. On the stump, she promises to take the country back to the good times of the 1990s and always praises her husband's White House leadership. Nevertheless, she has addressed, if obliquely, the issue of his fidelity, and has even made light comments about the matter.

Still, if Bill Clinton continues his recent unassailable behavior of engaging in humanitarian works, palling around with fellow redeemed president George H. W. Bush, making a concerted effort not to hog the attention when he is on the campaign trail with his wife, maintaining his good health, and providing a reassuring and rousing visual reminder that having him as the first First Gentleman might be beneficial and festive, he will indisputably be a boon to her campaign.

The Clintons' daughter, Chelsea, has always been an asset to her parents' political careers, even as she has striven to maintain a low profile. She was twelve when her father was first sworn in as president, after she had spent all her sentient years as the child of the Arkansas governor. She famously endured adolescence in the White House spotlight; attended a private school in D.C. to protect her from further exposure; served as a reassuring, stabilizing presence when scandal hit her parents, went across the country to

Stanford University, where she graduated in 2001; and went across the ocean to Oxford, where she got her master's degree. She is now a financial consultant living quietly in Manhattan. Her public appearances are rare but well timed. (She notably sat out the couple's famous *Sopranos* spoof, which remains a YouTube favorite.) Poised, lovely, and impressive, Chelsea Clinton will make herself available if her mother really needs her.

Making History

In an era when women have been chosen to lead countries such as Liberia and India, not to mention Germany and England, it seems high time for America to elect a woman president. Sounds great, now find one. There are, of course, a record number of notable women in political office. Governors Kathleen Sebelius of Kansas and Janet Napolitano of Arizona are considered ones to watch in the Democratic Party; Alaska Republican governor Sarah Palin generates buzz. There are more than a dozen female U.S. senators besides Hillary Clinton, and Nancy Pelosi is Speaker of the House. But only Clinton is currently positioned by fame, stature, and fund-raising ability as a viable candidate for the White House, in the 2008 and 2012 cycles. Her strength as a candidate,

> *"Hillary is the best non-incumbent candidate I've ever had the chance to vote for . . . If you want to restore America's standing in the world, please elect Hillary president."*
> —Bill Clinton

therefore, is even more exciting and historic, and appeals to voters of all ages (young people are more open to the idea, while older people would like to see a woman in the Oval Office during their lifetime); backgrounds (lower-income voters might expect more empathy and attention from a female leader, higher-income voters might have more sophisticated views on gender); races; and parties (plenty of Republicans want a woman elected president, even if she doesn't have an R after her name).

Clinton is well aware of this aspect of her campaign, but she is careful to balance it with hawkish (and stereotypically "masculine") statements about fighting terrorism and dealing with menacing countries such as Iran and North Korea, just in case anyone gets stuck on the clichéd notion of a female in a position of power—emotional, conciliatory, afraid to make tough decisions. She presents herself as a hardened leader, rarely indulges publicly in the type of girly chitchat she once hoped would soften her steely image, and generally does not engage in discussions of gender, no matter how tempting the bait, which shames her rivals into ignoring the issue as well.

On a personal level, she can be callous and harsh, and both chilly and chilling, certainly to her foes, but even, sometimes, to her loyal staff. That same staff, though, along with Clinton's many close friends, insist she is as caring and concerned as anyone they know, offering consolation about a sick parent or cheers on happy occasions with a regularity that would be impressive even if she were not one of the busiest people in the world. Additionally, her Senate and campaign workplaces are exceptionally family-friendly; employees are comfortable bringing in small children or requesting time off for family business. Her core team includes a circle of women who have stuck by her devotedly for years.

Areas of Potential Controversy

– Bill Clinton.

– Scandals galore past and possibly future: billing records, Whitewater, various shadowy controversies that will never fully die, and the potential for any new material investigative reporters or Republican foes can dig up.

– Her 2002 Iraq War vote and subsequent refusal to directly apologize for it.

– Her brothers, Hugh and Tony Rodham. Both have been involved in dubious business dealings, often taking advantage of their sister's connections. During the Clinton administration they tried to exploit their White House ties, such as with an embarrassing scheme involving the exportation of hazelnuts from the former Soviet republic of Georgia. And both Rodhams accepted money from clients in exchange for seeking presidential pardons from their brother-in-law.

Why Clinton Can Win a General Election

- She is Hillary Clinton. No candidate can match near-universal name recognition like that. She can get access to the airwaves and make news whenever she likes.
- Because she is a woman.
- If her historic candidacy can inspire women to turn out—particularly young, unmarried women who have never before voted—she could overwhelm any advantage that the Republican candidate has among men.
- Many voters seem to equate her eight years as First Lady with a readiness to be president. With no incumbent president or vice president running in 2008, Clinton might be seen as the closest thing to an incumbent prepared from day one to assume the awesome responsibilities of the

office. In the post-9/11 era, that could be a significant advantage, particularly if the Republicans nominate someone whose preparedness and experience can be challenged.

- When Senator Clinton first starting thinking about running for president, she followed the campaign blueprint of a certain two-term president: George W. Bush. Bill Clinton is a great politician, but his 1992 campaign and White House years were marked by chaos, infighting, leaking, and miscalculation. Hillary Clinton watched how candidate Bush, with the help of adviser Karl Rove, established a sharply organized and smoothly functioning team; managed to highlight the positive aspects of the presidency and legacy of his father, George H. W. Bush, while minimizing the negative; represented himself as a "compassionate conservative" who could win the general election and unite the country (during his 2000 race, at least—by 2004, the jig was up and he went straight for his base); controlled the Old Media by manipulating the New Media; and emphasized the advantages of front-runner status (expectations, endorsements, poll numbers, and support from the party's political establishment). Hillary Clinton has re-created all of this in her own campaign, insisting on a loyal and harmonious team; presenting Bill Clinton in the best possible light; aggressively responding to negative attacks from both the left and the right, not to mention from Democratic rivals and the press; and exploiting the conventional wisdom that her candidacy is inevitable, which she drapes about her campaign like a velvet mantle.
- Her skin is dragon-hide thick, her opposition research team is speedy and cold-blooded, her responses are polished and prepared, and her focus is unwavering, so she cannot easily be distracted from her goal.

- With a closely divided electorate and the negative views so many Americans already have of her, Clinton likely will have to define the election as a choice between her and the Republican candidate, rather than as a referendum on her own appeal. Clinton has learned to defend herself from attackers on all sides, but also has become accustomed to using opposition research and the politico-media Freak Show to characterize her opponents. In a "choice" election (remember 2004, when an increasingly unpopular George W. Bush was still able to defeat John Kerry), Clinton and her tenacious team could prevail.

- Though there are always fresh revelations about a presidential candidate's past in a general election, Clinton is less susceptible to being damaged by new data. Not only has she already been scrutinized for more than a decade and a half, but also the country feels it knows Hillary Clinton—the good and the bad. New information (unless it is of a particularly shocking or detrimental nature) will likely be absorbed into her familiar persona. For her opponent, about whom less will be known, new disclosures will have more impact and generate more drama.

- Her "listening tour" of New York state was a great success. She impressed residents with her earnest concern and concentration. She already has attempted to enact the idea on a nationwide scale in the nomination season, with Internet text and video messages and a nonstop schedule, and by spending time in places such as Iowa and New Hampshire at smaller, more intimate events where she can have "conversations" with individual voters.

- While she has not dominated the fund-raising sweepstakes as expected, she's no slouch in the cash-generating department. As the nominee, money would cascade into her coffers. New York is big and rich, and she has connections and supporters in Illinois, California, Texas, Florida, and other large states.

- Although she is not the best public speaker in the field (and certainly not in her family), she is a consistently strong television performer. She does not get intimidated or rattled by media questioners, and she moves smoothly from Sunday morning talk shows, to high-voltage press conferences, to *The Late Show with David Letterman*. And she can comport herself well in presidential debates, which may be decisive in 2008.

- She can handle hard work, and she does not have many hobbies. She will not demand undue time to jog, rest, socialize, or vacation. There will be, for example, no wind-surfing or baseball playoffs for Clinton during the 2008 calendar year, unless for a good photo-op.

- Her campaign team includes longtime aides Patti Solis-Doyle, Mark Penn, Harold Ickes, Mandy Grunwald, and Howard Wolfson, who are tough, hardworking, determined, and who know the way to win. And—it is worth repeating—she has the optimum political strategist in the country on her side: Bill Clinton.

Why Clinton Can't Win a General Election

- She is Hillary Clinton. Unlike any other first-time candidate in history, she starts the race with literally tens of millions of voters loathing her and determined to see her lose. There is no more ready-made cure for the diseases afflicting the demoralized Republican Party than Senator Clinton, inspiring Republicans to donate money, volunteer, and turn out to vote, united behind whoever their standard-bearer happens to be.

- Because she is a woman. It is possible that sexism will play a larger role than expected.
- The jaundiced view of her in the South and near West means it would be difficult for her to expand the Electoral College map for her party and put more than a handful of Red states in play. Male Republican voters could turn out against her in larger than usual numbers, creating an unbridgeable gender gap.
- Vast segments of the country want a president who can be a true unifier of more than their party base, and Hillary Clinton will have a difficult time convincing people that she is the (wo)man for that particular job, even if her Senate work suggests otherwise. Polarization has lately become one of the great concerns of the country, and to some, Clinton personifies this problem.
- Clinton Fatigue might be a chronic syndrome (not to mention Bush-Clinton-Bush-Clinton Fatigue).
- She is mistrusted by people on both the left and the right, occasionally based on the same series of events. One example is her posture toward the war in Iraq, starting with her 2002 vote authorizing military action. Some Democrats condemn her initial vote, her refusal to apologize for the vote, and her subsequent votes allowing for additional funding. Republicans complain that she has changed her position on the war since 2003 due to political pressure rather than a genuine shift in perspective. Continually fighting off attacks from both sides is a challenging proposition.
- Clinton doesn't enjoy campaigning, and it shows in her manner and in her voice, which tends to rise a few shrill levels when she is under stress.
- For much of the media, Old and New, nothing Hillary

Clinton does is ever good enough. She moves too fast or too slow. She does too much or too little. She is too liberal or too conservative. For all of her new and improved skill in handling the press, she has never been a media favorite.

- Bill Clinton could do something stupid (or at least spark the rumor machine).

The Best Case for a Clinton Presidency

- Hillary Clinton has learned how to seek centrist compromises from her no-nonsense tenure in the Senate. She could translate that practice to the White House, follow through on the unfinished agenda of the Bush years, and achieve results on the big issues—Iraq, immigration, the complex environment-vs.-energy tradeoffs, a major health care overhaul, tax and Social Security reform.

- She could use her 9/11 credentials as a senator from New York to rebuild a bipartisan consensus about the importance of fighting the war against terror and spending on homeland security, which has been squandered during the Bush years.

- The Clinton name is an asset in many parts of Europe, Africa, and Asia, and she has a great deal of experience meeting with foreign leaders, both from her time as First Lady and as a senator. As she pointed out during a July 2007 debate, "When I was First Lady, I was privileged to represent our country in eighty-two countries. I have met with many officials in Arabic and Muslim countries. I have met with kings and presidents and prime ministers and sheiks and tribal leaders. And certainly, in the last years during my time in the Senate, I have had many high-level meetings with presidents and prime ministers in Iraq, Afghani-

stan, Kuwait, Pakistan, and many other countries." She
would come into office already having personal relationships with many heads of state. Such alliances are vital to
diplomacy and the exercise of American power, and most
new presidents must expend an enormous amount of time
establishing them.

- As for being a woman, she said during the same debate,
"I believe that there isn't much doubt in anyone's mind
that I can be taken seriously . . . other countries have had
women presidents and women prime ministers. There are
several serving now—in Germany, in Chile, in Liberia, and
elsewhere—and I have noticed that their compatriots on
the world stage certainly take them seriously. It would be
quite appropriate to have a woman president deal with the
Arab and Muslim countries on behalf of the United States
of America."

- Hillary Clinton, especially when left to her own devices,
is a serious student and a diligent worker who is anxious
to do a good job. She is well aware of the taints of the Bill
Clinton administration missteps (even those in which she
was directly involved), such as the firing of the travel office, the health care fiasco, Whitewater, and the Ken Starr
investigation. She will try to avoid such calamities at all
cost. Far more disciplined than her husband, she will
likely set her sights on a second term at the get-go, and not
do anything too foolish, ambitious, or power-hungry to
give her enemies extra ammunition.

- Her husband would set off on a multicountry tour to repair damaged international ties, report back on areas of
need, establish new bonds with growing nations, spearhead humanitarian projects, and serve as shining proof

that the role of First Gentleman can be fulfilling, valuable, and respected.

The Worst Case for a Clinton Presidency

- She can be both cautious and stubborn, which could cause gridlock in Congress, tension in her cabinet, and unease in the populace.
- She could find herself completely unable to unite the country, producing four more years of the Bush-Clinton tribal warfare that has divided America into hostile camps.
- As a woman, she might find it frustrating to deal with those foreign leaders who are less inclined to accept gender equality.
- Her husband could embark on a series of scandalous activities that would make front-page news, humiliate and distract her, enfeeble her authority, and torpedo any hope of a second term.

What to Expect If Clinton Is President

- A White House like no other, with a record number of women throughout government. There likely would be an in-house attention to details and issues not generally considered by a male president. The staff would be diligent and proper, conscious of the much-criticized lax approach of the previous Clinton administration. Efforts would also be made to offer a pronounced contrast with Bush administration errors of insularity and complacency. Nevertheless, the air within the West Wing would be one of tension and timidity, with staffers careful not to ruffle Madame President.

- Hillary Clinton would try to build bipartisan coalitions to defeat special-interest gridlock on major issues; success or failure would depend in part on the strength and popularity of her administration.
- Should anything go awry, either in policy decisions or personal scandal, the Internet would double in size and trees would tremble in their roots at the prospect of unprecedented reams of newspaper copy.
- The national fascination with the Clintons would be revived in full force, and with Hillary Clinton in charge, there would be an onslaught of editorials, style articles, and cable television discussions dissecting every tiny detail, from wardrobe, to staff personalities, to decor, to foreign travel decisions, to lipstick choices, to the daily schedule of the First Husband. Hillary Clinton might give the national media one last chance to fall in love with her (but would not foster high expectations); the international press, meanwhile, would bombard her with flowers, candy hearts, and perhaps a few rotten eggs.
- Jeb Bush would instantly become the Republican frontrunner for the 2012 Republican presidential nomination.

Clinton's Own Words

"By and large the legal profession considers children—when it considers them at all—as objects of domestic relations and inheritance laws or as victims of the cycle of neglect, abuse, and delinquency. Yet the law's treatment of children is undergoing great challenge and change. Presumptions about children's capacities are being rebutted: the legal rights of children are being expanded."

—writing in the *Yale Law Journal*, June 1977

"[I would] continue to work for causes and issues I care about, in a setting like a university or foundation."

—on what she would do if she left the political arena

What Her Supporters Say

"I knew that Bill and Hillary were from Yale Law School and as far as I was concerned they were easterners. I was impressed with how bright they were. I remember thinking then that Hillary would make a wonderful lawyer and a wonderful political candidate wherever she ended up practicing law."

—longtime Clinton Arkansas adviser Betsey Wright

"The biggest mistake of the American press is thinking they know her. You know, people think she's such a big lib. I think she's extremely conservative. I think she has more in common with people in upstate New York than in New York City, in a lot of ways . . . [She is] patriotic and practical. She thinks it's important to spend money on social programs, but she wants to know that they work."

—Maggie Williams, Clinton's close friend and former chief of staff

What Her Critics Say

"I have been told about your charm and wit and let me say, the reports on your charm are overstated and the reports on your wit are understated."

—Congressman Dick Armey (R-Texas),
directly to Clinton during her initial testimony to
Congress on her husband's health care proposal in 1993

"We all believe she's wonderful. But we also believe that if she's the nominee, it sets up perfectly for the Republicans to win the

White House for another four years . . . Do we really want to re-hash Whitewater and all the stuff we had before?"

—Dick Harpootlian, former chairman
of the South Carolina Democratic Party

Clinton Facts and Stories

— She planned to spend the summer between college and law school working at a cannery in Alaska. She lasted a week; the dead fish were "purple and black and yucky-looking" and the conditions were unsanitary.

— She and her husband attended different churches when living in Little Rock (she is a Methodist, he a Baptist).

— The December 1984 issue of *Esquire* featured "The Esquire 1984 Registry," which included both Hillary and Bill among 272 under-forties, who represented the fully blooming baby boomer generation. Hillary Clinton was cited for her Ivy League education, her partnership in the Rose law firm, and her heading of the Arkansas Education Standards Committee.

— She was named by the *National Law Journal* as one of the one hundred most influential lawyers in America in both 1988 and 1991.

— Among her numerous accolades include being named one of the most powerful women by *Forbes* magazine and one of *Time* magazine's one hundred most influential people.

— A wax likeness of Clinton can be seen in Madame Tussaud's Wax Museum in New York City.

— The Clinton family pet is Seamus, a chocolate lab.

— The Clintons are driven in Secret Service vehicles but own a Ford hybrid.

— Hillary and Bill Clinton share a home in Chappaqua, New York, purchased in November 1999 just before they left the White House. They also maintain a residence in the exclusive Embassy

Row neighborhood of Washington, D.C., where she stays when in town on Senate and other business.

Quirks, Habits, and Hobbies

– She describes herself as a "lousy" cook.
– For exercise, she speed-walks.
– She likes crossword puzzles.
– She enjoys the music of Aretha Franklin, the Rolling Stones, Carly Simon, and U2.

The Undecided Voter's Guide Questionnaire

For what unhealthy food do you have the biggest weakness?

I'm a sucker for chocolate ice cream of any kind.

In what way would you hope America would most fundamentally change by the end of your time in the White House?

I hope that we get back to being a country that sets big goals again. Whether it was going to the moon and back or tearing down the vestiges of segregation with civil rights laws and voting rights laws, we were always on the forward march.

And that's what we need to do again. I will set a goal of universal health care coverage, of energy security and independence, of dealing with global warming, of ending the war in Iraq. I want to create a world where America is respected and seen as a force for good.

What is your most memorable childhood activity?

One of my favorite memories from growing up was how on Christmas mornings my father and the other fathers in the neighborhood would load us all into the car and take us ice skating on the Des Plaines River near where I grew up. We'd have this wonderful morning of gifts and family time together, and then we'd be outside spending time with our fathers.

Name someone you would like to see in your cabinet, or, at least, tell us what would be most distinctive about your cabinet?

I don't want a cabinet of "yes-people." A president needs to hear alternative views in order to come up with the best ideas for moving the country forward. I recently read Doris Kearns Goodwin's book about President Lincoln, *Team of Rivals*, a brilliant description of how Lincoln managed a cabinet of people who often had opposing viewpoints. And I think that's one of the reasons Lincoln is considered one of our greatest presidents.

What is your favorite way to relax (besides spending time with your family)?

Isn't the definition of relaxing spending time with your family? We love to play cards and word games and put together jigsaw puzzles. I also enjoy taking long walks.

Where is your favorite place to vacation?

We've been very lucky to visit some of the most interesting places in the world but we do have a soft spot for Martha's Vineyard.

Presidential Announcement

Hillary Clinton launched her presidential bid on the Internet on January 20, 2007, as an acknowledgment of and homage to the power of the New Media and the netroots. In a statement posted on her Web site and e-mailed to supporters, she offered the decisive opening line "I'm in. And I'm in to win," and recorded an accompanying video message to state her case. Smiling gauzily, resplendent in red and black, looking serene, she began what she called another "conversation," talking about the problems facing the nation. Leaning forward, she said, "So let's talk, let's chat, let's start a dialogue about your ideas and mine," and promised to offer more video conversations in the forthcoming days. Clinton held her first public rally of her campaign a week later in a school gym in Des Moines, Iowa, in front of two thousand enthusiastic people. She was glowing, confident, and lively, and joked about the media frenzy ("I want to have this as a one-on-one conversation, just you and me and about several hundred national press people"). She spent the weekend in Iowa at events in Cedar Rapids and Davenport, where she established her candidate persona by alternating between homey charm, 1990s nostalgia, anti-Bush rhetoric, and stalwart leadership. She also maneuvered the first-woman-president issue with nonchalant references to gender and snappy girl power remarks (when a woman in the audience shouted, "You go, girl!" she shouted back, "Go with me!"). Clinton made it clear she is up for the long, hard 2008 fight: "When you're attacked, you have to deck your opponents." Excerpts from her e-mailed statement:

E-mail announcement, January 20, 2007:
I'm in. And I'm in to win.

And I want you to join me not just for the campaign but for a conversation about the future of our country—about the bold but practical changes we need to overcome six years of Bush administration failures . . .

As a senator, I will spend two years doing everything in my power to limit the damage George W. Bush can do. But only a new president will be able to undo Bush's mistakes and restore our hope and optimism . . .

This is a big election with some very big questions. How do we bring the war in Iraq to the right end? How can we make sure every American has access to adequate health care? How will we ensure our children inherit a clean environment and energy independence? How can we reduce the deficits that threaten Social Security and Medicare? . . .

I grew up in a middle-class family in the middle of America, where I learned that we could overcome every obstacle we face if we work together and stay true to our values . . .

I have never been afraid to stand up for what I believe in or to face down the Republican machine. After nearly $70 million spent against my campaigns in New York and two landslide wins, I can say I know how Washington Republicans think, how they operate, and how to beat them . . .

Let's go to work. America's future is calling us.

Read More About Clinton

Hillary Rodham Clinton, *Living History* (New York: Simon & Schuster, 2003). Clinton's best-selling autobiography.

Hillary Rodham Clinton, *It Takes a Village, and Other Lessons Children Teach Us* (New York: Simon & Schuster, 1996). Clinton's analysis of the global and domestic needs of children and families, written during her tenure as First Lady.

http://www.hillaryclinton.com

JOHN EDWARDS

The Basics

Name: Johnny Reid Edwards

Born: June 10, 1953,
Seneca, South Carolina

Political party: Democrat

Spouse: Mary Elizabeth Anania
Edwards, married July 30, 1977

Children: Wade (deceased), Catharine,
Emma Claire, Jack

Religion: Methodist

Education: North Carolina State
University, B.S., 1974
University of North Carolina, Chapel
Hill, J.D., 1977

Career: Law clerk, 1977
Lawyer, Dearborn & Ewing,
1978–1981
Lawyer, Tharrington, Smith &
Hargrove, 1981–1993
Partner, Edwards & Kirby, 1993–1998
U.S. senator, North Carolina,
1998–2004
Presidential candidate, 2003–2004
(unsuccessful)
Vice presidential candidate, 2004
(unsuccessful)
Presidential candidate, 2006–present

IRAQ WAR

High Priority? ☑ *Yes* ☐ *No* ☐ *Maybe*

Record/Position: Having voted to authorize the war as a member of the Senate, has become an outspoken critic of Bush administration policy and of the failure of congressional Democrats to force a change in course. Supports a continued American military presence in the region to perform a limited mission, including dealing with potential genocide and civil war.

Quote: "I was wrong. Almost three years ago we went into Iraq to remove what we were told—and what many of us believed and argued—was a threat to America. But in fact we now know that Iraq did not have weapons of mass destruction when our forces invaded Iraq in 2003. The intelligence was deeply flawed and, in some cases, manipulated to fit a political agenda. It was a mistake to vote for this war in 2002."

WAR ON TERROR

High Priority? ☐ *Yes* ☐ *No* ☑ *Maybe*

Record/Position: Supports modernizing the Pentagon's force structure and changing Bush administration policy on Guantanamo Bay, habeas corpus, and interrogation methods. Wants to create a "Marshall Corps" of ten thousand professionals to work on stabilization and humanitarian missions in potential terrorist havens.

Quote: "The worst thing about the global-war-on-terror approach is that it has backfired—our military has been strained to the breaking point and the threat from terrorism has grown . . . By framing this as a 'war,' we have walked right into the trap that terrorists have set—that we are engaged in some kind of clash of civilizations and a war against Islam."

GOVERNMENT SPENDING/DEFICITS

High Priority? □ *Yes* ☑ *No* □ *Maybe*

Record/Position: Strongly believes that addressing priorities such as health care, poverty, and the environment are more important than short-term deficit reduction.

Quote: "Budget deficits make America less competitive. There's less money to invest in innovation and research and meet the challenges of education and health care. And there's more risk when we rely on another country for economic security."

ENERGY/ENVIRONMENT

High Priority? ☑ *Yes* □ *No* □ *Maybe*

Record/Position: Early in his campaign put forward a detailed plan to cap greenhouse gas pollution starting in 2010 with a cap-and-trade system, leading to an 80 percent reduction by 2050; to form an international treaty that decreases pollution; and to reduce American reliance on imported fossil fuels through development of renewable sources, efficiency, and conservation. Favors a limit on new coal-fired power plants. Calls on individuals to make personal changes to lessen energy consumption and does not rule out raising gas taxes.

Quote: "Our generation must be the one that says, 'We must halt global warming.' If we don't act now, it will be too late. Our generation must be the one that says 'yes' to alternative, renewable fuels and ends forever our dependence on foreign oil. Our generation must be the one that accepts responsibility for conserving natural resources and demands the tools to do it. And our generation must be the one that builds the New Energy Economy. It won't be easy, but it is time to ask the American people to be patriotic about something other than war."

HEALTH CARE

High Priority? ☑ *Yes* □ *No* □ *Maybe*

Record/Position: Wants to raise taxes to pay for universal health care by the end of his first term. Has proposed an ambitious plan that would cost between $90 billion and $120 billion a year and would require employers to either cover their employees or help finance their health insurance. Would make insurance more affordable through tax credits, expanding Medicaid and health care for children, reforming insurance laws, and enforcing cost controls. Would create regional purchasing pools to provide bargaining power, increase choices among insurance plans, and cut costs for businesses. Would require insurance companies to spend at least 85 percent of their premiums on patient care. Over time would make insurance mandatory and phase out private insurance.

Quote: "We have to stop using words like 'access to health care' when we know with certainty those words mean something less than universal care. Who are you willing to leave behind without the care he needs? Which family? Which child? We need a truly universal solution, and we need it now."

TAXES

High Priority? ☑ *Yes* ☐ *No* ☐ *Maybe*

Record/Position: Would like to raise the top tax rate on capital gains to 28 percent from 15 percent and increase income taxes on families earning more than $200,000 a year. Would use the money saved to help pay for tax-free savings accounts and expanded tax credits for lower-income workers. Would eliminate estate taxes for middle-class families and small businesses and estates worth as much as $4 million. Would eliminate or scale back offshore tax shelters and prohibit some private-equity firms from paying lower taxes on their profits. Proposes simplified tax payment for low-income and middle-class taxpayers using a new "Form 1."

Quote: "Hardworking families who pay their taxes shouldn't have to pay tax preparers, too. With 'Form 1,' there is only one thing you have to do—sign and return it."

JOBS/ECONOMY/TRADE/AGRICULTURE

High Priority? ☑ *Yes* ☐ *No* ☐ *Maybe*

Record/Position: Favors investments in the creation of new temporary jobs, including in rural areas. Supports rigorous labor and environmental standards in trade agreements. Proposes a ban on packer ownership to stop the spread of large corporate hog interests. Would limit farm subsidies to $250,000 per person, close loopholes in payment limits, and expand conservation programs.

Quote: "I believe we cannot go on as Two Americas—one favored, the other forgotten—if we plan to stay productive, competitive and secure. I want to live in an America where we value work as well as wealth. I know that together we can build One America—a place where everyone has a fair shot at the American dream."

ABORTION

High Priority? ☑ *Yes* ☐ *No* ☐ *Maybe*

Record/Position: A staunch supporter of abortion rights. Would seek Supreme Court nominees who support *Roe v. Wade*. In favor of insurance coverage and government funding for abortions.

Quote: "On the issue of abortion, I believe in a woman's right to choose, but I think this is an extraordinarily difficult issue for America. I think it is very important for the president of the United States to recognize—while I believe the government should not make these health care decisions for women—I believe they should have the freedom to make them themselves—this is a very difficult issue for many people. And I think we have to show respect for people who have different views about this."

EDUCATION

High Priority? ☑ *Yes* ☐ *No* ☐ *Maybe*

Record/Position: Wants to improve access to college for less well-off Americans by making it easier to get loans, prepare for college, and fill out applications. Favors integrating public schools based on wealth and not race.

Quote: "None of us believe that the quality of a child's education should be controlled by where they live or the affluence of the community they live in. We can build one school system that works for all our kids, gives them a chance to do what they're capable of doing . . . We can give our schools the resources that they need. We can provide incentives to put our best teachers in the subjects and the places where we need them the most."

STEM CELL RESEARCH

High Priority? ☑ *Yes* ☐ *No* ☐ *Maybe*

Record/Position: Favors increased funding for federal research.

Quote: "Stem cell research is not just another political issue. It's a moral issue, and where you stand is a test of moral leadership."

GAY RIGHTS

High Priority? ☐ *Yes* ☐ *No* ☑ *Maybe*

Record/Position: Rhetorically outspoken about equal rights, and opposed to a constitutional amendment banning gay marriage, although opposes gay marriage as well. Has pledged to eliminate laws that discriminate against gays and lesbians. Supports gays and lesbians serving in the military and the full repeal of the Defense of Marriage Act.

Quote: "It's a jump for me to get to gay marriage."

GUN RIGHTS

High Priority? ☐ *Yes* ☑ *No* ☐ *Maybe*

Record/Position: Supports gun ownership and the Second Amendment, but has advocated some limits, such as background checks at gun shows, the assault weapons ban, and the Brady law.

Quote: "It's very important for us as Democrats to understand that where I come from guns are about a lot more than guns themselves. They are about independence. For a lot of people who work hard for a living, one of the few things they feel they have any control over is whether they can buy a gun and hunt. They don't want people messing with that, which I understand."

WELFARE/POVERTY

High Priority? ☑ *Yes* ☐ *No* ☐ *Maybe*

Record/Position: Has made reducing poverty one of his signature issues. Wants to cut poverty by one-third within a decade, and end it in thirty years, by raising the minimum wage, creating one million temporary jobs over five years, making housing more affordable, strengthening labor laws, improving access to college and savings, and expanding the Earned Income Tax Credit.

Quote: "Poverty is not a New Orleans problem, a Pittsburgh problem, or an Appalachia problem. It is an American problem. And it's America's responsibility. And America needs a president who will lead on this issue, not turn his back on thirty-seven million forgotten Americans."

IMMIGRATION

High Priority? ☐ *Yes* ☐ *No* ☑ *Maybe*

Record/Position: Favors comprehensive immigration reform, with a path to legal status for undocumented workers and increased border enforcement, as part of his overall vision for the reduction of poverty.

Quote: "Of course we know there is a problem. We can address the problem at our southern border by assigning more personnel and equipping them with better technology to police the border . . . As for the people who are living here now who came illegally . . . the practical thing we can do is to provide a path to citizenship to those who are here illegally but are otherwise law-abiding. First, they will have to come forward and admit that they came here illegally and pay a fine. They will have to learn to speak English. Then they can move through the process for citizenship."

For all current issue positions, check out http://www.johnedwards.com/issues/.

Son of a Millworker

Johnny Reid Edwards was born in Seneca, South Carolina, the son of a millworker. That phrase—*the son of a millworker*—should be familiar to anyone who has ever heard John Edwards on the stump (to get it right, pronounce it with a ripe southern accent: *meeeeel-worker*). He moved through various South Carolina towns until his parents, Wallace Edwards and Bobbie Wade Edwards, brought the family to Robbins, North Carolina, in 1965. Eventually, after years working on the floor doing hard labor, Wallace Edwards became a supervisor in a textile mill, while Bobbie Edwards worked as a shopkeeper and a postal carrier.

Growing up itinerant and working class, Edwards watched his father struggle because he lacked a college degree. He remembers his father hastily shepherding the family out of a restaurant after seeing the menu prices, and trying to improve himself by studying math with a televised instructional program. The family at times lacked health insurance, he has recalled. Still, memories like these do not seem to have left John Edwards cynical, but rather, determined. They also have shaped how he approaches public policy

> *"You have to be yourself. You cannot fool people."*

issues. "I don't analyze these issues on some ideological spectrum," Edwards said after entering public life. "That's not how I think about them. I think about the issues that affect the lives of working people, regular folks."

The first member of his family to attend college, John Edwards graduated from North Carolina State University (with a B.S. in textile technology, in case he needed to fall back on the family trade) and got his law degree from the University of North Carolina at Chapel Hill. He drew a high draft lottery number just before the conflict in Vietnam ended, and was not called to serve. It was in law school that he met Mary Elizabeth Anania, the daughter of a navy pilot, who had been working toward a Ph.D. in American literature before switching her attention to the legal arena. The couple graduated, married, began their law careers (both first clerking for federal judges), spent five years at Nashville law firms, settled in Raleigh, and had two children, Wade and Cate.

At this point, John Edwards's life turned into a real-life John Grisham novel. As a trial lawyer, he became rich and famous, winning big-money verdicts against powerful corporations on behalf of injured children and ill-treated adults. His smooth, jury-friendly manner in the courtroom produced performances so legendary that other lawyers would gather to watch the master at work, and many of the opposing insurance company and corporate attorneys futilely offered him giant settlements before losing even greater amounts after jury judgments. Yet Edwards's life was struck by tragedy. In 1996, sixteen-year-old Wade, by all accounts a remarkable boy, was killed in a car accident. Spurred by loss, Edwards left the law and, a year later, ran for the Senate, winning his seat against the incumbent, Republican Lauch Faircloth, in 1998. In the meantime, he and his wife had two more children, Emma Claire and Jack. Edwards's Senate career included some high-profile work, and by 2000 he was seriously considered as a potential vice presidential running mate for Al Gore. Edwards had his eye on the top job, however, and in 2004, chose not to seek reelection to the Senate in order to run for president. Ultimately, he accepted the second slot on the ticket with John Kerry after his underdog bid for the nomination left him in second place. More personal sadness came with Elizabeth Edwards's diagnosis of breast cancer in November 2004, the same week he and Kerry lost the presidential race.

With President Bush back in office and his own Senate term at an end, Edwards spent the next few years making money, pondering poverty at his new nonprofit Center for Promise and Opportunity in North Carolina, visiting key campaign states such as Iowa and New Hampshire, and organizing his 2008 campaign. The return of Elizabeth Edwards's cancer, announced in May 2007, has thus far done little to slow down the couple's pursuit of the White House. Critics who say John Edwards is frangible are underestimating a man whose father taught him, "Don't ever start a fight, but don't ever walk away from one."

As much as Edwards talks about his humble origins, his experiences with poverty, his youthful obstacles, and his career-long battle for the rights of the underprivileged and needy, his life history before he entered politics has not been represented vividly in the public's mind. The concrete and ephemeral trappings of his current privileged life—his mansion, his millions, and his infamous four-hundred-dollar haircuts—have created a caricature of Edwards, that he and his followers find frustrating.

Edwards had an extraordinarily distracting mole removed from his upper lip after the 2004 campaign, making him—the hands tremble as the words are written—even more handsome.

Of the major candidates, only Republican Mitt Romney can match Edwards in the sheer drive to get to the White House or the amount of concentrated effort he has put into achieving his goal. His supporters see this as a desire to change America for the better. His critics—from the Democratic Party, the Republican Party, and the national media alike—instead see this as a combination of soulless ambition and phoniness that makes them recoil.

This time around, Edwards lacks the new-kid-on-the-block excitement that animated his candidacy in 2004. While he is still energetic and youthful-looking, his loss alongside John Kerry has taken some of the oomph out of his argument that Democrats can rely on his southern roots and populist style to win back the White House. Whereas he was once hailed as the second coming of Bill Clinton, with a comparably appealing bio and I-feel-your-pain manner but none of the personal baggage, he has struggled in the 2008 cycle to find his own place in the Democratic canon.

A Man without a Job

By the end of 2004, both Edwards's Senate career and vice presidential bid were over. This left him nationally famous, exceedingly wealthy, relatively young, and abruptly unemployed. After regrouping from his wife's first bout with cancer, he launched himself into the study of poverty, traveling around the United States and overseas to countries such as India, Uganda, and China, and setting up his Center for Promise and Opportunity. Not only was he able to burnish his credentials as an authority on the poverty issue, he was also freed from the shackles of the Senate, with its delicate votes, demanding schedule, constant controversies, and issue-defining decisions.

Edwards took smart advantage of lessons he learned from his 2004 presidential effort. As a second-time candidate he avoided many of the mistakes he made during his audacious first run for the most difficult job in the world after serving less than one term in Congress. He exploited his liberty from the Senate, while his major competitors for the Democratic nomination remained sitting members of that body. Since Edwards did not have to be in Washington casting votes for much of the year, he could be other places—at house parties in Iowa, in meeting rooms with union members, in conferences with academic leaders. He could distance himself from unpopular inside-the-Beltway routines and responsibilities, and he could confidently denounce the desperately unpopular Iraq War, and assertively apologize for his role in its inception. He also could allow himself to be lured into the lucrative world of hedge funds—Edwards joined Fortress Investment Group as a part-time senior adviser in the fall of 2005. So, free of Washington, financially re-freshed, and fully established as an antipoverty advocate, he was able to turn his attention full-time to running for president.

The New Old Candidate

After he was vanquished in the 2004 caucuses and primaries, dur-ing his first presidential try, Edwards and his political advisers dem-onstrated a singular determination and organized effort (if mostly under the radar) to compel John Kerry to tap him as his running mate in 2004. Edwards and many of those same advisers brought a similar energy to prepare for his 2008 run for the White House, in an attempt to address systematically any and all perceived short-comings.

- Not enough foreign policy experience? Head an effort at the prestigious Council on Foreign Relations to examine the United States' ties with Russia, and travel around the world to high-profile sites of strife and progress.
- Insufficient support from the Democratic Party's liberal wing? Become an outspoken critic of the Iraq War and spend countless hours on picket lines, at workplaces, and in meetings to build ties to organized labor, assisting with ballot measures on issues such as the minimum wage.
- Accused of being slick and insufficiently heartfelt with pol-icy commitments? Establish an academic center to study poverty, make the post-Katrina reconstruction of the Gulf Coast a signature issue, and drive the other Democratic candidates and the national debate by issuing detailed policy proposals on health care and other concerns.
- Hampered by an overreliance on fellow trial lawyers for financial and political support? Work early and often on

becoming a favored candidate among the Democrats' most outspoken and aggressive activists, including the Internet's netroots, liberal moneyed groups, and wealthy Americans met through hedge fund work.

- Defined as a Washington insider? Move the family back to North Carolina, peg your rivals as Washington senators, and take advantage of your freedom by launching your campaign almost immediately after the 2004 election. Log more time than anyone else in Iowa, New Hampshire, Nevada, and other key early voting states.

All of these deficiencies addressed, Edwards was able to formulate his campaign rationale. Perhaps the two most distinctive aspects of Edwards's candidacy have been his emphasis on eradicating poverty in America and around the world (not normally thought of as a politically winning issue) and the accelerated presentation of his plans on major issues such as health care, the environment, and Iraq, outstripping his rivals with specificity. Critics charge that in this second presidential attempt, Edwards has shifted to a new agenda comprised of more liberal stances. Their argument has some credibility, but it misses key points: Edwards has been an economic populist throughout his career in public service, and he contends that as times have changed, the solutions to the country's problems demand significant, updated proposals. His constant refrain that America's major challenges require bold, comprehensive solutions rather than tinkering around the edges has sometimes forced the other candidates to follow suit.

Trial by Jury

Everyone hates lawyers. People hate lawyers so much they appropriated and misinterpreted Shakespeare's famous line from *Henry*

VI, part II, "The first thing we do, let's kill all the lawyers," just so they could express their hatred in a more lyrical fashion. Particularly hated: trial lawyers. Most hated: personal-injury lawyers, who are blamed for out-of-control suits over coffee that is too hot or dry cleaning that is botched. But before he was a politician, Edwards was a personal-injury attorney who redefined the deplorable stereotype. It is no accident that he titled his autobiography *Four Trials*, and he has reason to be proud of some of his major cases and special clients.

There was little Valerie Lakey, a five-year-old girl whose intestines were sucked from her body when a cover came loose from a pool drain—a calamity that could have been prevented with a slight, inexpensive modification to the drain structure (and a problem of which the company was aware, as other children had been injured previously). Edwards fought the case with passionate daring and won a $25 million verdict against the drain cover manufacturer. At the time the biggest verdict in North Carolina history, the ruling also led to a law regulating such products. The Lakey family actively campaigned for Edwards when he ran for Senate, appearing in commercials and at events, speaking adoringly about the man who saved their family from financial ruin and their daughter from a life of further misery. Lakey was only one of many young children whose grievances Edwards avenged.

> *"I spent most of my adult life, before I went to the Senate, fighting for people who I believed played by the rules, and got hurt by people who didn't play by the rules."*

Then there was Jim Passe,

a patent lawyer and amateur magician who sued a transport company after an accident during the delivery of an 850-pound illusionist's levitation table broke his back and paralyzed him. The transport company said they were not liable because Passe had assisted with the delivery. Edwards, in part due to his sheer star power, helped get a settlement of $4 million (plus the cost of delivery) midway through jury selection. Following their win, the team repaired to Edwards's office, where Passe performed magic tricks.

These were just a few of Edwards's victories, which cemented his reputation as a personal-injury lawyer with a heart of gold and a record of green. This, some people said, is when the legal system works, when big-money verdicts make sense, when the little guy gets justice, when lawyers are seen as heroes rather than as sharks or leeches.

Americans may not be too crazy about trial lawyers, but they have no great love for the insurance companies and big businesses from whose deep pockets Edwards won numerous judgments over the years. Surprisingly, even when he was the Democrats' vice presidential nominee in 2004, there was no intensive national debate over the role of personal-injury lawyers in the U.S. legal system or the details of Edwards's own record in the courtroom. If the party nominates Edwards in 2008, it is unclear how such a discussion would play out, but it is safe to say that lawyers nationwide could not ask for a spokesman with a more sympathetic roster of past clients or a more silvery tongue with which to explain the profession, casting it as a voice for the vulnerable rather than as an opportunity for ambulance-chasing.

Edwards honed certain key skills in the courtroom—eloquence, passion, the capacity to connect with individuals, the ability to state his case. These all have helped him in his political career, in the Senate, and on the stump. He enjoys standing before a crowd, convincing, inspiring, commanding. Many politicians similarly thrive under the look-at-me spotlight of the campaign trail, but in this 2008 cycle, some presidential candidates seem to find the process exhausting or tedious, while others don't quite have the facility to form their message or influence their audience.

Edwards has smoothly transferred the pluses of his courtroom experience, but he cannot completely escape the minuses. To try a case, you need to know your own facts and arguments, those of your opposition, and the personalities of the judge and jurors. By all accounts, Edwards prepared in great detail for every big case when he was a personal-injury attorney. His former partner, David Kirby, called Edwards "a constant student. In a case dealing with a medical device, he'd purchase the operations manual, find out who the inventor was, and go interview him. By the time he entered the courtroom, he knew more about the operation of, say, a fetal heart monitor than the physicians he was about to question."

Being a politician is far more complicated than being a trial lawyer, particularly if you aspire to be the leader of the free world. People expect you to have a profound understanding of every major issue, foreign and domestic. You need to be willing to process new data all the time, and know it cold. This takes real discipline. As a national candidate Edwards has often been accused of preparing just enough to get by, and on occasion being caught falling short of even that standard. To be sure, candidates have won the White House with-

He changed his first name from "Johnny" to "John" early in his legal career (for reasons too obvious to state).

He can be superstitious—as a trial lawyer, he would wear special suits he believed would aid in victory.

out this discipline and serious study, but in this unusually competitive and consequential 2008 race, Edwards will need to recognize that glibness and rhetoric are not enough.

In any case, the law helped make Edwards confident, resilient, fast on his feet, and unflappable, not to mention rich. It is the trial lawyers' triple play of motivation: the thrill of victory, the lavish rewards of huge cash windfalls, and the chance to avenge the hardships suffered by individuals at the hands of unscrupulous, powerful business interests. John Edwards clearly loved all three elements, and they have provided invaluable aids in his run for the White House.

Family Joys and Tragedies

No fictional version of John Edwards's story would have heaped as much tragedy on him as his real life has supplied. Long before Elizabeth Edwards's breast cancer diagnosis in 2004, which made her the sympathetic face of and a national spokesperson about the disease, there was the loss of Wade.

Sixteen-year-old Lucius Wade Edwards was killed in 1996, when the Jeep he was driving flipped over in the wind (he was wearing a seat belt; obeying traffic rules; and, as was his habit, clean of alcohol or drugs). Losing a child is surely a catastrophic experience under any circumstances, but the Edwardses as a unit seemed particularly tight, and Wade seemed especially charismatic and beloved, by his family, by his friends, and by his community. Three weeks before he died, he visited the White House as a finalist in a national essay competition, in which he discussed democracy and voting rights. He wrote, "I have always gone with my parents to vote. Sometimes lines are long. There are faces of old people and young people, voices of native North Carolinians in southern drawls and voices of naturalized citizens with their foreign accents. There are people in fancy clothes and others dressed in overalls. Each has exactly the same one vote. Each has exactly the same say in the election. There is no place in America where equality means as much as in the voting booth."

For six months the Edwards family went into virtual emotional hibernation. John Edwards stopped going to his law firm; he would eventually return to work on just a few more cases before turning to politics. He had talked about running for public office on occasion, but, except for some campaign donations, he had never been involved in that world. This changed in the wake of Wade's death, although Edwards long resisted making explicit any causality, in part out of respect for his son's memory.

> Edwards and his wife have set up a number of scholarships and charities, some in honor of family members. They established the Wade Edwards Foundation, built the Wade Edwards Learning Lab for Raleigh students, and named a UNC–Chapel Hill scholarship for Elizabeth Edwards's father.

Wade's bereft friends continued to come to the Edwards home regularly after he died, and a traumatized Cate Edwards slept in her parents' room for months. Because very few of the politicians and political reporters who attempt to interpret John and Elizabeth Edwards knew them before Wade's death, it is difficult to understand what changes that tragic event wrought. Until the last few years, the Edwardses only rarely broached the matter in their public remarks. Some have suggested that they have since begun talking openly about Wade's death for politically expedient reasons, to garner sympathy and attention. But even those critics do not deny the strong family bond that connects the whole family, the life-changing grief they experienced, and the conviction that John Edwards's love for his late son was unqualified.

The family pulled together, and Elizabeth Edwards underwent fertility treatments to conceive Emma Claire (born in 1998 when Elizabeth was forty-eight) and Jack (born in 2000 when she was fifty), in part, she has said, because "our house was fairly joyless . . . And we said, well, kids give us happiness."

John Edwards's children are great assets to his campaign, as they were in 2004. Cate, capable and bright, is a graduate of Princeton and a student at Harvard Law School, who serves as a visible presence on the 2008 campaign, just as she did four years ago. Emma Claire and Jack, both blond, lively, and adorable, clearly feel comfortable acting like kids—clowning, climbing, asking questions, making demands—all in a way that reflects well on their parents, as evidence that politics doesn't trump parenting in the Edwards household. In part because of Elizabeth Edwards's health and their youthful portability, the younger children will be homeschooled and accompany their mother and father on the trail, where they will surely attract positive attention, a lot of "Aws," and some warm vibes for the Edwards campaign.

Elizabeth Edwards

Spousal influence is hard to measure, but it is safe to say that no wife or husband has been more involved in a presidential campaign than has Elizabeth Edwards. Beyond keeping a public schedule nearly as strenuous as that of a presidential candidate, Elizabeth Edwards is deeply engaged in decisions large and small. Even before her best-selling book, Oprah appearances, and cancer recurrence made her an important and iconic figure in her own right, she was not an afterthought or an appendage to the campaign, but one of its chief strategists. Most modern-day candidate spouses hover in the background, smiling and clapping and looking well-groomed and supportive, accepting sporadic interview requests pegged to a particular positive message or a special event. Elizabeth Edwards, even through her illness, has been a constant presence, giving stump speeches, talking to voters, agreeing to countless interview requests, and generally making herself accessible to all. When she offers up her own positions on the issues—which can be more liberal and confrontational than those of her husband—it makes headlines.

As a woman with her own career, ambitions, and sensibilities, she sometimes has been spared much of the particular negative attention brought to the modern political wife. While Elizabeth Edwards kept her maiden name of Anania when she married in 1977, she changed it to "Edwards" after Wade's death, she says, to honor his memory. That this name change coincided with her husband's decision to enter politics received little bad press or irritable speculation. Additionally, she has won praise for her own successful legal career and for her best seller *Saving Graces* as an individual rather than as her husband's accessory, while simultaneously making him look good for having such an accomplished wife. And she has been able to speak with confidence of her desire to see a better America, putting forth personal views and specific proposals, without appearing to crave political power for herself or generating the specter of that unwelcome "two for the price of one" label. She gives substantive policy speeches, and brings an experienced and sophisticated mind to internal campaign discussions about issues, the media, Democratic interest groups, political strategy, and scheduling. Reflecting her liberal views, she has been a frequent blogging presence on several Web sites and a strong proponent of gratifying the Internet's netroots. Increasingly, she has lashed out at her husband's opponents in a manner more direct and stinging than he would employ.

Four years older than John Edwards, she has a very clear idea of how he should present himself and his candidacy, with opinions ranging from the weighty to the symbolic. During his first presidential campaign, she relayed to *People* magazine some rules she had laid out for him: no pancake-flipping photo ops ("He doesn't flip pancakes at home, so why do it now?"); no wearing hats ("He's not much of a hat person"); no dancing ("In a photo, it's going to look like some oddball movement"); no costumes ("I don't like costumes"); and be yourself, despite the above advice ("She always says, 'Listen to your own voice,' " says John). She takes a self-deprecating approach when referencing her husband's much-discussed cuteness, despite her own peaches-and-cream beauty.

> Elizabeth Edwards still wears the eleven-dollar ring that John gave her when they got married, and the couple continues to celebrate their July 30 wedding date each year by dining at Wendy's, just as they did on their first anniversary.

Those in her orbit whom she respects praise her as one of the strongest and most inspirational people they have ever known. Those who fall out of favor have described a scary and unforgiving figure.

A national debate was set off by the Edwardses shared decision to continue the presidential campaign despite her cancer recurrence. Many around the county, in public venues and in private homes, asked themselves what they would do under similar circumstances. But John and Elizabeth Edwards have been clear and comfortable about their choice, and unless she faces further health problems, are unlikely to change their plan.

Six Years

Edwards came to the Senate with a little halo over his head in Democratic circles, as a handsome, genial, bright young man who had beaten an incumbent Republican in a southern state by running as an economic populist. In his Senate campaign, Edwards emphasized the patients' bill of rights and the need to reduce the influence of lobbyists in Washington. He quickly became a favorite of the Democratic Senate leader, Tom Daschle of South Dakota, and of old lion Edward Kennedy of Massachusetts. Edwards was assigned a leading role in helping manage the Democrats' side of President Clinton's impeachment trial, and he helped with the negotiations over the patients' bill of rights and campaign finance reform.

He served most prominently on the Judiciary and Intelligence committees, although none of his efforts led to significant legislation. During the last years of his term, he spent a good portion of time on the presidential campaign trail.

Almost immediately, he was portrayed as a Bill Clinton 2.0, a possible vice presidential candidate for 2000, and, inevitably, a presidential candidate. These days, when he makes reference to his time in the Senate, he is usually apologizing for his October 2002 vote to sanction the president's authority to go to war in Iraq. Otherwise, he rarely mentions his Senate record and does not seem anxious to harvest more copious notices for his term. Instead, he adopts the image of a Washington outsider prepared to fundamentally change the nation's politics.

Areas of Potential Controversy

– Edwards's work as a trial lawyer and continued reliance on campaign contributions from the profession.

– Edwards's post-Senate business dealings including a big payday from a hedge fund that has engaged in some controversial practices. Hedge funders are the new trial lawyers.

– Edwards's shift on the Iraq War has won him some fans on the left, but raises the question of opportunistic positioning.

– Edwards's failure to vote regularly as a citizen before he entered politics.

Why Edwards Can Win a General Election

- In the last forty-two years, the only Democrats who have been elected president have been white, southern men. Hillary Clinton and Barack Obama are not white, southern men. For all the progress in our country's culture and attitudes, many Americans still seem to feel most comfortable with a white male as their leader.

- Edwards's past experiences, which balance and perhaps eclipse his current life of privilege, have animated his pursuit of social justice: growing up in a family of humble means and engaging in blue-collar labor; dealing with the vestiges of a racially segregated South; representing injured clients in courtrooms against corporations and insurance companies; and the twin tragedies of the accidental death of a child and the life-threatening cancer of his wife. His political opponents relentlessly caricature him as a soft dilettante, but the evidence of his life history suggests that John Edwards is hard and resilient.

- Edwards helped drive the early portion of the race for the Democratic nomination in at least four ways: by offering early detailed plans on issues such as health care, rural development, and the environment; by taking strongly liberal positions, such as advocating against free trade agreements; by pushing firmly against the Bush administration's Iraq policy; and by traveling frequently to Iowa, thereby ensuring the influence of that state's early caucuses in choosing a nominee. This instinct for agenda-setting could make him a formidable opponent for any Republican.

- Generally in the modern era, presidential campaigns have been won by the most likable candidates and by the candidates who perform well on television, and John Edwards has the personal skills to excel in both of those areas. As a speaker and as a leader, Edwards is a masterful mixture of optimism about American's future and anger at those forces he believes threaten that bright vision.

Why Edwards Can't Win a General Election

- In 2004, Edwards demonstrated little appeal in the Republican Red states (he failed to win his North Carolina home county or hometown). He didn't seem to move the needle all that much in the Democratic Blue states, either. While he has a good résumé, a compelling life story, an earnest manner, and a captivating family, he has been known to turn people off. Many who remain unmoved by Edwards, even those who bear him and his party no ill will, describe him as inscrutable, insincere, and hollow.

- Republicans will peg him as a one-term Senate know-nothing, a lightweight pretty boy, a White House loser, an ambulance-chaser, a flip-flopper, and an out-of-touch millionaire. Voters will see negative ads featuring Edwards's sprawling mansion, unseemly for a politician who claims to revile "Two Americas" and who rails against poverty and threats to the environment.

- The Edwardses live in a big house. A very big house. In 2006, the family moved into a newly built home on a 102-acre estate near Chapel Hill. The main house is more than 10,000 square feet, a recreation building (which includes a basketball court, a squash court, a swimming pool, and a tower) is more than 15,000 square feet, and the place overall is estimated at more than 28,000 square feet. The property is said to be the most valuable in the county. John Edwards is a wealthy man—a *self-made* wealthy man—and there is no reason why he shouldn't have a nice, spacious home. (Journalists and visitors report that it is exceedingly livable and unpretentious.) His previous houses, in Washington, D.C., and in North Carolina, were large and expensive, and the media attention given to those properties also has been excessive. The (often ill-paid) press seems to demonstrate a certain real-estate envy when reporting on rich politicians, particularly Democrats. In 2004, voters were made well aware of John Kerry's multiple manors (Nantucket! Beacon Hill! Sun Valley!). Even Bill Clinton's relatively modest postpresidency Chappaqua home has been dissected and assessed, from the size of the garden to the color of the paint. Thus, when the Edwards family settled into their new residence, they did so under a cloud—not of termites, but of negative press, with editorials, criticisms, and jokes about John Edwards's "Two Americas" platform. Elizabeth Edwards found herself in a public fight with a Republican neighbor. Late-night comedians joined the game; Jay Leno said of John Edwards on

The Tonight Show, "Well, I think we know which America he's living in, huh?"

Edwards points out that the Democratic Party has been led by millionaires, from the Roosevelts to the Kennedys, whose personal wealth did not stand in their way of taking populist public policy positions or hamper their ability to champion and inspire the economically less well-off. And Republican presidents are not traditionally cash-poor either.

- Republicans would most likely paint Edwards as effete, as they did effectively with Michael Dukakis, Al Gore, and John Kerry (but not, significantly, with Bill Clinton, the only recent Democrat to avoid such a brand). The groundwork has already been laid for Edwards in this regard: an infamous YouTube video showing a mirror-brandishing Edwards and a meticulous makeup artist fussing with his hair before a television appearance (set to the tune of "I Feel Pretty"); the bad penny of a four-hundred-dollar haircut (Edwards was pilloried after it was revealed that a house call from a Los Angeles–based hairstylist not only cost a whopping four-hundred dollars, but also was accidentally charged to the campaign fund—Edwards reimbursed the money, but still was criticized as vain, extravagant, and shady); his subsequent squabble with the offended hairstylist, and the label of "Breck Girl," famously applied to him by an anonymous Bush campaign adviser in 2003.

- Edwards's popularity in 2004 was boosted because many voters considered him to be a decent guy. This time he will have to balance the advantages of that reputation with the need to engage in the rough and tumble of politics—thorny for anyone to pull off.

- Elizabeth Edwards's health, despite her positive outlook and strong determination, might be a factor. John
  Edwards's supporters observe that he has proven himself
  capable of succeeding and thriving in a public role even
  while dealing with unthinkable private hardship.

The Best Case for an Edwards Presidency

- Like Bill Clinton, Edwards's direct familiarity with middle-
  class life and a desire to extend economic opportunity to
  every American could be inspirations to many. As president, Edwards might begin to make unprecedented ad-
  vances in tackling the issue of poverty. He can relate to the
  poor, the rich, and the in-between.
- Edwards has pledged to spend some of his first months as
  president traveling the world trying to repair the damage
  done by the Iraq War and other Bush administration policies. His youthful image and ardent wish to forge alliances
  might be just what the nation needs to regain its international footing. At least in personal interactions, he would
  be unlikely to step unnecessarily on any foreign toes.
- Edwards's resolution to raise the necessary revenue to create a universal health care system in America equal to those
  in all of the world's other industrialized democracies, would
  set off a much-needed national debate on how to solve a
  problem that almost everyone agrees must be addressed.
- He is smart, committed, hyper-rational, vigorous, and enthusiastic.

The Worst Case for an Edwards Presidency

- With limited national security experience and virtually no
  executive experience, Edwards might have trouble manag-

ing the federal government during a crisis or even day
to day.

- He might wrestle with the impulse to fight for the lower
and middle classes while neglecting to protect the conditions necessary for a thriving business community.

- Although he served in Congress, Edwards was not there
long enough to get a full understanding of how the legislative process truly works. Many Democrats on Capitol
Hill resent his young-man-in-a-hurry ascent in national
politics. And Republicans in Washington and around the
country feel he has never reached out to them, nor do they
think he could bring the country together after the divisive Bill Clinton and George W. Bush years. This potential
problem has only been exacerbated by the liberal rhetoric
of his current campaign.

- He has on occasion cut corners, politically and intellectu-
ally. That doesn't work well in the Oval Office, where
every decision is important. Should he fail to commit
to careful study and meticulous work, he could make
mistakes; eloquence cannot save a president from bad
decisions.

What to Expect If Edwards Is President

- John Edwards would bring a feeling of youth and change
to the White House.

- He would try to realize his plan to end the Iraq War, aiming for major troop withdrawals over a twelve- to eighteen-
month period.

- An Edwards White House would place its main focus
on domestic issues. He would call for a universal health
care plan to create a dual public-private system, with the

option to put the country on a path to a single-payer, government-financed health care system. He also likely would raise income-tax rates for the wealthiest Americans, push policies that would empower labor unions and provide more government assistance to the poor and working class, and pursue aggressive environmental policies to lessen America's reliance on fossil fuels. He also would support a path to citizenship for illegal immigrants.

- His campaign manager, former Michigan congressman David Bonior, would likely play an important role in an Edwards White House. Several advisers who worked in Bill Clinton's administration and in Edwards's presidential campaigns would also be expected to have influential roles, including strategists Jonathan Prince and Jennifer Palmieri.

- Elizabeth Edwards would serve as his chief adviser, and likely would be involved in every major (and minor) decision, on policies foreign and domestic. She would probably write another book and continue to give innumerable interviews on topics of policy, life in the White House, and her health. Daughter Cate Edwards would return to Harvard Law School to get her degree, and then likely would accept a job in Washington, D.C., to be near her family. Emma Claire and Jack would continue to be cute and endearing, and would no doubt enjoy scampering around their historic new home.

- Media and in-house photographers would become used to the sight of the fanatically fit John Edwards running daily on the White House grounds, throughout the capital, and around the country.

Edwards's Own Words

"I was wrong to vote for this war. Unfortunately, I'll have to live with that forever. And the lesson I learned from it is to put more faith in my own judgment."

"George Bush goes down to that big ranch of his, with that big belt buckle . . . He pretends to know what it's like for you and me."

"Why, you lookin' for a haircut?"
—when asked by a reporter about his modish flop top back in 2003, long before the haircut debacle of 2007. Edwards consigned it to "some guy on Capitol Hill," but the reporter followed up, writing, "Turns out it's Ian McWilliams of Bravado Hair Design, a hot stylist whose clients have included Bill Clinton, Chelsea Clinton and Al Gore."

"I came to genuinely understand how smart and decent all kinds of regular American people are and will surely continue to be, even at the worst moment in their lives. I also learned how our great system can often discount the hardships and genuine suffering of such people, and how it can sometimes seem to forget their struggle almost completely."

"It is time to ask the American people to be patriotic about something other than war."

What His Supporters Say

"You have to see John in action and see how much he cares about the people he represents to understand what a fine person he is . . . I am certain he would take that passion and use it in the Senate to help everyone in the state."
—Sandy Lakey, mother of Valerie, on his 1998 Senate run

"I never want him to have another unhappy moment as long as he lives. And if there's anything that he wants, I want it for him."

—Elizabeth Edwards

What His Critics Say

"It's not every day that you run against a very slick, very glib, very talented, very presentable personal-injury lawyer. They know how to sell."

Republican strategist Alex Castellanos,
whose client lost his U.S. Senate seat to Edwards in 1998,
and who now advises Mitt Romney's presidential campaign

"When he has had the opportunity to reduce taxes and return money to the taxpayer, he just says 'no' . . . If Senator Edwards had his way, the government would be much larger and personal wealth far smaller."   —Tom Schatz, president of council
for Citizens against Government Waste

Edwards Facts and Stories

– He has two younger siblings—sister Kathy and brother Blake.
– He says he was drawn to the law as early as elementary school, and recalls writing a paper, "Why I Want to Be a Lawyer," about the profession as a child. Sample line: "I would like to protect innocent people from blind justice."
– He played football and basketball at North Moore High School, and still especially enjoys playing and watching the latter sport. He once said that his hidden talent is his jump shot.
– Summer jobs in high school included soda jerk, carpet layer, railroad cross painter, and millworker.
– He was raised a Baptist, but is now a Methodist (his parents are still Baptists but have publicly supported their son's religious choice).

– He grew up in a Republican household but became a Democrat.

– His grandfather was a boxer who was paralyzed during a fight.

– He made the law review, as did his wife, at UNC–Chapel Hill.

– He conquered his fear of heights by climbing Mount Kilimanjaro with his son, Wade, in 1995.

– For years following Wade's death, he wore his son's Outward Bound pin on his lapel (although he was initially unwilling to comment on it).

– He spent more than $6 million of his own money on his 1998 Senate race.

– He named his son, known as Jack, John Atticus Edwards (after the Roman intellectual, not the hero of *To Kill a Mockingbird*).

– He was designated as one of the "sexiest men alive" by *People* magazine in 2000. Seemingly ambivalent about this honor, Edwards proved adept at poking fun at himself, making frequent self-deprecating comments about performing unglamorous household duties: "I'm wipin' my son Jack's butt and changin' his diaper . . . And my wife comes up to me, and leans over and whispers in my ear . . . 'You don't look too sexy right now!' "

– In addition to "sexiest man," Edwards has been called "a populist Adonis," a "golden god of a southern Democrat," and "the Michael Jordan of politics," and has been compared to John F. Kennedy, Robert F. Kennedy, Bill Clinton, Mickey Mantle, Robert Redford's character in *The Candidate*, Jimmy Stewart's character in *Mr. Smith Goes to Washington*, a Ken doll, and Olympian Bruce Jenner.

– In 1993, he founded his Raleigh firm, Edwards & Kirby, with partner and friend David Kirby; Edwards sold his share for about $5 million in 2002.

– His relationship with former running mate John Kerry can best be described as prickly.

– Daughter Cate Edwards is the designated guardian of her two younger siblings.

Quirks, Habits, and Hobbies

– John Edwards loves Diet Coke so much his ten-can-a-day habit was featured prominently in innumerable profiles, and the drink was stocked in every campaign vehicle, television studio, and debate green room. He has since scaled back his consumption considerably.

– Edwards loves to run, for exercise and stress relief, and has competed in a few marathons. He prefers to run alone, and insists on running daily—this need is a significant factor in how he schedules his sleep, events, and travel.

– He looks young. Ridiculously young. Boyish, wrinkle-free, floppy-maned, trim, bright-eyed, with nary a gray hair. Photographs of him from two decades ago are virtually indistinguishable from photographs of today.

– His musical tastes include bluegrass, Bruce Springsteen, Dave Matthews, Sting, Vince Gill, and U2.

– Family cars reportedly include a Ford Escape hybrid, a 2004 Chrysler Pacifica midsize SUV, and a 1994 GMC truck.

The Undecided Voter's Guide Questionnaire

For what unhealthy food do you have the biggest weakness?

Cheeseburgers.

In what way would you hope America would most fundamentally change by the end of your time in the White House?

I hope we can build One America with universal health care, good wages and real retirement security.

What is your most memorable childhood activity?

Playing football with my father.

What is the biggest single difference between men and women, besides physiology?

Women complain less than men.

What is your most strongly held superstition?

When you see a penny on the ground sitting heads up, you have to pick it up for good luck.

Name someone you would like to see in your cabinet, or, at least, tell us what would be most distinctive about your cabinet.

I will pick the strongest and most talented people, regardless of party.

What is the worst thing you did as a teenager?

I drove before I had a license.

How are you most different as a person than your parents?

I am a more aggressive person.

What is your favorite way to relax (besides spending time with your family)?

Running (about 4 to 5 miles per day).

Where is your favorite place to vacation?

North Carolina beaches.

Presidential Announcement

In 2003, John Edwards appeared on *The Daily Show* to announce his run for the White House. As he told host Jon Stewart, "I'm announcing my candidacy for the presidency of the United States on your show . . . Now they promised me that you wouldn't make fun of me if I announced on your show." Edwards returned to the program in November 2006 to let it be known he was going to try again; Stewart pointed out, "You know, you announced that you were going to run for president on this program in 2003. Here you are again sitting here in 2006, it's almost a situation comical in its synchronicity." Edwards's plans for 2008 came as a surprise to no one, as he had been plainly running since 2005. He gave his official 2008 announcement on December 28, 2006, in the Katrina-ravaged Ninth Ward of New Orleans, wearing a simple shirt and jeans. His announcement took place in the middle of a busy news week, sandwiched between the death of President Gerald Ford and the hanging of Iraqi dictator Saddam Hussein, and was somewhat diluted because his campaign Web site accidentally posted the information a day early. But Edwards nevertheless managed to get himself in the race before other leading candidates, garner decent media coverage, and launch his campaign with a well-attended three-day tour of the early-nomination states Iowa, New Hampshire, Nevada, and South Carolina. Excerpts from his statement:

December 28, 2006
Ninth Ward, New Orleans, Louisiana
New Orleans, in so many ways, shows the Two Americas that I have talked about in the past and something that I feel very personally. And it also exemplifies something that I've learned since the last election, which is that it's great to see a problem and to understand it; it's more important to actually take action and do something about it.

That's why I'm in New Orleans, is to show what's possible when we as Americans, instead of staying home and complaining about somebody else not doing what they're supposed to, we actually take responsibility, and we take action. And I don't mean we take action after the next election. I mean we take action now . . .

You know, my own view is that actually the biggest responsibility of the next president of the United States is to reestablish America's leadership role in the world, starting with Iraq . . .

So whether it's poverty, energy, health care, demonstrating that we are once again the beacon for the rest of the world—which is what we need to be, not just for us but also for them, because when America doesn't lead, there is no stability.

We are the stabilizing force in the world. We are the preeminent power in the world, and we need to maintain that power. We need to maintain our strength. It's what gives us the capacity to lead. But we also have to show that we have a responsibility to humanity, and the world needs to see that from us. They need to see our better angels again, because it will affect the way they respond to us and it will affect our ability to lead.

Read More About Edwards

John Edwards with John Auchard, *Four Trials* (New York: Simon & Schuster, 2003). Edwards's account of his life as a trial lawyer, featuring some of his celebrated and defining cases.

Elizabeth Edwards, *Saving Graces: Finding Solace and Strength from Friends and Strangers* (New York: Broadway, 2006). Elizabeth Edwards's story of her life and her battle with cancer.

http://www.johnedwards.com/

BARACK OBAMA

The Basics

Name: Barack Hussein Obama Jr.

Born: August 4, 1961, Honolulu, Hawaii

Political party: Democrat

Spouse: Michelle Robinson Obama,
married October 3, 1992

Children: Malia Ann, Natasha (Sasha)

Religion: Protestant

Education: Occidental College,
1979–1981

Columbia University, B.A., 1983

Harvard Law School, J.D., 1991

Career: Writer and analyst, Business
International Corp., 1984–1985

Community organizer, Harlem,
New York, 1985

Executive director, Developing
Communities Project, Chicago,
1985–1988

President, *Harvard Law Review*, 1991

Executive director, Illinois Project
Vote, 1992

Senior lecturer, University of Chicago
Law School, 1993–2004

Lawyer, Davis, Miner, Barnhill &
Galland, Chicago, 1993–1996

State senator, Illinois, 1997–2004

U.S. House candidate, Illinois, 2000
(unsuccessful)

Career (*cont.*): Keynote speaker, Democratic National
  Convention, Boston, 2004

 U.S. senator, Illinois, 2005–present

 Presidential candidate, 2007–present

IRAQ WAR

High Priority? ☑ *Yes* ☐ *No* ☐ *Maybe*

Record/Position: An early opponent of the American invasion and
  congressional authorization before he was elected to the Senate. In
  his first years as a senator, regularly voted to fund the war and was
  not as aggressive as some other Democrats about forcing the Bush
  administration to change course.

Quote: "We live in a more dangerous world, partly as a consequence of
  Bush's actions, primarily because of this war in Iraq that should have
  never been authorized or waged. What we've seen is a distraction
  from the battles that deal with al-Qaeda in Afghanistan. We have
  created an entire new recruitment network in Iraq, that we're seeing
  them send folks to Lebanon and Jordan and other areas of the region."

WAR ON TERROR

High Priority? ☐ *Yes* ☐ *No* ☑ *Maybe*

Record/Position: Supports efforts to limit nuclear proliferation to keep
  weapons out of terrorists' hands, and intensive tactics to capture al-
  Qaeda terrorists around the world. Would step up diplomatic talks
  and would allocate the amount of aid to allied countries based on
  their commitment to fighting terror.

Quote: "When I am president, we will wage the war that has to be won.
  The first step must be to get off the wrong battlefield in Iraq and take
  the fight to the terrorists in Afghanistan and Pakistan."

GOVERNMENT SPENDING/DEFICITS

High Priority? ☐ *Yes* ☐ *No* ☑ *Maybe*

Record/Position: Has not made macro deficit reduction a major goal, but
  has supported reducing the influence of lobbyists (who can win

government spending for clients). Championed an online searchable database to track federal grants, contracts, and loans. Supports more scrutiny of government contracts and of earmark spending for individual members of Congress. Rejects privatization of Social Security but has said options such as raising the retirement age or payroll taxes should be considered.

Quote: "There are some things we have to do at home to get our house in order. Number one is we shouldn't be running up budget deficits . . . You've got to pay interest on it, so you've got horrendous budget deficits that we are piling on, and that our children and grandchildren are going to pay the interest on. It's inexcusable, and it makes us uncompetitive."

ENERGY/ENVIRONMENT

High Priority? ☑ *Yes* ☐ *No* ☐ *Maybe*

Record/Position: Says reducing greenhouse gases is one of his most important domestic goals. Co-sponsored the Climate Stewardship and Innovation Act to cap emissions from industrial plants and oil refineries and has encouraged religious leaders to join the environmental movement. Has called for more restrictions on carbon in fuels and tougher auto fuel efficiency standards.

Quote: "Today, there are two kinds of car companies—those that mass-produce fuel-efficient cars and those that will. The American auto industry can't afford to be one of those that will anymore. And America can't afford to follow the world. For the sake of our economy, our security, and our planet, we must lead it."

HEALTH CARE

High Priority? ☑ *Yes* ☐ *No* ☐ *Maybe*

Record/Position: Intends to implement a health care overhaul by the end of his first term. Would create a subsidized public health insurance plan that funds prevention and chronic care management, with benefits comparable to what federal employees currently enjoy. Private insurance plans would still be available. Would have the federal government assume the costs of the most expensive cases, keeping premiums low. Advocates the increased availability of generic drugs, reduced power for the drug and insurance industries, and the modernization of health care records and billing. Opposes an individual mandate requiring everyone to obtain insurance.

Quote: "We can't afford another disappointing charade in 2008, 2009. It's not only tiresome, it's wrong."

TAXES

High Priority? □ *Yes* ☑ *No* □ *Maybe*

Record/Position: Proposes repealing the Bush income tax cuts that benefit the wealthiest Americans who make more than $250,000, which are due to expire in 2010, and raising some taxes on private-equity and hedge fund managers.

Quote: "There's no doubt that the tax system has been skewed. And the Bush tax cuts—people didn't need them, and they weren't even asking for them, and that's why they need to be less, so that we can pay for universal health care and other initiatives . . . What people really want is fairness. They want people paying their fair share of taxes."

JOBS/ECONOMY/TRADE/AGRICULTURE

High Priority? □ *Yes* □ *No* ☑ *Maybe*

Record/Position: Favors public-private partnerships to create opportunities for low-wage workers, as well as government programs for training, transportation, tax credits, and loans to benefit those trying to establish themselves in the workforce. Has a mixed record on trade deals.

Quote: "Over the last few decades, fundamental changes in the way we work and live have trapped too many American families between an economy that's gone global and a government that's gone AWOL. Too many rungs have been removed from the ladder to middle-class security, and the safety net that's supposed to break any falls from that ladder has grown badly frayed."

ABORTION

High Priority? ☑ *Yes* ☐ *No* ☐ *Maybe*

Record/Position: A staunch supporter of abortion rights. Would seek Supreme Court nominees who support *Roe v. Wade*. Is in favor of insurance coverage and government funding for abortions.

Quote: "I think that most Americans recognize that this is a profoundly difficult issue for the women and families who make these decisions. They don't make them casually. And I trust women to make these decisions in conjunction with their doctors and their families and their clergy. And I think that's where most Americans are."

EDUCATION

High Priority? ☐ *Yes* ☐ *No* ☑ *Maybe*

Record/Position: Supports federal assistance for higher teacher pay, extended summer school, and increased student aid for college. Thinks merit pay for teachers is a good idea but only if teachers themselves support it.

Quote: "Our education system is not keeping up with the demands of an information society. We've got to revamp our education system."

STEM CELL RESEARCH

High Priority? ☑ *Yes* ☐ *No* ☐ *Maybe*

Record/Position: In favor of relaxing federal restrictions on research. Voted for the Stem Cell Research Enhancement Act of 2005, which was vetoed by President Bush.

Quote: "All over the country, patients and their families are waiting today for Congress and the president to open the door to the cures of tomorrow. At the dawn of the twenty-first century, we should approach this research with the same passion and commitment that have led to so many cures and saved so many lives throughout our history."

GAY RIGHTS

High Priority? ☐ *Yes* ☐ *No* ☑ *Maybe*

Record/Position: Believes that marriage should be between a man and a woman, but has expressed doubts about his own position. Supports same-sex civil unions and opposed a constitutional amendment to ban gay marriage. Favors a full repeal of the Defense of Marriage Act.

Quote: "[I am] open to the possibility that my unwillingness to support gay marriage is misguided . . . I may have been infected with society's prejudices and predilections and attributed them to God."

GUN RIGHTS

High Priority? ☐ *Yes* ☑ *No* ☐ *Maybe*

Record/Position: Supports a ban on semiautomatic weapons, increased state restrictions on some types of firearms, and a requirement for child-safety locks. Has opposed liability limits on gun manufacturers.

Quote: "My experience has been, based on my relationships with gun owners in Illinois, is that most people are entirely comfortable with sensible approaches to gun control."

WELFARE/POVERTY

High Priority? ☑ *Yes* ☐ *No* ☐ *Maybe*

Record/Position: As a state senator, helped pass the Illinois earned-income tax credit. Supports a minimum-wage increase, efforts to promote more responsible fatherhood, and government programs to make low-income housing more affordable.

Quote: "At the dawn of the twenty-first century we also have a collective responsibility to recommit ourselves to the dream; to strengthen that safety net, put the rungs back on that ladder to the middle-class, and give every family the chance that so many of our parents and grandparents had. This responsibility is one that's been missing from Washington for far too long—a responsibility I intend to take very seriously as president."

IMMIGRATION

High Priority? ☐ *Yes* ☐ *No* ☑ *Maybe*

Record/Position: Favors comprehensive immigration reform, with a path to legal status for undocumented workers and increased border enforcement. Supports a guest worker program that puts American workers at the front of the line for available jobs.

Quote: "Today's immigrants seek to follow in the same tradition of immigration that has built this country. We do ourselves and them a disservice if we do not recognize the contributions of these individuals. And we fail to protect our nation if we do not regain control over our immigration system immediately."

For all current issue positions, check out http://www.barackobama.com/issues/.

Dreams

Intelligence has no color. Neither does charisma. Nor do passion, dedication, or drive. But when Barack Obama began attracting media attention two decades ago, his race was a factor in his celebrity. He was admired as a black community organizer in his early twenties, honored as the first black president of the illustrious *Harvard Law Review*, recognized as an up-and-coming black leader in the Illinois state Senate, heralded as the Democratic Party's black star of the future at the 2004 national convention, and welcomed as Congress's only current black senator in 2005. Now, as the 2008 presidential campaign gets under way in earnest, voters are considering his record more than his race.

Obama is, by any measure, a remarkable man. He has a brilliant and curious mind, a refined and lyrical writing style, a relaxed and self-deprecating sense of self. His résumé indicates a sincere commitment to making society better and to taking on tough problems, motivated not just by ambition, but also by optimism and conviction. No other person seeking the presidency in 2008 has generated the widespread excitement Obama has inspired. It is difficult to imagine a fortysomething white politician with a limited policy portfolio stirring this sort of adulatory media and public enthusiasm. Such a politician would be seen as an up-and-comer, a rising star. There would be talk of higher office, perhaps even a place on the presidential ticket. But journalists and pundits would not likely scramble to find glowing new superlatives, or affix labels such as *rock star* and *superhero*. All things considered, Obama benefits from the color of his skin. It makes him distinctive, as does his exotic name. It energizes those intrigued by the historic aspects of his candidacy and those who hope his election might help heal the nation's scarred and shocking racial past. It has helped him with fund-raising, with endorsements, and with attention.

But more than race has catapulted Obama into the political stratosphere. He is a highly gifted and conscientious politician. Perhaps his greatest strength is his likability. While he is not without enemies, few deny he is a compelling figure whose election would be hailed at home and abroad as a historic advance. Those are the chief reasons why a man with two years' experience in national office before announcing his run, who was virtually unknown until 2004, and who is still nothing more than a smiling face and unusual name to many people (even to some who intend to vote for him) has a chance to be the next president of the United States. For some, the interest is purely in the man and his image, rather than in his political career or his ideas. Obama's own personal appeal has turned the dual challenges of race and inexperience into assets. He is new, he is change. One need not know very much about him to see that.

His newness is bound with the problem of greenness, and some gently suggest that Obama is too young and too untried, that his time for the presidency can come in four, eight, twelve, or even sixteen years, when he will be older, seasoned, and primed, and less prone to the kinds of gaffes that have hurt his campaign. Yet others worry that as time goes by, Obama might, in perception or reality, gradually lose the fresh quality that inspires people the most. When challenged on his readiness for office and his overarching

"Once people know my background as a community organizer, as a civil rights attorney, as somebody who taught constitutional law, as a state legislator, as well as a U.S. senator we will do well."

objective to smash the mold of national politics—in everything from foreign affairs to the legislative process to how people relate to the federal government—Obama has not backed down. He has called his own campaign an "improbable quest" to bring about change to address both the cynicism that many American feel about government and the biggest problems facing the country—the war in Iraq, health care, the environment. Despite his establishment credentials, Obama puts himself forward as the leader of a new generation determined to run a different kind of presidential campaign aimed at "reclaiming the meaning of citizenship, restoring our sense of common purpose, and realizing that few obstacles can withstand the power of millions of voices calling for change." When his critics call him naïve or vague, Obama responds that they are too tied to the status quo to understand or accept the power of his effort to lead a movement to restore hope. Obama has made a good first impression on the nation, but by definition, this is the only presidential cycle when he can be novel, with all that represents. The candidate who has caused Obamamania to sweep the nation is seizing the day, despite of the risks. "I love to body surf," he has said. "If you're on a wave, you ride it. You figure at some point you're going to get a mouthful of sand. It doesn't last forever."

Still, many remain convinced that Obama simply does not have enough of the requisite credentials as a chief executive to lead, or a sufficient practical knowledge of foreign policy to conduct global diplomacy, manage a war, or prevent another terrorist attack on American soil. That his policies are too liberal for a divided nation (and even for an unsettled Democratic Party). That his cerebral manner is unsuited to the active and demanding role of president. That his unconventional background and youthful indiscretions—he has been open about experimenting with cocaine—will turn off mainstream voters. And some feel that, regardless of polls or wishful thinking or public progress, there are people in America who will not vote for a black man.

Whether Obama can break this biggest barrier remains to be seen. Leadership has no color. And the candidate who says he embodies change hopes to lead an America that continues to evolve regarding race relations and tolerance. Perhaps one can wistfully anticipate a time when politicians such as Obama will be measured on their records alone, the positives and negatives alike, and not on the color of their skin. Perhaps that time is 2008.

Hope

Barack Obama is fond of saying, "My father was from Kenya, which is where I got my name, and my mother is from Kansas, which is where I got my accent." It is a charming line that neatly sums up the diverse elements of Obama's heritage. Yet his background is far more complicated and intriguing than that of most presidential candidates, layered as it is with multicultural influences and societal challenges. He has often felt like an outsider, but has found a way to survive and thrive in many demanding situations, and has become expert at winning people over.

"Barack" means "blessed" in Swahili.

His maternal grandparents, Stanley and Madelyn Dunham, both white, grew up in small Kansas towns, and lived in Wichita, where they married and had one child, daughter Stanley Ann Dunham (named thusly because her father hoped for a son). Mr. Dunham, a furniture salesman, moved the family to the Seattle area and then Honolulu; Ann Dunham attended the University of Hawaii in preparation for a career as an anthropologist.

Obama's father's family was from the Luo tribe near Lake Victoria in the western part of Kenya. Barack Hussein Obama Sr. came to Hawaii to study economics, and after marrying Ann Dunham, continued his education in a Ph.D. program at Harvard, leaving his wife and baby behind in Honolulu. The couple divorced when Barack Jr. was two; Obama Sr. eventually returned to Kenya to work in the Ministry of Finance, and later remarried (he had been married once before meeting Dunham, and Senator Obama has five half brothers and one half sister from his father's side).

Dunham also married again; her second husband was an Indonesian man named Lolo Soetoro, another fellow student from the University of Hawaii. She and her son moved with him to Jakarta, where he worked in the oil industry. Obama lived there from ages six to ten, attending government schools with mostly Muslim students, and a private Catholic school. Obama's memories of the city, at the time still undeveloped and rustic, are dense and colorful. He attempted to learn the local language, adapt to the customs, and befriend the village children. He has said that his experiences in Indonesia "left a very strong mark on me living there because you got a real sense of just how poor folks can get."

Shortly after his half sister, Maya Soetoro, was born in 1971, Obama was sent back to Hawaii to attend the prestigious Punahou School, to reintegrate into American culture and prepare for college in the States. His mother and sister initially came with him, but Dunham preferred traveling abroad to traditional domesticity, and Obama's grandparents were happy to look after him. When Obama was ten, his biological father came to Hawaii for a month-long visit, but the two never again met in person; Obama Sr. died in 1982, in a car accident in Kenya, when his son was twenty-one.

As a teen, Obama tried to figure out a balance between assimilation and acceptance, going by the nickname Barry, which he had picked up as a small child, making a point of his mother's race so he could better blend in with his white, wealthy classmates, struggling with the pressures of adolescence, and eventually drinking, and experimenting with drugs, including cocaine. As he wrote in his memoir *Dreams from My Father*, "Pot had helped, and booze; maybe a little blow when you could afford it." After his early life of foreign travel and cultural variation, he began to sort out his identity as a black person living in America.

> *"I come from a lot of worlds and I have had the unique opportunity to move through different circles."*

He graduated from high school and enrolled at Occidental College in Los Angeles on a scholarship. While his work was strong and he was involved in student programs and activism, he has said he was not sufficiently focused on academics. As he continued to dabble in illegal substances, he recognized that he was sliding into the worrisome pattern that has plagued many young black men in America. He decided he needed a bigger school and a more stimulating environment. He later explained, "Some of the problems of adolescent rebellion and hormones were compounded by the fact that I didn't have a father. So what I fell into were the exaggerated stereotypes of black male behavior—not focusing on my books, finding respectability, playing a lot of sports . . . It wasn't until I reached college that I started recognizing that I had bought into a set of false assumptions about what it meant to be black." He transferred to Columbia University in New York City, where he was quiet and studious, and majored in political science and international relations. After receiving his degree, he spent a year at the publishing firm Business International Corporation, and then worked for a short period as an activist in Harlem.

At that point, Obama made a fateful decision. Looking for a community activist job in a classified listing, he came upon one in Chicago. He got the position, at an annual salary of thirteen thousand dollars, working for a church-based community organizing group, and moved to the midwestern city that would become his political, religious, family, and personal base. For the next three years, he spent long days in coalitions with neighborhood ministers in a section of Chicago beset by low employment and high crime. He worked to improve neighborhood infrastructures, health care, government services, job training, and tenant's rights. Paradoxically, the most difficult aspect of the job—finding compromise in a system that seemed to live by feuds and factional disputes—only helped him develop what has become Obama's political calling card. As one writer observed, "Chicago politics tends toward polarization. Depolarization is Obama's stock in trade." A few years later, looking back on his introduction to Chicago, Obama said, "I have worked and lived in poor black communities and I can translate some of their concerns into words that the larger society can embrace."

> *"I feel like I've walked through a door a whole lot of other people worked hard to open."*
> —on being the first black president of the *Harvard Law Review*

It was during that time that Obama joined the church he belongs to today, the predominantly African-American Trinity United Church of Christ on Chicago's South Side. Although his father was a Muslim and he was exposed to that faith while he lived in Indonesia, Obama is a Protestant, and religion began to play a more prominent role in his life from this time onward. Eager to build his résumé and broaden his opportunities, Obama decided to leave Chicago to attend Harvard Law School. He graduated at twenty-nine with his second Ivy League degree, a ream of glowing newspaper profiles, and a book contract, having made history as Harvard's first black president of its prestigious *Law Review*. He also met his future wife, Michelle Robinson, during a summer internship at a Chicago law firm.

Audacity

Barack Obama's friends and supporters point out that after he graduated from Harvard, he could have done anything he liked—in particular, he could have made a fortune at a topflight law firm. Instead, he returned to Chicago and spent six months as executive director of Illinois Project Vote, which registered more than one hundred thousand minority and low-income people for the 1992 elections. He then joined the University of Chicago faculty as a part-time senior lecturer and became an associate at a politically connected law firm specializing in civil rights law and housing contracts.

In 1996, Obama ran for Illinois state Senate. As he later said, "When I was in college, I decided I wanted to be part of bringing about social change, and politics was really an extension or progression from that broader set of goals. Some of that is based on the values my family gave me. Some of it is based on my status as an African American in this country. And some of it is informed by my having lived abroad and having family in underdeveloped countries where the contrast between rich and poor is so sharp that it is hard to ignore injustice." Obama's race aside, the ability to rise up successfully in the rough, competitive world of Illinois politics without family connections or the taint of personal or political corruption is an achievement. As he now jokes on the stump, referencing the reactions he got when he decided to run for office, " 'You seem like a nice guy, you have a fancy law degree, you make a lot of money, you've got a beautiful, churchgoing family, why would you want to go into something dirty and nasty like politics?' " Obama also showed he could throw a political elbow when needed—the incumbent in that race had planned to run for a different office, but she decided she wanted to keep her seat and tried to get Obama to step aside. He not only refused, but also used legal challenges to force her name off the ballot.

When Obama got to the state Senate, he learned some useful lessons. Illinois is in some ways a microcosm of America with big cities and rural areas, so Obama was able to get a sense of the process and personalities of a big-time legislature. Since he served in the minority for most of his tenure, he had to learn to be realistic. He put together compromises, sometimes with conservative members of the other party, rather than merely scolding them in the press to appease his liberal base. He took on serious issues (health care, criminal justice and death penalty restructuring, campaign finance and lobbying reform) and moved up quickly to a leadership role where he used his skills at reconciliation to bring together factions within the Democratic caucus, as well as members of both parties. He tried to balance the needs and interests of his local constituents with wider statewide interests. And he demonstrated an understanding of the interplay between the "inside" game of politics (working quietly with colleagues and adversaries behind the scenes) and the "outside" game (dealing with the media and the public). He was a reformer who sought change, but tried to do so without unduly alienating the devotees of the status quo who dominate most every legislative body in America.

Obama did provoke some grumbling during his state Senate days. Critics on the left felt he compromised too much in his dealmaking with conservatives, and that he dodged some votes on contentious issues such as abortion. He missed a key gun violence law vote when he was in Hawaii (although most of his detractors backed off when they learned he extended his stay because his young daughter was ill). Critics on the right were uncomfortable with his positions on the death penalty and racial profiling, maintaining that such views exposed his liberal agenda and instincts. And he undermined his reformer image by assertively securing earmarked spending projects for his district and by occasionally helping his financial contributors win government contracts.

In 2000, Obama challenged incumbent African-American congressman Bobby Rush for his seat in the U.S. House. For neither the first nor the last time, Obama's fancy education, heritage, and manner caused his opponents to question his "blackness," with some of Rush's supporters calling him "a white man in blackface." Rush easily retained his seat, and Obama, somewhat chastened, returned to Springfield.

But just three years later, Obama launched a run for an even bigger office, the U.S. Senate. The retirement of Republican Peter Fitzgerald created an open seat, but Obama would have to fight his way through a crowded Democratic primary field, featuring state-wide officeholder Daniel Hynes and multimillionaire businessman Blair Hull. If he won the nomination, Obama would then have to tackle Republican Jack Ryan, also a multimillionaire business-man, in the general election. Obama got some lucky breaks—and made some luck of his own. Both Hull and Ryan ultimately self-destructed over disclosures of embarrassing divorce details. Obama campaigned energetically throughout Illinois, extended his strong state fund-raising base into a national one, and forged a multiracial coalition of support. He won 52 percent of the vote in the primary, well ahead of Hynes, and, after winning the nomination, was tem-porarily able to campaign unopposed after Ryan withdrew from the race in June 2004.

The search for a Republican candidate to replace Ryan dragged on for a comically long time, with several wealthy businesspeople and former Chicago Bears' coach Mike Ditka flirting with the idea but ultimately backing away. In the interim, Obama grew stronger, raising money, campaigning around the state, and building up the snowball of national and international press coverage that would peak with his delivery of the keynote address at the Democratic National Convention in Boston that summer. All the attention might have overwhelmed someone with less poise and assurance, but Obama, expressing bemusement, kept his bearings. "I haven't changed," he said at the time. "It's the situation that's changed. I'm still just me."

The Illinois Republican Party recruited Alan Keyes, a magnetic former Reagan administration official and 2000 presidential candidate from Maryland. Keyes, a conservative African American, waged a messy and underfunded campaign marked by vitriol and personal attacks. Obama deliberately avoided a negative approach, and won with 70 percent of the vote, becoming the only African American in the Senate and just the third since Reconstruction.

> *"There's not a liberal America and a conservative America—there's the United States of America. There's not a black America and white America and Latino America and Asian America—there's the United States of America. . . . We are one people."*
> **—at the Democratic National Convention, July 2004**

In his U.S. Senate career, Obama has been active for a freshman, seeking to sponsor bills and striking the occasional bipartisan deal, such as with Republican senator Richard Lugar of Indiana on legislation involving nuclear proliferation. As a senator envoy, he has traveled to Europe and the Middle East, and his trip to Africa in 2006 attracted special notice and an international frenzy. As he remarked, "Obviously, I've got a personal connection to Africa that makes the trip special. I also have a deep, abiding interest in what happens to the African continent as a whole." Obama has a consistently liberal voting record, as do all but a handful of Senate Democrats. But evaluating Obama's fitness for the presidency is difficult. Like John F. Kennedy, Obama has been marked as a potential presidential candidate from the day he was elected to the Senate, with his every move scrutinized. It is only appropriate, therefore, to grade this phase of his career with an "Incomplete."

When he got to Washington in 2005, Obama went out of his way to keep as low a profile as possible. Still, the newly minted freshman made an impact. Many of his colleagues were impressed by his quiet intelligence, his star quality, and his fund-raising ability. He received more requests for speeches, interviews, and other public appearances than virtually any member of Congress in American history—literally hundreds a month. The press and public clamor was too much for him to ignore completely, and yet, even after he began his presidential bid, many of his fellow senators (with the occasional exception of those running against him for the Democratic nomination) put aside their jealous tendencies and enjoyed the Obamapolooza along with everybody else.

Obama originally took himself out of the running for both president and vice president for the 2008 race, but it is an indication of the national media's often reverential coverage of his career that he paid no discernible price for his artful about-face announcement on *Meet the Press* in October 2006 that he was considering a run.

Several factors contributed to

> Obama has cited Abraham Lincoln and Martin Luther King as his political heroes. He also likes to quote Lyndon Johnson's comment, "Every man is trying to live up to his father's expectations, or make up for his mistakes."

Obama's change of heart. First, the tour for his 2006 book *The Audacity of Hope* generated the kind of national publicity that few political figures ever see, suggesting a ready-made army of donors and supporters around the country. He was heavily in demand to campaign and raise money for Democrats in 2006, and made appearances in more than twenty states, including a particularly electrifying performance in Iowa at a political steak fry hosted by Democratic senator Tom Harkin. Second, many of Obama's Senate colleagues discreetly told him he would make a dynamic candidate, adding that they had concerns about the leading Democratic contenders. Third, a study by his advisers indicated that windows of opportunity for potential presidential candidates do not open very often, regardless of age, and that Obama's chance might not come around again anytime soon, if ever.

The Content of His Character

Obama's soft-spoken manner and people-pleasing instincts have caused some observers to think he is not very ambitious. This is clearly wrong. He expressed an interest in politics and the presidency as early as childhood; gained acceptance to elite universities; prevailed in the heavily contested, famously cutthroat competition to be president of the *Harvard Law Review*; ran for the state legislature without much political background; challenged an incumbent U.S. House member; wrote two books; won a U.S. Senate seat; and had the, yes, *audacity* to run for the presidency. This is a wily man of long-standing, well-packaged, but no doubt potent ambition.

Ambition is to be expected in a candidate, but action is important in a leader. Obama's lack of executive and national security practice and his relative unfamiliarity with federal issues temper some of the enthusiasm his adherents feel about his potential presidency, but close observers have an additional concern. Throughout his career, and even now as a presidential candidate and an orator, Obama gravitates toward the ethereal and the abstract. His mind is supremely analytical, which benefits an advocate, a writer, and a legal scholar, but not necessarily a candidate for president or a commander in chief.

As Bill Clinton—also a former constitutional law professor—discovered, the White House is a place for action, not introspection. Clinton got off to a slow start in his presidency in part because he miscalculated the pace of the presidency. The pressures of the job did not allow for reflection and equivocation. Those afflicted with what Jesse Jackson has called "the paralysis of analysis" still can thrive in some settings by moving to act as needed, often after careful deliberation. But in the constant wild rush of the White House, where every decision reverberates and consequences are global, a presidency must constantly move forward, sharklike, or fail.

Interestingly, in part because of his intellectual, thoughtful nature, Obama appeals more to upscale, wealthy voters than to the less well off. Early in his campaign, Obama struggled for the support of those he fought for as an activist and whose needs he prioritized as a politician. Even when he talks about his years as a community organizer in Chicago, Obama does not always seem to be imbued with the soul and spirit of the effort. Obama's failure to become *the* candidate of the party's liberal wing is manifested in the criticism he has endured on Internet blogs. Yet Obama's most zealous fans believe he can eventually unite the Eugene McCarthy and Bobby Kennedy wings of the Democratic Party, bringing together antiwar, clean-government types with pure economic populists.

One of Obama's great strengths is his capacity to see all sides of an issue and talk about them empathetically. This quality appeals to his listeners, who sense that he is tolerant, objective, and rational.

It also lends him a welcome nonpartisan aura. But such a reflective approach also can be a weakness, when it prevents Obama from taking a definitive point of view. His well-received book *The Audacity of Hope* is filled with his analyses of difficult issues in an on-the-one-hand-on-the-other-hand fashion. This can be a frustrating or negligent trait in a politician. Along with his lack of seasoning in world affairs, it could cause concern that he might not know what to do in a time of crisis.

Face of the Future

Obama has made a few enemies over the years but not many. He endured some criticism before his presidential run, but not much. The attributes that attract many Americans now—his engaging manner, his obvious respect for differing points of view, his intellect and humor—have brought about the academic and professional success he has enjoyed since young adulthood.

America has become vastly polarized, and voters want a candidate who can unite the country after sixteen years of Bill Clinton and George W. Bush. Many, including independents and even some Republicans, see this potential in Obama, even without full knowledge of his background, his bipartisan achievements in the Illinois legislature, or his platform. Part of the reason, clearly, is his race, coupled with his persona. Many Republicans who disagree with Obama's posture on most issues say they are pleased he is running for president. A few even admit they would be curious, and not unhappy, to see him win. Those Republicans include some of George W. Bush's top campaign advisers, as well as rank-and-file party members from around the country.

Although he has occasionally flouted some of the Democratic Party's sacred cows—pondering changes to Social Security, tweaking unions, criticizing some African Americans for their inconsistent voting or parenting choices, expressing compassion for Palestinians—in the main, Obama is a conventional liberal Democrat. He argues for nonpartisanship—even postpartisanship—yet he has rarely backed that up with performance. In the Senate, he has been part of the occasional effort at bipartisan compromise, but as a presidential candidate, he has mostly been part of the negativity that currently dominates the country's politics, even as he has regularly called for an end to the politics of the past.

In 2002 he directly and vociferously denounced the Iraq War, calling the planned venture "dumb," and presciently argued that the invasion's aftermath would be difficult and dangerous. At the time, this was a politically risky move, as poll numbers indicated Americans felt favorably toward the offensive. (It should be noted that this was long before he began his tenure in the Senate, and therefore was not faced with a vote.) By 2006, when his presidential candidacy was in the offing and the Iraq War was widely reviled, he enjoyed highlighting his consistency on the issue, and attacking those who had initially supported military action. Yet as a senator, he has not been a leading force for pulling troops from Iraq and ending the war; he repeatedly voted for additional funding, and did not join the loudest voices on the Senate floor calling for accelerated withdrawal.

Obama has been a smoker on and off throughout his life, though he has made a commitment to kicking the habit once and for all. His wife told *60 Minutes*, "One of my prerequisites for entering into this race is that he couldn't be a smoking president . . . America, keep an eye on him and call me if you see him smoking."

Furthermore, he has been more of a follower than a leader when it comes to pressuring the Bush administration to change course. His condemnation of those Democratic rivals who voted to authorize the war in 2002 has therefore lost potency as the race has moved forward. And as a presidential candidate who wants to represent the future, he cannot spend too much time railing about the past.

Michelle Obama

Even in a presidential cycle overflowing with impressive candidate spouses, Michelle Obama makes a powerful impact. Graceful, striking, brilliant, and accomplished, she has audiences murmuring that she should consider running for public office as well. But she is neither a natural politician nor a natural political spouse. She is dubious about the carnival aspects of political life, and has had to learn to relax at events, project her voice on the stump, and accept the constant intrusion of the press. Yet, as she has said, "If politics were my passion, I'd find out how to do it and make it work. But it's not mine. It's Barack's, and so it's a good balance because I have a bunch of different passions that don't necessarily conflict." Now an elegant, fluent campaign speaker, Michelle Obama serves as a strong advocate for her husband's candidacy, eloquently explaining his dedication to public service and his plans to heal the country, but happy to humanize him by describing his tendency to leave dirty socks on the floor; complaining about his history as a cigarette smoker ("that is the dark underbelly of Barack Obama; that and the sock thing"); and winking at her husband's deific image ("not a perfect person; close, but not perfect"). She makes a point to stress this last theme, often reminding supporters, "He's a gifted man, but in the end, he's just a man."

Barack Obama, meanwhile, adopts the well-received, if slightly grating, role of meek, docile husband, portraying his wife as a no-nonsense, all-knowing arbiter. A favorite line on the stump, which has various incarnations depending on the crowd, is "I did what every wise man does when confronted with a decision: I prayed on it, and I asked my wife."

Born Michelle LaVaughn Robinson, she has described herself as "Chicagoan through and through." Both her parents were Windy City natives, and she has aunts, uncles, and cousins all over the area. Her father, the late Frasier Robinson, was a city pump operator and her mother, Marion, worked as a secretary. She grew up on Chicago's South Shore, was a disciplined and active student at a magnet high school, followed her older brother to Princeton University on scholarship (he is now head basketball coach at Brown University), and then got her law degree at Harvard. She went to work at the posh Chicago firm Sidley Austin Brown & Wood, specializing in marketing and intellectual property, where she and Obama met in 1989, when he interned during a summer break from law school and she was assigned to supervise him. Tiring of the rarified air of the law firm, she left for a job in Chicago mayor Richard Daley's office, and has since worked as executive director of the nonprofit group Public Allies, as an associate dean of students at the University of Chicago, and as vice president at University of Chicago Hospitals. She has also served on a number of boards, including the Chicago Council on Global Affairs and TreeHouse Foods.

> Michelle Obama's college thesis was titled "Princeton-Educated Blacks and the Black Community."

Child-rearing is serious business for Michelle Obama as well, she organizes the schedules of their two daughters with piano, ballet, gymnastics, tennis, potlucks, school events, soccer, and chores for everyone, and she is unwilling to let the campaign encroach too much on such domestic endeavors. Of potential physical threats to her high-profile husband, she told *60 Minutes*, "I don't lose sleep over it, because the realities are that, you know, as a black man, Barack can get shot going to the gas station, so you can't make decisions based on fear and the possibility of what might happen. We just weren't raised that way."

Perhaps it is superficial to point out that the Obamas are good-looking, but the country places an emphasis on physical appearance, even for politicians, particularly in the modern age. (The comeliness of John and Jackie Kennedy has been discussed for decades.) There are quite a number of attractive candidates and spouses in the 2008 race, but those young, dishy Obamas certainly make a handsome pair (and a tall one—she is five feet eleven, he is six feet one). Their charming daughters, Malia and Sasha, complete the picture.

Just as Barack Obama manages to convey a healthy ambition to be president combined with a refreshing distance from the swaggering spectacle of the race, so, too, does Michelle Obama strike a sensible balance on the campaign trail. She is neither a Stepford spouse with a frozen grin and programmed patter, nor an overly aggressive surrogate, pushing her policy views, ready for a fight (although she has been known to complain about the opposition on occasion). Rather, she delivers speeches of substance, describing her husband in an unadorned and compassionate manner, and expressing her hopes for a stronger, more tolerant America. Michelle Obama is a powerful asset on the trail, aided at times by Malia and Sasha, who are, in their father's words, "gorgeous, healthy, and mischievous."

So Much, So Soon

Barack Obama is a young man, particularly for a national politician (if he were a pro tennis player or a reality television star, perhaps he would look a little long in the tooth). Most of his competitors are about a decade and a half older than he, and a full generation removed. Obama is not intimidated; on the contrary, he likes to emphasize this distinction, to contrast himself as a man of the future, of change, of energy. He rarely appears callow, having matured quite early. Additionally, he has had fewer years to modify his views with shifting times, basically remaining the same, in outlook, style, and philosophy. In a race in which flip-flopping is a sin and You-Tube is the confessional, a consistent record is an asset.

America has had several presidents with about the same amount of experience in elective office as Obama—some successful and some less so. In the last century, Theodore Roosevelt, Woodrow Wilson, Herbert Hoover, Jimmy Carter, and Ronald Reagan all had relatively brief prepresidency political careers. Others have been similarly young. President Kennedy was only forty-three when he was elected, although he had served a full term in the Senate and several in the House before that. President Clinton assumed the job at forty-seven, but previously had been governor of Arkansas for more than a decade. Obama has been on the national scene for just a few years. Can one make a leap from phenom to leader of the free world, when the country is facing major problems?

As with most other 2008 candidates, Obama has failed to lay out specifics in many major areas of interest to voters. The press and his critics often link the issue of his inexperience with the shortage of policy particulars he has presented. Obama and his supporters argue that no one is truly and discernibly prepared for the role of president before taking office and that he has begun to detail his plans. They also insist that sterling judgment and a range of real-

He loves Scrabble, and has said "when it comes to Scrabble I just can't help myself . . . I've got a competitive nature."

life skills matter more than Washington credentials, a governorship, administrative expertise, or reams of policy papers.

There is little Obama can do to fully address doubts about his readiness for the hardest job in the world. It likely will be his conduct over the next several months, as much as his arguments about the applicability of his professional history, that may or may not convince skittish voters that he can command the Oval Office.

Areas of Potential Controversy

– The details of Obama's admitted transgressions, such as his use of illegal drugs as a youth and a real-estate deal with shady Chicago businessman Antoin Rezko.

– The regrettable tradition of corrupt practices in Chicago and Illinois politics, which might taint him by actual or implied association.

– Stock investments he made along with some of his campaign contributors in speculative investments shortly after becoming a U.S. senator.

– The unexplored periods of his life before he entered public office.

– The accusation that he took more than the literary license he acknowledged in *Dreams from My Father* to flavor the truth.

– His name is Barack Hussein Obama, which is often twisted to evoke dictators and terrorists. Childish, perhaps, but for those who wish to subtly imprint his exotic background and scare off voters who might prefer a more traditional candidate, that name packs a wallop.

Why Obama Can Win a General Election

- America wants change. Obama is perceived as an agent of change, superficially because of his age and race, practically because of his unwavering anti–Iraq War stance, and intrinsically because of his platform and values. If 2008 is a "change" election in which voters want to turn the page, nothing says change more than a youthful black man who talks relentlessly about the importance of change—generational change, attitudinal change, policy change, change for change's sake.

- Without political or historical baggage, and with what could be an unprecedented Internet-fueled grassroots army, Obama could maximize the advantages that the Democratic nominee is expected to have after eight years of George W. Bush. By hammering issues such as the Iraq War and duplicity in the White House, he might win handily.

- Obama could cause energetic minority turnout in some major Blue states such as California, Michigan, Pennsylvania, New York, and New Jersey, allowing Democrats to secure their electoral votes without significant effort. Obama's appeal to younger voters could bring many of them to the Democratic column. A nomination win for Obama will have launched the process of affecting the electorate itself, drawing to the polls the young, alienated, and disenfranchised in the general election as well.

- Electing a black candidate would likely inspire many elements of the Democratic Party's base, including labor unions, gay and lesbian groups, and civil rights groups, to immerse themselves in the election and to work hard for Obama.

- In some southern and midwestern states, Obama's celebrated candidacy could boost African-American turnout disproportionately, with most of the votes going to the Democrat. This could put typically Red states such as Ohio, Louisiana, North Carolina, Tennessee, Virginia, and Florida in play. Obama understands how to reach out to rural and suburban white voters—parts of southern Illinois, where Obama is now a popular figure, are closer, geographically and culturally, to Tupelo, Mississippi, than to Chicago.

- Throughout his public career, Obama has proven he can attract a first-rate staff of advisers, who tend to be tight-knit and to keep their office clashes out of public view. He has hired talented and highly regarded Democratic consultants such as David Axelrod, who say they find him personally inspirational and are deeply committed to seeing him win.

- He is likable and confident. One of the traits credited to George W. Bush when he first contemplated a run for the White House was how comfortable he was with himself. Obama is Bush's equal in that regard, but without the Bush swagger that has produced some complaints of personal machismo or policy stubbornness in the White House.

- Obama's ease in any social situation will allow him to campaign in a wide variety of venues. Already he has appeared to positive reviews at Rick Warren's Saddleback Church in California, on *Monday Night Football*, on Jay Leno's couch, and several times on his friend Oprah Winfrey's program. There is almost no cultural, educational, high-culture, pop-culture, or sports entity in America that would not like to book Barack Obama for an event in the next year. Most candidates have to fight for that kind of publicity and access to voters.

- The national media would give his campaign tens of millions of dollars' worth of favorable coverage. One of the reasons the widely circulated "I've Got a Crush on Obama" YouTube video received a great deal of attention from political reporters was that it expressed the secret harbored by some in the press—they are sweet on him.

- If the major party candidates choose to fund their general election campaigns with private donations rather than with the fixed public amount to which they are entitled, Obama's impressive fund-raising strength would serve him well. He has been a fund-raising whirlwind, both in the amount raised and in the number of donors enlisted. Just seven weeks after launching his campaign, he broke fund-raising records, raising large contributions from rich supporters and small donations from grassroots and Internet fans. His home base, Illinois, is a wealthy state. He is popular in the coastal bastions of glamour and money, New York and California. He can continue to charm major donors in person at private fund-raisers, while also romancing Internet supporters, whose more modest donations nevertheless add up fast and furiously. He also has been able to raise additional funds with a line of merchandise: Obama tees, pins, and stickers are unusually successful. He has become both a pop-culture icon and a hip fashion statement.

Why Obama Can't Win a General Election

- Obama's life story mixes conventional candidate imagery with the unconventional—and even unprecedented. While he has amassed Ivy League degrees, statewide elective office in a big state, conspicuous recognition as a star in his party, and multimillion-dollar fund-raising tallies, he is of biracial heritage, has admitted to using cocaine, and has a complicated family history.

- Obama's strongest primary and general election opponents in his 2004 Senate race were eliminated by personal scandals, so he has never been tested in a tough statewide or national election. While he has faced brickbats already in the nomination contest with more to come, the general election is sure to feature months and months of unrelenting Republican attacks. The man Maureen Dowd of the *New York Times* has dubbed "Obambi" might not be up to the fight. He is so dismissive of the conservative politico-media attack machine that has won many elections for the Republicans in the age of the Freak Show that he might be unprepared for its sway. As he wrote in *The Audacity of Hope*, "By nature, I'm not somebody who gets real worked up about things. When I see Ann Coulter or Sean Hannity baying across the television screen, I find it hard to take them seriously . . . I've never believed there are a bunch of people out there who are pulling all the strings and pressing all the buttons." If Obama becomes the Democratic nominee and still holds this quaint opinion, he will need to watch a lot more Fox News, keep a closer eye on the Drudge Report, and monitor Rush Limbaugh if he is to have a chance to win.

- The "experience" concern is not to be minimized on any level, including campaign skills. Obama has worked hard, but he has never been under the pressure he will face in the presidential race. He asserted in May 2007 that ten thousand people had died in a Kansas tornado disaster, when in fact only twelve had been killed. He chalked it up to a fatigue-driven misstatement. A small moment, perhaps (and certainly innumerable politicians have mixed up their facts or made silly mistakes), but also one that might give pause to those concerned about how much sense and readiness one can store up in a handful of decades. At a minimum, it showed that Obama is susceptible to erring when he is tired. But he also can blunder when he is alert, displaying a lack of instinct and judgment—no matter how bright he may be, no matter how fast a learner, nothing can make up for on-the-job knowledge and practice. Sloppy responses to foreign policy questions during the slew of summer 2007 Democratic debates resounded in the media for weeks afterward, and set off a war of words with his opponents. This could prove fatal to his chances for 2008.

- In the nomination process, Obama's race is probably a plus, given the makeup of the Democratic electorate. In the general election, however, his race would be a more nebulous factor. The hidden antiblack vote, including from whites and from Hispanics and Asians who could resent Obama's rise, might outweigh any increase in turnout from African Americans. This could put must-win states such as Ohio, Michigan, Iowa, Wisconsin, and Pennsylvania out of reach. And Obama's black support might not be quite as overwhelming as his advisers contend. Even Obama has observed some black unease with his candidacy. "It's interesting that the people who are most hesitant about this oftentimes are African Americans because they feel protective of me," he has said. "They're either concerned about the attacks I'd be subjected to or they are skeptical oftentimes that America is prepared to elect a black president."

- Obama has not been immune to the type of question-able and foolish business decisions that beleaguer so many politicians. He involved himself in a controversial real-estate transaction involving the purchase of his current home and the adjacent parcel of land, sold to him by longtime financial backer Antoin Rezko, who was later indicted on charges of corruption. Obama has admitted, "I am the first one to acknowledge that it was a boneheaded move . . . given that he was already under a cloud of concern," which makes one wonder why Obama made such a dubious choice in the first place.

- Obama is not always the world's most mesmerizing speaker. Daringly, he eschews applause lines (the red meat of the conventional candidate stump speech), dismissing them as indulgent pandering and a waste of time. But without those expected cues and pauses, an Obama appearance can seem a little droning and draggy. Many Americans are likely to be surprised at how soft-spoken and cerebral Obama normally is in public. Obama's moments in the sun (his 2004 convention speech, his presidential announcement in Springfield) have shown him as a fiery and fired-up orator, but that is not how he usually presents himself, even to large crowds. While Obama initially can light up a room with his charisma, it is hard to sustain that electricity during an hourlong town hall meeting, and it may not spark at all for those who only see him on television.

- He was until recently a smoker; even those who love (or crave) a relaxing burst of nicotine recognize that such behavior is dangerous.

The Best Case for an Obama Presidency

- Abroad, the world could see an America turning away from internationally unpopular policies with a president very different in ideology and background from President George W. Bush. Obama could use his diverse cultural perspective to reach out to countries around the world.

- At home, the crucible of race—the enduring American puzzle—would have a chance to be addressed in an unprecedented fashion.

- He would enact a fundamental change in the way Washington does business that he has promised on the campaign trail, such as reducing the influence of special interests, lobbyists, and campaign donations on the political process.

The Worst Case for an Obama Presidency

- The worst fears about Obama's inexperience, inaction, and inadequate instincts on national security might be realized. Obama might lack the personnel and management abilities required of a president. He might dither, ponder, and fret instead of making tough decisive choices, leading to peril and chaos.

- Elements of the right and center might be appalled by the liberal causes he would pursue, leading to Clinton-Bush-style polarization.

- The job causes serious stress, and he might smoke like a chimney.

What to Expect If Obama Is President

An Obama presidency would, at least initially, energize the nation, get some young people to focus on politics, and open a new discussion about race in America. Interest groups and journalists would count the number of minorities on his staff. Close attention would be paid to the résumés and expertise of his cabinet, and how Obama would acclimate to the power and authority of the office.

The White House press corps would swoon at press conferences, at least for the first six months. Media coverage of his international trips would return to the wall-to-wall levels of interest not seen since the Cold War.

Michelle Obama, as the first career-oriented First Lady of the twenty-first century, would make a profound choice between her professional aspirations and the manner in which she could apply her legal acumen and private skills to the duties of the East Wing. Women across the country would likely mimic her stylish appearance. The Obama daughters, who no doubt would be protected from the spotlight by their parents, nevertheless would provide adorable photo ops at the inauguration; at Christmas, Easter, and other holidays; and in unexpected John-John-under-the-desk moments.

The city of Chicago—its architecture, its food, its fashions, its neighborhoods—would enjoy its biggest blaze of distinction since Mrs. O'Leary's cow.

The state of Hawaii—its beaches, its food, its people, its tourist trade—would enjoy its biggest moment in the sun since Steve McGarrett last said, "Book him, Dan-O."

The search would be on for the Obama summer White House location.

Obama's Own Words

"I stand here knowing that my story is part of the larger American story, that I owe a debt to all of those who came before me, and that in no other country on earth is my story even possible."

—in his keynote speech at the Democratic National Convention, July 2004

"When I'm in rural Illinois and see some elderly white couple, I see my grandparents. When I watch black girls playing Double Dutch on Chicago's South Side, those are my daughters."

"In some ways, because it has happened so quickly or maybe because I don't have much sense, I haven't had the opportunity to get too freaked out about it."

—on his sudden skyrocket to political fame

"This is something I'm not enjoying about the presidential race. Me getting screwed I'm fine with. Suddenly everybody who's ever touched my life is subject to a colonoscopy on the front page of the newspaper."

"I have high expectations for myself. And I usually meet them"

What His Supporters Say

"He's very unusual, in the sense that other students who might have something approximating his degree of insight are very intimidating to other students or inconsiderate and thoughtless. He's able to build upon what other students say and see what's valuable in their comments without belittling them."

—Harvard Law School professor
Laurence Tribe, in 1990

"The true test comes when he is elected and he gets in there and starts having to make tough decisions. This is being looked at as sort of 'happily ever after.' But we will need prayers and help when we are in the belly of the beast."

—Michelle Obama, on her husband's Senate race

"I know people might find this hard to believe, but Barack is doing this because he feels he is personally blessed with so much that he owes it to society not to just sit back and be idle."

—Michelle Obama

"Barack is more comfortable without a plan. His whole life wasn't a plan."   —Michelle Obama

"He was the kind of [basketball] player to pass the ball, even if he was the best one on the court. But if push came to shove and the team needed to win, he wasn't afraid to take the big shot. That's the kind of leader we need in this country."

—Hill Harper, actor and Harvard Law classmate,
on Obama's basketball and leadership skills

"Barack is the most unique political talent I've run into in more than fifty years. I haven't been this excited about a candidate since Adlai Stevenson first got me into politics."

—former Illinois congressman, judge, and Clinton
administration White House counsel Abner Mikva,
who also has said, "He has restored 'liberal' to the
vocabulary. He knows how to build bridges with people
who don't necessarily agree with him."

"I know him personally. I think that what he stands for, what he has proven that he can stand for, what he has shown, was worth me going out on a limb for and I haven't done it in the past because I haven't felt that anybody—I didn't know anybody well enough to be able to say, I believe in this person."

—Oprah Winfrey, on endorsing Barack Obama,
her first time ever endorsing a political candidate

What His Critics Say

"You can think big, but remember, you shouldn't always say everything you think if you're running for president, because it has consequences across the world."   —Senator Hillary Clinton

Obama Facts and Stories

– Although he is now "skinny," according to his own description, not to mention gangly, lanky, rangy, and gaunt, he was downright chubby as a child.

– In Indonesia, Obama's family had a variety of pets, including a turtle; an ape named Tata; and some crocodiles, which were kept in a concrete tub.

– He has said his favorite childhood TV show was *I Spy*. Now he watches C-SPAN when he has time.

– He worked in a Baskin-Robbins as a teenager in Hawaii, and as a result is not an ice cream fan.

– As a student in the 1970s, he signed his last name in yearbooks with a large O decorated with an Afro.

– When he arrived in New York City to attend Columbia University, he spent his first night sleeping on his luggage in an alley because there was a mix-up with his new landlord.

– He has said an alternate career would have been as an architect.

– He speaks Spanish and a "smattering" of Swahili.

– His half sister, Maya Soetoro-Ng, is a history teacher who lives in Honolulu.

– His grandfather Stanley Dunham, whom he called "Gramps," died in 1992. His grandmother Madelyn, whom he calls "Toots," remains in Hawaii.

– His mother died of cancer in 1994; he writes movingly of her in his books.

– His brother-in-law Craig Robinson, who like younger sister

Michelle, attended Princeton University on a scholarship, was the school's fourth-leading scorer in its basketball history. He is a frequent campaign speaker for Obama.

– He was named one of the "40 Under 40" by *Crain's* Chicago in 1993.

– He was named one of the world's most influential people by *Time* magazine.

– He was named one of the most influential black Americans by *Ebony* magazine.

– He received a Grammy Award in 2006 for the audio recording of his book *Dreams from My Father*.

– He received an NAACP Image Award for his book *The Audacity of Hope*, in 2007.

– Both *The Audacity of Hope* and the reissued edition of *Dreams from My Father* have been best sellers.

– He has appeared on *The Oprah Winfrey Show*. Icon and media mogul Winfrey is a major supporter.

– As a student and activist, Obama was teased (good-naturedly) for his tattered jeans and ratty sweaters; in recent years (particularly after winning a seven-figure advance for his recent book) he has updated and improved his wardrobe.

– Obama has carried a passbook belonging to his Kenyan grandfather. According to Obama, his grandfather "was a cook and he used to have to carry this passbook to work for the English. At the age of forty-six it had this description of him that said, 'He's a colored boy, he's responsible and he's a good cook.' "

– The walls of Obama's Senate office are hung with photos of Nelson Mandela, Abraham Lincoln, Martin Luther King Jr., John F. Kennedy, Mahatma Gandhi, Thurgood Marshall, and Muhammad Ali.

– Obama and his wife and daughters live in a four-bedroom home in Hyde Park, on the South Side of Chicago, financed in part with proceeds from his book advance.

Quirks, Habits, and Hobbies

– Although he has listed fried chicken and chili among his favorite foods, as a child in Indonesia, according to his memoir, he sampled "dog meat [tough], snake meat [tougher], and roasted grasshopper [crunchy]."

– The Obamas currently have no pets, but, according to the parents, the children are aiming to leverage the 2008 race to get a dog.

– His favorite sport to play is basketball.

– He told the Associated Press that his worst habit is frequently checking his BlackBerry.

– Musical favorites include Miles Davis, Sting, Thelonius Monk, Aretha Franklin, and Stevie Wonder (who serenaded Obama during an event at the AME Church in Los Angeles in spring 2007). Obama told *People* magazine that "I'm old-school, a jazz guy, but I'm current enough that I've got a little bit of Jay-Z, the Fugees and Beyoncé." Michelle Obama reported, "Marvin Gaye is one of his favorites. He loves to sing 'Let's Get It On.' You need to get him to get up and do that. He's not shy, if you sort of coax him."

– He drives a Chrysler 300C sedan, and said his first car was "A Ford Granada. It was a terrible car. It was a tin can. The thing would rattle and shake."

– He reads the Harry Potter series aloud to his older daughter. He also enjoys E. L. Doctorow, Toni Morrison, Philip Roth, and John le Carré.

– He likes to joke about his unusual name and the mispronunciations he endures: "Alabama" and "Yo Mama" are particularly popular.

The **Undecided Voter's Guide Questionnaire**

For what unhealthy food do you have the biggest weakness?

French fries.

In what way would you hope America would most fundamentally change by the end of your time in the White House?

I hope it will be said that we restored civility to our public discourse, and used the White House to forge a new sense of unity and common purpose among the American people; that we opened up government and changed the tone and nature of politics in Washington so we finally could get important things done on challenges like universal health care and energy independence that had languished for decades.

And I hope that we will have regained respect and our moral leadership in the world, making America more secure through the responsible and intelligent use of our military when necessary, but also through aggressive diplomacy and new initiatives to bring hope and opportunity to the forgotten corners of the earth.

What is your most memorable childhood activity?

Body surfing at Sandy Beach in Hawaii.

What is the biggest single difference between men and women, besides physiology?

I won't touch that.

What is your most strongly held superstition?

I'm not superstitious.

Name someone you would like to see in your cabinet, or, at least, tell us what would be most distinctive about your cabinet.

I want a cabinet filled with people of competence, integrity, and independence—most importantly, no yes-men.

What is the worst thing you did as a teenager?

Drugs.

How are you most different as a person than your parents?

I'm less sentimental than my mother and more invested in my family than my father.

What is your favorite way to relax (besides spending time with your family)?

Reading a good book.

Where is your favorite place to vacation?

Hawaii.

Presidential Announcement

Barack Obama made his official announcement on February 10, 2007, at the Old State Capitol in Springfield, Illinois, where Abraham Lincoln held office and, later, as president, delivered his 1858 "House Divided" speech against slavery. The day was brilliantly bright and frigidly cold, but the event drew an astonishing number of observers and supporters, men and women, diverse in race and ethnicity, estimated at more than fifteen thousand. It was only a few weeks earlier that Obama had indicated his intention to consider a run for the White House. After being introduced by Democratic

Illinois senator Dick Durbin, his chief campaign booster, Obama made his entrance, to the blossoming chords of U2's "City of Blinding Lights." He shook hands with his fans; flashed a dazzling smile; and greeted his wife and daughters, who joined him briefly on stage (sensibly, they were bundled up in hats and scarves, unlike Obama, who wore only a coat, although he reportedly had a portable heater secreted nearby), and left him to his remarks. People in the crowd beamed and cheered, waving "Obama 08" signs and glossy head shots of their candidate. He summarized his biography, talked about the troubles in Washington with special interests and partisanship, condemned the Iraq War, and made reference to God and his personal faith. Obama spoke clearly, with deliberation, poise, and passion. Nor was he shy about drawing comparisons between himself and everybody's favorite Civil War president, saying, "The life of a tall, gangly, self-made Springfield lawyer tells us that a different future is possible. He tells us that there is power in words. He tells us that there is power in conviction. That beneath all the differences of race and region, faith and station, we are one people. He tells us that there is power in hope." Upon finishing his speech, Obama did as many modern-day presidential candidates do when officially launching a campaign, and headed straight to Iowa. Excerpts from his statement:

February 10, 2007
Old State Capitol, Springfield, Illinois

I recognize there is a certain presumptuousness—a certain audacity—to this announcement. I know I haven't spent a lot of time learning the ways of Washington. But I've been there long enough to know that the ways of Washington must change.

The genius of our founders is that they designed a system of government that can be changed. And we should take heart, because we've changed this country before. In the face of tyranny, a band of patriots brought an empire to its knees. In the face of secession, we unified a nation and set the captives free. In the face of depression, we put people back to work and lifted millions out of poverty. We welcomed immigrants to our shores, we opened railroads to the West, we landed a man on the moon, and we heard a king's call to let justice roll down like water, and righteousness like a mighty stream.

Each and every time, a new generation has risen up and done what's needed to be done. Today we are called once more—and it is time for our generation to answer that call.

For that is our unyielding faith—that in the face of impossible odds, people who love their country can change it.

That's what Abraham Lincoln understood. He had his doubts. He had his defeats. He had his setbacks. But through his will and his words, he moved a nation and helped free a people. It is because of the millions who rallied to his cause that we are no longer divided, North and South, slave and free. It is because men and women of every race, from every walk of life, continued to march for freedom long after Lincoln was laid to rest, that today we have the chance to face the challenges of this millennium together, as one people—as Americans.

All of us know what those challenges are today—a war with no end, a dependence on oil that threatens our future, schools where too many children aren't learning, and families struggling paycheck to paycheck despite working as hard as they can. We know the challenges. We've heard them. We've talked about them for years.

What's stopped us from meeting these challenges is not the absence of sound policies and sensible plans. What's stopped us is the failure of leadership, the smallness of our politics—the ease with which we're distracted by the petty and trivial, our chronic avoidance of tough decisions, our preference for scoring cheap political points instead of rolling up our sleeves and building a working consensus to tackle big problems . . . And if you will join me in this improbable quest, if you feel destiny calling, and see as I see, a future of endless possibility stretching before us; if you sense, as I sense, that the time is now to shake off our slumber, and slough off our fear, and make good on the debt we owe past and future generations, then I'm ready to take up the cause, and march with you, and work with you. Together, starting today, let us finish the work that needs to be done, and usher in a new birth of freedom on this earth.

Read More About Obama

Barack Obama, *Dreams from My Father: A Story of Race and Inheritance* (New York: Three Rivers Press, 2004). Obama's memoir of his early life and the marriage and legacy of his white mother and black father.

Barack Obama, *The Audacity of Hope: Thoughts on Reclaiming the American Dream* (New York: Crown, 2006). Obama's memoir of his political life and his thoughts on current American society.

The *Chicago Tribune*'s multipart series about their adopted hometown son, http://www.chicagotribune.com/news/politics/chi-obama-life-storygallery,0,1773480.storygallery??track=sto-relcon.

http://www.barackobama.com/

MORE DEMOCRATS

JOE BIDEN

The Basics

Name: Joseph Robinette Biden Jr.

Born: November 20, 1942,
Scranton, Pennsylvania

Political party: Democrat

Spouse: Jill Tracy Jacobs Biden,
married June 17, 1977

Children: Naomi Christina (deceased),
Joseph R. III, R. Hunter (with
Neilia Hunter Biden, married
1966, died December 18, 1972),
Ashley Blazer (with Jill Biden)

Religion: Roman Catholic

Education: University of Delaware,
B.A., 1965
Syracuse University, J.D., 1968

Career: Partner, Biden and Walsh,
Wilmington, Delaware 1968–1970
Member, New Castle County Council,
Delaware, 1970–1972
U.S. senator, Delaware, 1973–present
Presidential candidate, 1988
(unsuccessful)
Adjunct professor, Widener University
School of Law, 1991–present
U.S. representative to the General
Assembly, UN, 2000
Presidential candidate, 2007–present

Speed Racer

Joe Biden runs at full speed. He thinks fast and talks fast. He is full of ideas, energy, and enthusiasm. He won his U.S. Senate seat at just twenty-nine, and made his first run for the presidency twenty years ago, when he was forty-four years old. What slows him down is his own spirited, impetuous personality. It gets him into trouble, distracts from his message, and sometimes lends a cartoonish quality to his otherwise impressive political stature.

In his 2007 autobiography, Biden explains two of his childhood nicknames, both relevant today. "Joe Impedimenta. My classmates hung that nickname on me our first semester of high school [Latin class] . . . It was one of the first big words we learned. Impedimenta—the baggage that impedes one's progress. So I was Joe Impedimenta. Or Dash. A lot of people thought they called me Dash because of football. I was fast, and I scored my share of touchdowns . . . [but] they called me Dash because of [my] stutter . . . That impedimenta ended up being a godsend for me. Carrying it strengthened me and, I hoped, made me a better person. And the very things it taught me turned out to be invaluable lessons for my life as well as my chosen career."

Biden has needed that strength of character because he has endured great tragedy. A month after he was elected to the Senate in 1972, a car accident killed his wife, Neilia Hunter Biden, and baby daughter Naomi, and critically injured his two young sons, Beau and Hunter. He rarely discusses this catastrophe and when he does so, it is always with poignant composure. He began his Senate career in a shroud of grief, and with the help of his sister Valerie, divided his time between tending to his sons in Delaware and performing Senate business in Washington. His sons recovered, and eventually he remarried, to educator Jill Jacobs; they have a daughter, Ashley. That second marriage, like his tenure in the Senate, has lasted more than thirty years.

Biden grew up in a middle-class family and, unlike most senators, has never gotten very rich. Although he has become one of the world's leading diplomat-legislators and a fixture on network television talk shows, he continues to prioritize his working-class constituents in Delaware as he makes public policy decisions. He sees himself as a regular guy, and, even after all these years in Washington, he is down to earth and accessible.

He considered running for president as early as 1984, and threw his hat in the ring for 1988. His candidacy came to an embarrassing halt when it was revealed that he plagiarized a speech by British Labour Party leader Neil Kinnock; further disclosures included his unattributed use of a Robert Kennedy quote and another accusation of plagiarism while in law school. Biden's withdrawal from the presidential race in September 1987 was followed by even more bad news. In February 1988, he suffered two brain aneurysms, nearly died, and spent seven months recuperating, with titanium clips in his head.

Once healthy and back in the Senate, he contributed two decades of solid work and rehabilitated his reputation, emerging as a respected statesman. When the old controversies now arise, he addresses his errors in judgment with contrite candor, and the specifics are largely downplayed by Democrats and the media as blips in the broad span of his accomplishments. He recently said of his tainted 1988 run, "I didn't deserve to be president. I wasn't mature enough." That was then: Biden, and indeed others in his party, now believe he does deserve to be president, and in many ways, is the most qualified candidate in the race, regardless of low poll numbers or weak fund-raising tallies.

Nevertheless, Biden's biggest problem remains that personal quirk, or flaw—his loose tongue, which is connected to his frisky brain. His intelligence is marred by a lack of discipline and an occasional imprudence of speech. His rather headstrong, careless nature has led him to make new mistakes, such as remarking "You cannot go to a 7–Eleven or a Dunkin' Donuts unless you have a slight Indian accent. I'm not joking," or describing Senator Barack Obama as "articulate and bright and clean and a nice-looking guy." That quote hit the news cycle on January 31, 2007, the same day Biden announced his decision to run again for the presidency, and supplanted every molecule of good press he might otherwise have received.

One might argue that a headstrong, careless nature is not well suited to the presidency. But Biden's gaffes and blunders seem to be confined to his personal conduct, and have not had any measurable impact on his actions in the Senate. On the campaign trail, Biden can deliver coherent, incisive, and inspiring remarks, at a small house party, a large rally, or on television programs, and impress everyone as a smart, creative, thoughtful leader with great ideas and a commitment to solving problems. Then, once in a crowd of supporters, or in a gaggle of journalists, he can trip up with awkward statements, goofy smiles, and endless chatter. Media stories seldom fail to cite this last trait; two examples include a July 2007 *New York Times* story headlined "In Iowa Yard, Biden Talks (and Talks) about Experience," and a March 2006 *GQ* profile titled "Joe Biden Can't Shut Up."

Biden is well aware of his problem, and his advisers have begged him to rein himself in. These days he is the first to poke fun at his big mouth; he usually opens his appearances on late-night talk shows and news programs with a self-deprecating joke. He earned raves during a Democratic presidential debate when asked this question: "Can you reassure voters in this country that you would have the discipline you would need on the world stage, Senator?" His reply: "Yes." The audience responded with stunned silence and then delighted laughter and applause.

To some degree, Biden must be forgiven his moments of bad judgment and loquaciousness. He brims with enthusiasm for discussing his thoughts and strategies—he is a font of excellent, well-considered proposals. When he touts himself as the most accomplished person in the race, he makes an excellent case even though he lacks executive experience. In the Senate, where he chairs the Senate Foreign Relations Committee, he has proven to be a skilled and resourceful legislator, particularly on issues of war and foreign policy. He has taken nearly a dozen trips to Iraq, surreptitiously inspecting the scene before the war began and returning regularly throughout the conflict. He has been one of the leading voices in favor of dividing Iraq into three sectarian states, with a central capital, so that most American troops can be withdrawn without undue delay. He also played a leading role on landmark legislation involving funding for the United Nations and limiting the spread of chemical weapons. He has been chairman of the Judiciary Committee, spearheading legislation on drug laws, anticrime legislation, and the Violence against Women Act. He is mostly an activist liberal, but a hardheaded one who is unafraid to criticize his party when he thinks it falls short. For example, he has complained that some Democrats are too reluctant to discuss the role of faith in public life.

Many political players and members of the press speculate that Biden is aware of his uphill path to the Democratic nomination, and is in reality positioning himself for secretary of state, a job he was expected to get in a John Kerry administration. He is highly qualified for that assignment as well, as a bona fide expert on international relations. In addition to formulating an exit strategy in Iraq, he took the lead on addressing the conflict in Bosnia during the Clinton administration, and can talk with clarity, command, and passion about genocide and the crisis in Darfur. He knows diplomats and public officials around the globe from his years traveling abroad as part of America's foreign policy elite. "I know most of the world leaders," he says. "Not because I'm an important guy, but because I've just come up with them."

But at the moment, Biden is running for the top job, with the determination and optimism that has buoyed him throughout his life.

Why He Has a Chance

When he keeps his goofier side in check, Biden comes across as a reliable and shrewd leader. His three and a half decades in Congress, working with seven presidents, is a plus. He still has many friends in Iowa and New Hampshire from his aborted 1988 presidential run. The country could be well served by a relentlessly energetic foreign policy expert. Despite having spent virtually his entire career in the Senate, he does not come across as an insulated Washington insider. With his Irish Catholic background, real-guy manner and bank account, and unpretentious perspective, he seems instead like a defender of the people, an idealized image of a politician.

Voters often give Democrats credit when they risk talking tough, and Biden isn't shy. He treats President Bush with caustic disdain—he has unapologetically deemed him "brain dead," and has hurled a slew of other insults the president's way. He lashes out freely at the Republican Party as well, with stinging outrage and precision.

Biden Facts and Stories

– Joe Biden was born in Scranton, Pennsylvania, and grew up in Wilmington, Delaware, the eldest of four children, and the son of the late Joseph Robinette Biden Sr. and Jean Finnegan Biden.

His mother now resides with him and Jill Biden. His father passed away in 2002.

– In the wake of the car accident that killed his first wife and daughter, Biden began a daily routine he continues to this day: he commutes round-trip by train between his home in Wilmington, Delaware, and Washington, D.C. All of those ninety-minute, hundred-mile trips have made Senator Biden a major advocate of public transportation.

– Son Beau Biden (formally Joseph R. Biden III), is attorney general of Delaware, elected in 2006, and a captain in the Delaware National Guard. His unit was notified in August 2007 that it will likely be deployed to Iraq in 2008. Hunter Biden is a Washington attorney who served in the Clinton administration.

– Biden has five grandchildren.

– His sister Valerie Biden Owens has been his top campaign adviser in all of his races.

– He does not smoke or drink.

– He loves to sketch and design homes, and says an alternate career would be as an architect.

– Biden remains a man of comparatively modest means; he and his wife sold one house to finance their sons' college educations, and took out a second mortgage to pay for their daughter's tuition. He has jokingly begged people to buy his book so he can pay off his children's student loans.

– His owns a 1967 Corvette, a gift from his father, who was a car salesman.

About Biden

"He's a man of immense character and integrity, as decent as any-one I've ever met in this business. I think he would make a very knowledgeable, experienced, and effective president."

—Republican senator Chuck Hagel of Nebraska

Read More About Biden

Joe Biden, *Promises to Keep: On Life and Politics* (New York: Random House, 2007). Biden's autobiography.

http://www.joebiden.com/

CHRIS DODD

The Basics

Name: Christopher John Dodd

Born: May 27, 1944,
  Willimantic, Connecticut

Political party: Democrat

Spouse: Jackie Marie Clegg,
  married June 18, 1999

Children: Grace, Christina

Religion: Roman Catholic

Education: Providence College, B.A.,
  1966
  University of Louisville School of Law,
  J.D., 1972

Career: Volunteer, Peace Corps,
  Dominican Republic, 1966–1968
  Member, U.S. Army Reserve and
  Connecticut National Guard,
  1969–1975
  Lawyer, Suisman, Shapiro, Wool &
  Brennan, New London,
  Connecticut, 1973–1974
  U.S. congressman, Connecticut,
  1975–1980
  U.S. senator, Connecticut,
  1981–present
  Chairman, Democratic National
  Committee, 1995–1997
  Presidential candidate, 2007–present

Experience Matters

Chris Dodd is the embodiment of a classic northeastern, liberal, Democratic career politician. He has been a U.S. senator for Connecticut more than twenty-five years, a job once held by his father, Thomas J. Dodd. He has been involved in public service his entire adult life: he spent two years in the Peace Corps, enlisted in the U.S. Army Reserve and Connecticut National Guard, entered the House of Representatives in 1975, joined the Senate in 1981, and served as Democratic National Committee chair for several years during the Clinton administration. He tends to favor big-government solutions to America's problems and has been a force on the Senate Banking and Foreign Relations committees. On the surface, Dodd, a white-haired Washington insider, is perhaps not the most fresh-faced candidate in the race. But he is confident he is the most qualified, because, as he says repeatedly, "this time around, experience really does matter."

There are two kinds of senators—those who become famous, and those who don't. Chris Dodd so far falls into the second category. Despite his decades in the House and Senate, his high-profile legislative accomplishments, and his reputation as a delightful man and a great talker, Dodd has not penetrated the public consciousness in the 2008 race or joined the top tier of candidates. Even when he was the Democrats' national party chairman, he remained mostly an inside figure. He has always been somewhat overshadowed by the people around him—his imposing father; his larger-than-life crony Ted Kennedy; and his prominent, outspoken Connecticut colleague Joe Lieberman. Now he is overshadowed by a host of intriguing presidential competitors.

Most underdog candidates convince themselves that all they have to do is meet every voter in the country and they'll win. In Dodd's case, it might be true. He has been remarkably popular in his home state, and is considered highly articulate and gracious by his colleagues and staff. He has an understated charisma, and, as he points out, "Celebrity and the amount of money you've raised is becoming less and less important . . . No one can name a horse in the Kentucky Derby until Derby Day . . . The issues of who can win and who can govern, who could lead the country in the direction we hope it will go in is going to become more and more important. And you can't acquire those skills overnight. I could become well-known in 24 hours, I could raise money if I'm the nominee . . . I know how to do this. I've done it for others and I've done it for myself." But Dodd will have to find a different strategy to separate from the pack, whether it means honing his killer instincts, breaking through with his story of solid experience and competence, or just having some old-fashioned luck.

Dodd was born in Connecticut to an Irish Catholic family, and moved to Washington in 1959 when his father was elected to the Senate. He attended prep school and then entered Providence College, his father's alma mater. Inspired by the ideal of national service and volunteerism, he joined the Peace Corps, and was assigned to the Dominican Republic, where he erected buildings, learned Spanish, and "grew up quickly." Dodd, who often cites his Peace Corps years as some of the best of his life, has since gone many times to Latin America, and takes a particular interest in issues related to the region.

Thomas Dodd, a reserved man who spent eighteen months as a lead prosecutor in the Nuremberg tribunals after World War II, and served in Congress, saw his Senate career blighted with a 1967 censure for alleged financial impropriety. He lost his 1970 reelection bid, suffered a heart attack, and died in 1971, four months after leaving the Senate. Chris Dodd had been in the Dominican Republic as the scandal unfolded, but worked in the 1970 Senate campaign, and was deeply affected by his father's somber end. As Democratic Hawaii senator Daniel Inouye, a colleague of both father and son, once remarked, "Sometimes, I think almost everything Chris Dodd does down here [in Washington] is meant to vindicate his father." Dodd married a speechwriter from his father's 1970 campaign, finished law school, worked briefly in a law firm, and ran successfully for Congress in 1974 (observers had conflicting views about whether the Dodd name hurt or helped—certainly, the Watergate scandal was beneficial to a Democrat aiming to topple a Republican incumbent). Six years later, Dodd won his father's old Senate seat.

In the Senate, Dodd is widely viewed as a leader who doggedly pursues his legislative goals by patiently building coalitions. He is credited with finding the right balance between the prosaic nitty-gritty details of public policy and the poetry required to sell ideas to the public. As an internationalist, he has been at the center of several high-profile foreign policy issues over the decades, most visibly fighting to end American military assistance to the Nicaraguan Contras in the 1980s and working with President Clinton to facilitate the Good Friday peace agreement in Northern Ireland in the 1990s. He has also pursued major domestic legislation, notably on banking and family issues. Dodd calls himself the "Children's Senator," having spent seven years leading the effort to pass the Family Medical Leave Act, which lets employees take unpaid leave after the birth of a child or to care for a sick relative. Bill Clinton often calls the law one of the proudest achievements of his presidency, and Dodd has since pushed to expand the measure's provisions. He spearheaded child care legislation, sought funding for autism research, is a longtime supporter of early childhood education, and was named "Senator of the Decade" by the National Head Start Association in 1994. That same year, he just narrowly missed becoming the Democratic Senate minority leader.

Dodd follows a clean line of Democratic voting, almost without fail. He supports abortion rights, a pathway to earned citizenship for illegal aliens, universal health care, gay rights, and election reform. He has put forth one of the most aggressive energy and environmental plans of any of the candidates, proposing to reduce greenhouse gas emissions and curb dependence on foreign oil, in part by increasing taxation on carbon emissions.

He has become increasingly outspoken against the Iraq War, and, though he voted to authorize military action in 2002, he now blames the Bush administration for using "fabricated" evidence to induce congressional support. He has pressed for a plan to set an end date of early 2008 for military funding.

Like most members of Congress, Dodd sometimes puts aside his ideological emphasis in favor of more parochial constituent and contributor interests. He has been a longtime advocate for the insurance and banking industries, many of which are based in his homestate and have given him a lot of campaign cash, leading some to wonder if this has sometimes motivated his legislative actions more than his usual populist, liberal posture. When he was appointed chairman of the Senate Banking Committee in 2006, there was some apprehension about how he would find a proper balance and how it might affect his presidential platform. Dodd says his approach to government regulation of the financial sector is "fair and open," indicating he would both protect individuals and allow the free market to flourish, with his decisions impossible to predict or pigeonhole. But critics suggest that in some cases he has tilted too far in favor of the financial community—for instance when he opposed certain regulation of hedge funds.

Dodd sometimes spoofs his senior statesman facade (he laughs about his "snow on the mountaintop" and made a YouTube campaign video mocking his white-haired image with the help of a white hare), but he is known as a witty, captivating man and is the father of two young daughters. Ending a twelve-year marriage in 1982 without any children, he led a bachelor's life, enjoying rowdy outings with fellow senator and onetime partier Ted Kennedy. In the late 1980s, Dodd began dating Jackie Clegg, then a Republican congressional staff member; they married in 1999, following a decade-long courtship. Grace, named after both their mothers, was born on September 13, 2001; Christina was born on March 1, 2005. He often jokes on the campaign trail, "I'm the only presidential candidate who gets mail from AARP and diaper services." He has adjusted happily to late-in-life fatherhood: "It is great. You always want to be polite when people pull out the pictures. I've always sort of gone through the motions pretending to be interested. Now I am flashing pictures all over the place." He has said that the birth of Grace two days after September 11, with the smoking flank of the Pentagon visible from the hospital maternity ward, is what made him think seriously about running for president, after two decades working contentedly in the Senate.

Why He Has a Chance

Dodd offers a reliable, traditional image of a seasoned New England Democrat. He has a sterling résumé, a kindly manner, and a sensible approach. In a race populated with complicated biographies, new faces, and eccentric personalities, Dodd's steadfast persona could be a plus.

He is said to have a sly and clever sense of humor and an ease with people of all ages and backgrounds. If he lets these traits fully emerge on the campaign trail, they could help him stand out.

He is bold, proud of his party, and unperturbed by the ups and downs of the political game. After the massive GOP midterm victory in 1994, when Republicans were crowing and Democrats were cowering, he marched into the Senate press gallery and announced, "My name is Chris Dodd, and I am a Democrat." That take-charge attitude and partisan pride is well suited to the current political environment.

Dodd Facts and Stories

– Dodd has five siblings, with whom he is very close (teasingly, they address him as "Senator"). His eldest brother, Thomas J. Dodd Jr., served as the U.S. ambassador to Uruguay and Costa Rica during the Clinton administration. Other siblings include a teacher, a photographer, and a mother of five. A younger brother suffered a stroke nearly a decade ago and now lives with him. Chris Dodd has said that his siblings have avoided political careers because of their father's anguish over his Senate censure.

– He was present at John F. Kennedy's inaugural address.

– He is fluent in Spanish, thanks to his two years in the Peace Corps in the Dominican Republic.

– He married speechwriter Susan Mooney in 1970; they were divorced in 1982. Before remarrying in 1999, he dated celebrities such as Bianca Jagger and Carrie Fisher. The *Hartford Courant* once referred to Dodd and Ted Kennedy as the Playboys of the Western World.

– His wife, Jackie Clegg, is a Mormon. Their daughters were baptized in the Catholic Church and blessed in the Church of Jesus Christ of Latter-Day Saints, and are learning about both religions.

– Utah native Clegg is about a decade and a half younger than her husband and comes from a family of stalwart Republicans.

– He has kept his father's old desk and chair in his office.

– He had a cameo in the 1993 Kevin Kline film *Dave*.

– He told the Associated Press that his favorite meal to prepare is "an August New England dinner: lobster, corn, and tomatoes."

– He drives a 2007 Ford Escape hybrid.

– He plays tennis and rides a bicycle for exercise.

– He announced his candidacy on the *Imus in the Morning* radio program on January 11, 2007.

– He lives in East Haddam, Connecticut, with his family.

About Dodd

"Chris Dodd can take you apart and leave you smiling."

—Democratic strategist Harold Ickes

Read More About Dodd

Chris Dodd and Lary Bloom, *Letters from Nuremberg: My Father's Narrative of a Quest for Justice* (New York: Crown, 2007).

http://www.chrisdodd.com

DENNIS KUCINICH

The Basics

Name: Dennis John Kucinich

Born: October 8, 1946, Cleveland, Ohio

Political party: Democrat

Spouse: Elizabeth Harper Kucinich,
married August 21, 2005

Children: Jacqueline Kucinich
(with Sandra Lee McCarthy)

Religion: Roman Catholic

Education: Cleveland State University,
1967–1970

Case Western Reserve University,
B.A., 1973

Case Western Reserve University, MA,
1974

Career: Member, Cleveland City
Council, 1970–1975

Clerk of courts, Cleveland Municipal
Court, 1976–1977

Mayor, Cleveland, Ohio, 1977–1979

Radio talk show host, 1979

Member, Cleveland City Council,
1981–1982

Media consultant, 1982–1994

State senator, Ohio, 1994–1996

U.S. congressman, 1997–present

Presidential candidate, 2003–2004
(unsuccessful)

Presidential candidate, 2006–present

The Road Already Taken

In 2003, Ohio congressman Dennis Kucinich announced that he would run for president of the United States. He was seen as the ultimate fringe candidate, offbeat and quirky, but engaging and articulate, with an explicit antiwar, pro-workers' rights, pro-universal health care, anticorporate message. He provided a passionate voice and a vibrant dash of comic relief throughout the grim, angry 2004 campaign. After winning only 1 percent of the vote in the Iowa caucuses and New Hampshire primary, and failing to make his mark in other states, Kucinich finally threw his support to John Kerry and continued his career in Congress. But he remained a presence on the national stage, as a champion of liberal principles and a vocal opponent of the Iraq War and the Bush administration.

Few were surprised when Kucinich said he would try again for the White House in 2008, and he was greeted as a campaign veteran with interesting ideas and an established, if small, following. Nevertheless, members of his party and the press consider his chance at the presidency relatively slim—but Kucinich does not care. He has absolute confidence in his values and is indifferent to pundit opinions and poll numbers. He wants to spread his message far and wide, even if it doesn't get him to the White House. He relishes all sorts of media attention, whether for his antiwar rhetoric, his lively debate performances, or his eccentric image.

And Kucinich has much to contribute to the political dialogue. His platform has distinctive elements and thoughtful ideas and reflects the views of many in the nation. He is an economic populist in the spirit of his longtime ally Ralph Nader and the quintessence of a full-fledged, old-school liberal presidential candidate—an endangered species since Bill Clinton shifted the party to the center and "liberal" became a dirty word, eschewed by Democrats and mistrusted by many voters. Kucinich's ideological record is unwavering—the liberal organization Americans for Democratic

Action has rated him at the top of the charts for his voting record. Some of his policy proposals are unique in the Democratic candidate field, and he doesn't mind being different.

There is a tendency to portray Kucinich in fantastical terms. Media profiles compare him to a wizard, a sprite, an elf. To be sure, he presents an atypical figure for a politician—he is a slight five feet seven inches with merry, button eyes and conspicuous ears. He follows a vegan diet (which omits all animal and dairy products) and has said of his nutritional regimen, "It's consistent with a desire to help participate in sustaining the planet . . . And it also sustains my health, which creates a reciprocal relationship between self and world."

His personal life is unconventional as well. By 2004 Kucinich was twice divorced, with a grown daughter, and single after the breakup of a long-term relationship. He declared himself on the market for a girlfriend as well as for votes, and subsequently participated in a "Dating Game" segment on *The Tonight Show with Jay Leno* (he was paired with actress Jennifer Tilly). In May the following year, he met Elizabeth Harper, a striking, six-foot-tall redhead from England, when she visited his office as a representative of the reform group American Monetary Institute. He proposed marriage at their next encounter, and they wed three months later. Elizabeth Kucinich shares her husband's philosophy, vegan diet, and hopes for the future. She dismisses curious comments about the disparity in their ages (she is about three decades younger) and heights: "Who cares? I like wearing high heels so I'm used to being taller than most men I stand next to." She also mirrors her husband's mind-set—when pondering life as First Lady, she remarked, "Can you imagine what it would be like to have real love in the White House and a true union between the masculine and the feminine?"

Kucinich's campaign style is also unusual. He is a skilled ventriloquist, and has been known to provide levity by bringing out his dummy to answer questions and discuss Washington politics. In February 2007, to illustrate his independence from special interests at an AFSCME labor event for Democratic candidates, he twirled in front of his podium, arms outstretched, and shouted, "A president with no strings!" He revolved slowly, calling out "No strings!" as fans in the audience yelled back,"No strings!" He continued to chant "No strings!" as he twirled off the stage. That is Kucinich: a wizard, a Prince Charming, and an autonomous marionette.

Yet his life hardly began as a fairy tale. He grew up in a poor Ohio family, the oldest of seven children. His father, Frank Kucinich, was a truck driver who struggled to make ends meet, and moved the family twenty-one times before Kucinich turned seventeen. Money was so tight they occasionally were homeless; Kucinich has said matter-of-factly that he slept in "a few cars" during his youth. He often mentions that he wore the same pair of turquoise and black striped trousers every day for more than a year—"like something out of a psychedelic prison"—until a concerned teacher bought him some new ones. He has recalled his gratitude for the help of acquaintances when his family was in trouble. He lived in an orphanage for five months as a teen when his parents could not look after him, and left home for good before his eighteenth birthday. Kucinich was a hardy soul; despite his size, he made third-string quarterback at the private Catholic school Saint John Cantius (which he paid for with earnings from part-time and summer jobs).

Despite all those hardships, young Dennis had weighty ambitions. When he was fourteen, he wrote, "Throughout high school I've done quite a bit of creative writing and have enjoyed it. Someday I intend to be an author, but I consider this secondary. My main ambition is, and will be, a career in national politics." He added, "and I'm going to aim for the very top." As a college student, he took jobs while enrolled full-time at Case Western University. At just twenty-three, he won a seat on the Cleveland City Council, after a first attempt at age twenty-one.

In 1977, at thirty-one, Kucinich ran for mayor of Cleveland and won the job, along with the nickname "boy mayor." He soon acquired less favorable monikers such as "Little Runt" and "Dennis the Menace." He angered everyone from the business community to the City Council to the media. He refused to sell the city's electric company, Municipal Light, to alleviate Cleveland's budget woes; engaged in vituperative public squabbles, such as firing his police chief live on the evening news; and struggled to save the floundering city. He survived assassination attempts and a recall election (holding his job by only 236 votes), and lost his 1979 reelection campaign to Republican George Voinovich (later Ohio governor and now a senator), leaving Cleveland in fiscal chaos. Kucinich served another year as councilman, then slunk away from Ohio politics, traveled west, and experienced financial hardship, losing his house and holding a variety of jobs. But he found spiritual enlightenment during his trips to California and New Mexico, where he met with sages and alternative healers and contemplated matters of war and peace.

Back in Ohio, he ran unsuccessfully for Congress in 1988, but his political aspirations were bolstered by the revelation that his refusal to sell the electric company as mayor had ultimately saved taxpayers an estimated $200 million. In 1994, with a lightbulb as his campaign logo and the smug slogan, "Because he was right," Kucinich won a seat in the Ohio state senate. Two years later, he was elected to Congress (his campaign motto: "Light up Congress with Kucinich"). He served the first decade of his congressional career in the minority, with Republicans controlling the House, limiting his effectiveness. He was a reliable liberal vote on most foreign and domestic issues, but the circumstances did not allow him to author or help pass any major legislation. He was a bystander in the wars between centrist Bill Clinton and the Republican majority, and his status did not improve in the Bush administration. Still, he appeared regularly on the House floor, giving impassioned speeches to national C-SPAN audiences about welfare, education, and health care. In his district, Kucinich has been popular, easily winning reelection, although his liberal social policies disturb some of his Catholic and conservative constituents. His love of the national spotlight does not seem to have alienated his hometown support.

In February 2002, Kucinich delivered a speech titled "A Prayer for America" to the Southern California chapter of Americans for Democratic Action. Infused with religious and patriotic energy, it began, "as a prayer for our country, with love of democracy, as a celebration of our country. With love for our country. With hope for our country. With a belief that the light of freedom cannot be extinguished as long as it is inside of us. With a belief that freedom rings resoundingly in a democracy each time we speak freely. With the understanding that freedom stirs the human heart and fear stills it. With the belief that a free people cannot walk in fear and faith at the same time." Kucinich then enumerated the ways in which he believed the Bush administration had erred, and lamented the damage to the American spirit. It so inspired his audience that it launched a grassroots effort for his 2004 presidential bid.

Kucinich has been an unwavering opponent of the war in Iraq. He voted against authorizing military action in 2002, and has since called it an "illegal war," demanding that troops be withdrawn and the United Nations sent to resolve the conflict. He has made the end of the war a centerpiece of his presidential platform. In the spring of 2007, he introduced articles of impeachment in the House against Vice President Dick Cheney for his alleged conduct related to the war. He also has said he would cut the Pentagon budget and talks of creating a Department of Peace, to promote domestic and international harmony.

He supports single-payer health care, tax increases on the wealthy, and the regulation of corporations. He opposes free trade agreements, such as NAFTA and the United States' membership in the World Trade Organization. He considers gay marriage a "civil rights issue," supports abortion rights (he was prolife before running for president in 2004), and has sponsored legislation promoting stem cell research. His years of financial struggle have made him outspoken and heartfelt about the issue of poverty in America.

Kucinich is deeply spiritual. He was raised a Catholic, and has immersed himself in a variety of religious and mystical pursuits. During an interview with the faith-centered Web site Beliefnet, he told the reporter, "I'm meditating now. This conversation with you is a meditation . . . it is a constant flowing in and flowing out of spiritual principles, connection to thought, which is derived from spirit. It's the way I live every moment." His Catholic upbringing has influenced his ideal of "nonviolence as an organizing principle in our society."

Why He Has a Chance

Kucinich, despite his ethereal, earnest persona, is a hip, compelling fellow. His vegan lifestyle; stunning, groovy wife; unusual life story; and grave integrity appeal to many young voters who might turn out to support their impish hero. He has never required much money to campaign (he is accustomed to doing without cash when necessary), but he has raised a steady stream of donations from Internet supporters and liberal fans.

Kucinich represents an ideology similar to that of Ralph Nader, who found measurable success as a presidential candidate with the Green Party. A number of Americans embrace this platform, yet the top-tier 2008 candidates have not incorporated all of these positions. Kucinich considers himself the natural leader of this sector of voters, who he says are the new center of the country's political spectrum.

His political viewpoint is guided in large part by his spirituality, which could appeal to Red state voters. Faith is very important in his life, but he does not impose his religious beliefs on others, which could satisfy more secular citizens.

He is utterly sincere and unshakable in his views. Voters are bloodhounds when it comes to hypocrisy and pandering, and Kucinich is refreshingly principled.

As he often says on the campaign trail, "I come to the political system as an advocate for people, not an advocate for any special-interest group. That is what distinguishes me from anyone else in this race."

Kucinich Facts and Stories

– His father Frank, was of Croatian descent; his mother, Virginia, of Irish heritage.

– Daughter Jackie Kucinich (from his second marriage) is a political reporter who lives in Washington, D.C.

– He has been good friends with actress Shirley MacLaine since the 1970s. She has provided spiritual counseling and financial support, and is Jackie Kucinich's godmother.

– His brother Gary Kucinich has also been a member of the Cleveland City Council.

– He did not serve in the military, because of a heart murmur.

– During his break from politics in the 1980s and early 1990s, he worked as a lecturer, a media consultant, and a television reporter.

He also has been a caddy (as a teenager to earn tuition money), a copy editor, and a hospital orderly.
– The Kucinich family does not allow shoes to be worn in their home.
– He has said his favorite song is John Lennon's "Imagine."

About Kucinich

"Dennis Kucinich has dedicated his life to creating the context in which people can come together to work through their differences and to celebrate their humanity. He's a leader with a clear vision for America, a clear vision of hope, a clear vision of peace, a clear vision of social and economic prosperity."

—Democratic National Committee
vice chair Lottie Shackelford

Read More About Kucinich

Dennis Kucinich and Studs Terkel, *A Prayer for America* (New York: Thunder's Mouth Press, 2002).

http://www.dennis4president.com/

BILL RICHARDSON

The Basics

Name: William Blaine Richardson III

Born: November 15, 1947,
  Pasadena, California

Political party: Democrat

Spouse: Barbara Flavin Richardson,
  married August 15, 1972

Children: None

Religion: Roman Catholic

Education: Tufts University, B.A., 1970
  Tufts Fletcher School of Law and
  Diplomacy, MA, 1971

Career: Staffer, U.S. House of
  Representatives, 1971–1972
  Legislative management officer,
  congressional relations, State
  Department, 1974–1976
  Staffer, Senate Foreign Relations
  Committee, 1976–1978
  Executive director, New Mexico state
  Democratic Party, 1978
  Principal, Richardson Trade Group,
  Santa Fe, New Mexico, 1978–1982
  U.S. congressman, New Mexico,
  1983–1997
  U.S. Ambassador to the United Nations,
  1997–1998
  Secretary, U.S. Department of Energy,
  1998–2001

Career (*cont.*): Senior managing director, Kissinger McLarty,
   Washington, DC, 2001–2002
  Governor, New Mexico, 2003–present
  Presidential candidate, 2007–present

The Major Leagues

Everything Bill Richardson does, he does with gusto. When he decided to break the Guinness world record for greatest number of handshakes during an eight-hour period, he shook 13,392 hands while campaigning at the New Mexico state fair. He loves to eat, and is often seen with a heaping plate of food in one hand and a glass of wine in the other. He enjoys a fine cigar. His dress shirts often come untucked and are occasionally stained, his thick shock of dark hair can flop untidily across his forehead. Richardson contends that these comfortably messy qualities are assets—that voters like a regular guy. Indeed, Richardson is a very likable man, with a lively charm and a sparkle in his eye, who cracks jokes throughout his stump speeches, is not afraid to poke fun at himself, and who manages to offer stern assessments of his opponents without sounding mean-spirited or unduly political.

But Bill Richardson is far from a regular guy. He had an unusual childhood marked by privilege and discrimination. He was born in Pasadena, California, to William Blaine Richardson II, the son of an American father and a Spanish mother, and María Luisa López-Collada Márquez, a Mexican native. His father, an American citizen, was born in Nicaragua, raised in Boston, and lived in Mexico City, but traveled with his wife to Pasadena during both of her pregnancies so the children's births would occur on American soil. Bill grew up in Mexico City, where his father was a wealthy and influential banker. At home, Bill learned English but spoke Spanish with his mother, and practiced both American and Mexican customs.

When he was thirteen years old, he was sent to the tony Middlesex boarding school in Concord, Massachusetts. He initially had trouble fitting in with the largely white, East Coast student body, but he maintained his good humor, excelled at sports, and was a star at baseball. He also met future wife Barbara Flavin, a Concord local, during these years. He went on to Tufts University, where he got his bachelor's and master's degrees, and after graduation jumped right into a political career. He worked as a Capitol Hill staffer in Washington, D.C., then moved to New Mexico—in part because of its large Hispanic population—and became executive director of the state Democratic Party in 1978. He ran for Congress in 1980 and lost, but won the seat in 1982 and spent fourteen years working for his constituents on Native American concerns, the preservation of state wildlife, and on national issues such as global warming and the environment. He helped pass NAFTA, was chief deputy whip of the House Democratic leadership, and developed a friendship with then president Clinton, who made him U.N. ambassador in 1997, and secretary of the Department of Energy in 1998. Richardson's work in the cabinet enhanced his expertise in the environment, renewable energy, gas prices, and nuclear power.

While in Congress, Richardson began his daring, almost cinematic, approach to foreign diplomacy. He engaged in delicate negotiations over hostages and peace deals in Iraq, North Korea, Zaire, Nigeria, Yugoslavia, and Kenya. He also traveled to Nicaragua, Guatemala, Peru, India, and Bangladesh. Sometimes he was sent as an emissary of the U.S. government, but in other cases he went as a swashbuckling freelancer out to break through the bureaucracy and do some good. In 1994 he was on the ground in North Korea after an army helicopter was shot down over restricted airspace; one pilot died but the other survived, and Richardson brought them both home. In 1995 he went to Baghdad to negotiate in person with Saddam Hussein for the release of two American contractors who were being held hostage after inadvertently crossing the Kuwaiti border into Iraq. In 1996 he met with Cuban president Fidel Castro and maneuvered the release of three dissidents, and went to Sudan to win freedom for three Red Cross workers held by government rebels. Richardson touts these achievements on the campaign trail as evidence that he is ready to solve the world's diplomatic problems from the White House. He has been nominated four times for the Nobel Peace Prize: in 1995, 1997, 2000, and 2001.

With the end of the Clinton administration, Richardson took a break from public life, working as an adjunct professor at Harvard's Kennedy School of Government and joining the Washington consulting firm Kissinger McLarty. The hiatus did not last long. After being mentioned as a possible vice presidential running mate for Al Gore in 2000, Richardson was elected governor of New Mexico in 2002, and has been hugely popular in the job, winning reelection in 2006 with 69 percent of the vote (and an impressive 40 percent of the Republican vote). He has cut taxes, fought poverty, facilitated opportunities for businesses, streamlined the budget, provided life insurance for members of the National Guard (a move that was duplicated around the country), and improved the education system. He also served as chairman of the Democratic Governors' Association, and was the subject of speculation once again as a possible running mate for John Kerry in 2004. Richardson continued his diplomatic missions, negotiating the release of a Pulitzer Prize–winning New Mexican journalist from Sudan in 2006, and returned to the country in 2007 with the Save Darfur coalition to broker a cease-fire, which lasted for a number of weeks. He traveled to North Korea in April 2007 to bring back the bodies of American soldiers killed in the Korean War.

Richardson is a Hispanic politician, with a vanilla last name. It is safe to say he would be far more famous if he had a traditionally Latin surname. "How is an Hispanic named Richardson?" he often asks. "Well, that is also a slight problem I have with the electorate, because you know I am running for president, and Hispanics don't know I'm Hispanic. In fact, most people don't know who I am—I'm just kidding." That said, he has not been a leading light for the Latin community, and beyond his home state and its surrounding area, has not developed a dominant following among Hispanics nationally. Richardson talks about his heritage with great pride, but takes a practical approach to assimilation and compromise. He supports a path to citizenship for illegal immigrants, but calls for them to learn English, pay back taxes, and undergo background checks. Otherwise, he has not spent much time on other political issues related specifically to the community. He lives by the creed "be mainstream, but retain your culture."

Richardson presents himself to Democratic voters as the only westerner in the race, with a superior hands-on understanding of regional issues related to water, energy, and public lands. He has also put forth national security and energy independence as the two leading issues, and says a priority is regaining America's international standing and getting out of Iraq "in an efficient and honorable way." He advocates a "Hero's Health Card," providing easy access to medical care for all military veterans; he is prochoice, and supports the death penalty and gun rights. He describes himself overall as "a progressive moderate." Watchdog groups have given him high marks for being fiscally responsible with New Mexico's budget. Richardson sometimes tries to make the case that he is the most conservative Democrat in the race, but he has been unable to solidly establish that credential.

Despite his earnest domestic work and daredevil international triumphs, Richardson has made his fair share of errors, professional and verbal, ranging from the grave to the preposterous. During Richardson's term as secretary of energy, Taiwanese-born Los Alamos scientist Wen Ho Lee was accused of stealing nuclear secrets from the laboratory, was fired by Richardson from his job, arrested, and held in solitary confinement for nearly a year. He was eventually released and cleared of espionage. Richardson received a share of the blame for the lax security and bumbling investigation, and was widely criticized for his blustery behavior at the height of the episode. Richardson was caught up in a different kind of controversy after he interviewed Monica Lewinsky for a job, at the behest of the White House.

In 2007 as a presidential candidate Richardson got himself in trouble on a number of occasions. He admitted that he harbored some special sympathy for besieged former attorney general Alberto Gonzales purely because Gonzales is Hispanic. He identified his model Supreme Court justice as Byron White, who wrote the dissent against *Roe v. Wade,* and he seemed somewhat unfamiliar with White's tenure when quizzed later. At a debate hosted by the Human Rights Campaign, a gay and lesbian group, he suggested he believed homosexuality was a choice rather than a biological trait, drawing derision from a key party constituency, despite his long record in support of gay and lesbian rights.

He speciously indicated that he had parlayed his prowess as a teenage baseball player into a major league draft offer from the Kansas City Athletics, and also was muddled and contradictory in identifying his favorite baseball team. On the May 27, 2007, edition of *Meet the Press*, he and moderator Tim Russert exchanged thirty volleys over whether he supported the Red Sox or the Yankees. Richardson stammered the word "no" a total of eighteen times during his responses, and finally insisted he was a definitive fan of both teams, explaining that while Mickey Mantle was his hero and playing center field for the Yankees was his lifelong dream, his "favorite team has always been the Red Sox."

Richardson usually handles these flubs and mistakes with an anxious apology and an admission that "I am not perfect." But he has turned off some potential voters, and has limited his positive buzz from Democratic activists and the media who equate such slips with the question of competence. Richardson is playing in a national arena now, and he had better make sure his pitching arm is limber and his batting form is solid.

Why He Has a Chance

Richardson is the only Democratic candidate who has served as a governor. Governors, with their executive experience and facility with both minor details and macro problems, typically do well in presidential campaigns.

He has a record of solving international problems through force of personality and will, and knows politicians, diplomats, and military leaders around the globe.

He loves to campaign—he enjoys meeting people, relishes the spectacle, and sees the process as an important, extended party. He is garrulous, unapologetically ambitious, cheerful, and unpretentious, tossing around nicknames and sassy insults. His friends in Washington and New Mexico speak about him with great warmth.

He is Hispanic, and while his ethnicity has not fully registered with voters, it offers the public a chance to break down some new barriers. He identifies himself as the first Hispanic Democrat to run for the presidency.

Richardson's signature television ad, which received a good deal of attention when it first started airing in spring 2007, was set in a personnel office, with Richardson applying for a job. His faux interviewer read Richardson's qualifications aloud from a faux ré-sumé:

> "Mm-hmm. Huh. Okay, fourteen years in Congress; U.N. ambassa-dor; secretary of energy; governor of New Mexico; negotiated with dictators in Iraq, North Korea, Cuba, Zaire, Nigeria, Yugoslavia, Kenya; got a cease-fire in Darfur; nominated for the Nobel Peace Prize four times. So what makes you think you can be president?"

Ba-da-bum. That is Richardson's argument in thirty seconds.

Richardson Facts and Stories

– His parents met in Mexico City when his mother worked as his father's secretary. His mother, now in her nineties, still lives in Mexico City. His father passed away in 1972. His sister, Vesta, is eight years his junior. As a child, he attended church every Sunday (for which he credits his grandmother), attended catechism, and received Communion. He has said God continues to play an important role in his life.

– He has had to contend with rumors of inappropriate behavior with women; Richardson denies them adamantly, and points to his solid marriage of more than thirty years. He and his staff have chalked up some of the negative chatter to his physical style with supporters in the office and on the campaign trail. He has promised that his wife, Barbara, who has been described as this election's least-known candidate spouse, will increase her visibility as his campaign progresses. The couple has no children.

– He received a Vietnam draft deferment because of a deviated septum.

– He owns a gun.

– He is perpetually on a diet.

– He likes to watch boxing, play tennis, and ride his horse,
Sundance.
– He drives a Jeep Wrangler.
– Bill Clinton is a close friend.
– He was named one of the twenty-five most influential Hispanics
by *Time* magazine in 2005.
– He announced his presidential candidacy on May 21, 2007, in
Los Angeles. He said of his rival candidates, "Some are rock stars.
I am not, but I have a proven record."
– He and Barbara Richardson live in Santa Fe with their cats,
Squeaky and Jane.

About Richardson

"If there's one word that comes to mind when I think of Bill Richardson, it really is energy."

—Bill Clinton, upon naming Richardson
secretary of the Department of Energy in 1998

Read More About Richardson

Bill Richardson with Michael Ruby, *Between Worlds: The Making of
an American Life* (New York: Plume, 2007).

The *Albuquerque Journal* five-part series about Bill Richardson's life,
http://www.abqjournal.com/richardson/531607nm01-21-07.htm.

http://www.richardsonforpresident.com

PART III: **THE INDEPENDENT**

MICHAEL BLOOMBERG

The Basics

Name: Michael Rubens Bloomberg

Born: February 14, 1942,
Boston, Massachusetts

Political party: Independent

Spouse: None

Children: Emma, Georgina (with
Susan Brown)

Religion: Jewish

Education: Johns Hopkins University,
B.S., 1964
Harvard Business School, M.B.A., 1966

Career: Trader, Salomon Brothers,
1966–1973
Partner, Salomon Brothers, 1973–1981
Founder, Innovative Market Systems,
1981–1986 (renamed Bloomberg L.P.)
CEO, Bloomberg L.P., 1986–present
Mayor, New York City, 2002–present
(reelected 2005)

Mayor Mike

When Michael Bloomberg was sworn in as mayor of New York in January 2002, he began his first job in elected office. Bloomberg is not a career politician. He is one of the country's most accomplished businesspeople, who relatively late in life decided to apply his executive skills to the political arena. He is difficult to define, and in some ways is an unlikely potential presidential candidate. He has been a Democrat, a Republican, and an independent, all in the space of a decade. He is, in his own words, "a five-foot seven-inch billionaire Jew." He is mostly fiscally conservative and mostly socially liberal. He considers the apparatus of Washington, D.C., petty, ineffectual, and self-indulgent.

A Bloomberg candidacy offers several advantages others cannot. He is one of the world's wealthiest people, with a fortune estimated at well over $5 billion and likely more than double that amount. Special interests have no hold over him. He has no obligations to any party or political machine. He has made few enemies in the political world. Should he decide to run for president, he could easily spend $500 million or more on the race and hardly notice a dent in his bank account. Once in office, his advisers say, he would answer to no one except the American people. He is a pragmatic, innovative problem-solver, not an ideologue, and his guiding principle seems to be competence, not political philosophy. In polarized America, the Bloomberg paradigm just might hold the key to the Oval Office.

America has never sent an independent candidate to the White House, but it seems that every four years, the electorate searches for someone outside the Republican and Democratic parties to enter the race. Some independent candidates have enjoyed a degree of success—Texas billionaire Ross Perot was a legitimate contender in 1992 (eventually winning one in five votes), and Ralph Nader had an impact in 2000. Americans are dissatisfied with the insularity and constant clashes of the two-party system. Political theorists and strategists see an opening for a real independent to capture those voters turned off by polarization. Few potential contenders have generated as much interest as Bloomberg. He is not a fiery populist but a cool technocrat who believes the federal government needs less ire and more efficiency. If he decides to run, it will be because he thinks he can win, rather than merely to influence the debate or the outcome.

Bloomberg and his advisers recognize the difficulty of an independent candidacy. The major party candidates have institutional advantages for winning the Electoral College. Some of Bloomberg's positions—he is a strong advocate of gun control, same-sex marriage, and liberal immigration laws—would make it difficult for him to compete for the electoral votes of conservative states. And his temporary membership in, and fiscal support for, the Republican Party, could cause trouble for him in Democratic-leaning states. Bloomberg has said he intends to finish out his second term as mayor and then in 2009 retire from public life to focus on philanthropy full-time. But behind the scenes, his advisers have kept the campaign buzz alive and have laid the logistical groundwork to make a presidential run possible.

His lack of ideological fervor partly explains why Bloomberg has received little backlash for switching political parties, not once, but twice. After a lifetime as a Democrat, he joined the Republican Party in 2001 so he could compete in its less contested New York mayoral primary. In June 2007 he changed his status to independent, leading many to speculate that he was preparing to run for president. Most politicians would be savaged for such apparent opportunism. Yet Bloomberg was never fully comfortable in the Democratic Party, with its tolerance of union rules and penchant for taxation. Meanwhile, his many liberal positions on social issues made him an awkward fit with the Republican Party. His designation as an independent is compatible with his emphasis on non-partisan solutions to economic problems, and with his views on foreign policy and government regulation.

When Bloomberg entered the contest for mayor of New York City as a Republican—the term-limited Rudy Giuliani was finishing his tenure—he opened up his wallet and launched a full-scale effort. But primary day fell on September 11, 2001, and the race was thrown into chaos. The primary was rescheduled, and Giuliani became the most famous mayor in the world. Some wanted to extend Giuliani's term because of his renewed popularity, apparent competence, and symbolic appeal, but those attempts failed. Bloomberg won the Republican nomination, eventually received Giuliani's endorsement ("If he can have half the success with New York City that he has had in business, New York is going to have an even greater future," the outgoing mayor said), and spent $73 million of his own money to win a narrow victory over the Democratic nominee. In January 2002, Bloomberg took the reins of a city filled with skittish citizens, beset by a battered economy, and blighted by a smoldering wound where the World Trade Center once stood. Accepting a token annual salary of one dollar, Bloomberg set up shop at City Hall, eschewing the grand private office for a desk on the main floor surrounded by his staff and replicating the environment he first encountered as a stock trader at Salomon Brothers. As Bloomberg explained, "My whole business life has been out in the open."

In his first term as mayor, he managed the economic crisis brought about by September 11 and other circumstances by raising property taxes and making spending cuts. He worked with local, state, and federal officials and the White House to secure funds to rebuild lower Manhattan and protect the city from future terrorist threats. In contrast to Giuliani, he smoothly managed race relations and dealings with unions and the Democratic-dominated City Council. He commandeered the unruly public school system and saw some results, and enforced a stringent smoking ban in bars and restaurants. The ban was initially controversial, and Bloomberg was accused of infringing on civil rights and causing potential harm to the restaurant industry. But the measure was a success, and has since been adopted in other cities, including that nirvana of cigarettes and laissez-faire, Paris.

Bloomberg followed Giuliani's example and appeared at crime scenes, city disaster sites, and public events, making himself available for press conferences and briefings despite his instinctive annoyance with an intrusive media. He sparked some bureaucratic mutterings and saw his poll numbers drop precipitously, but persevered. He made few mistakes of real consequence, avoided scandal, and ultimately proved to be beholden to nothing but the job, as he had promised.

He won reelection easily in 2005, thanks to a solid record, a contented populace, and another $75 million or so of his own funds, spent mostly on a blizzard of television and radio advertising. In his second term, he vowed to tackle New York's growing environmental problem by pledging to introduce hybrid taxis and impose traffic congestion fees, and by planting more trees. He has been a big advocate of public transportation, and commutes to City Hall by subway (even if his city-appointed SUV sometimes carries him from his home to the most convenient subway stop). He has joined with fellow iconoclast California governor Arnold Schwarzenegger to tackle global warming. He has maintained Giuliani's emphasis on quality-of-life issues such as reducing crime and maintaining clean streets. As a companion law to his smoking ban, he barred trans fats from New York restaurants as a long-term method to cut health care spending. Critics say he has not made sufficient progress on homelessness, housing, education, and lowering taxes. Still, New York is a tough city to govern, and Bloomberg, despite some setbacks, has been almost uniformly judged a success—in some ways, a better mayor than Giuliani, on whose work Bloomberg has built.

Bloomberg has largely supported the Bush administration's policies in Iraq and the war on terror, and points to lower Manhattan as the first battlefield of the conflict. He has made room for some foreign policy experience during his mayoralty, traveling to Israel, Mexico, and Great Britain. He supports abortion rights and same-sex marriage, explaining, "I just think that the government shouldn't be in certain businesses. I don't think it's the government's business to tell you things about your personal life." That civil liberties position partly accounted for his open opposition to the nomination of John Roberts as Supreme Court chief justice. Bloomberg has become one of the nation's most outspoken proponents of gun control, and formed the group Mayors against Illegal Guns, traveling the country and to the halls of Congress to build support, and becoming one of the National Rifle Association's biggest enemies. He considers taxes a "necessary evil" and believes many bureaucratic woes can be solved by the application of new technology, a philosophy that made him immensely rich in the private sector.

Bloomberg is a genial man who socializes with New York's most prominent and cultured residents. Dapper in his well-cut clothes, confident in his power and flair, he mingles happily at galas and cocktail parties, attends swank dinners, and savors the New York nightlife. He comes off as brash but earnest, arrogant but solicitous, brilliant but unaffected. His closest friends include luminaries in the worlds of business, entertainment, and the arts. He has long been a trustee of some of the city's most fashionable and influential cultural organizations, such as the Metropolitan Museum of Art, Lincoln Center, and the Central Park Conservancy, and is a member of the American Academy of Arts and Sciences. He does not conceal his great wealth—he owns homes in Bermuda, London, Vail, and North Salem, New York, and has remained in his own East Side, 7,500-square-foot, multimillion-dollar town house rather than move into the designated mayor's residence, Gracie Mansion. He is a pilot who has his own airplane. He plays golf whenever he can. But he is neither pompous nor ostentatious, and is exceedingly generous with his money. He is consistently rated by *Forbes* as one of the most charitable of the billionaire set, giving away more than $150 million annually in recent years. In a way, Bloomberg's mayoralty is an extension of his philanthropy.

Bloomberg was born in Boston and grew up in Medford, Massachusetts, the son of William Bloomberg, a bookkeeper, and Charlotte Rubens Bloomberg, a homemaker. He received a bachelor's degree in engineering from Johns Hopkins and a business degree from Harvard, and, after graduating in 1966, went to work at Salomon Brothers in an entry-level position. He was promoted to equities trading, and made partner in 1973, relishing the excitement of Wall Street and the luxuries it provided. He met British-born Susan Brown in 1973; they married and had two daughters, Emma and Georgina.

In 1979 he was transferred to Salomon's information systems division where he worked with computers; he considered the move a demotion, and was let go in 1981 with a $10 million severance check. He invested the money to start Innovative Market Systems, a company that provided up-to-date market data to Wall Street firms through a computerized information system. In 1983, he sold a 30 percent stake to Merrill Lynch for $30 million, and the venture took off—he renamed it Bloomberg L.P. in 1986, and the computer terminals used by his clients became known as Bloomberg Boxes. His success was enormous, and his business expanded exponentially. He indulged in the New York social scene and divorced his wife in 1993, although the couple stayed close friends. He spent several years reveling in bachelorhood. (In 1996, he said, "I like the theater, dining, and chasing women. Let me put it this way: I am a single, straight, billionaire in Manhattan. What do you think? It's like a wet dream.") His companion since 2000 has been the willowy, glamorous, and politically connected Diana Taylor, currently the managing director of a financial securities firm, and a fixture in the nonprofit community and on the society charitable circuit. Bloomberg has said of his paramour, "She's got beauty, she's got brains, she's got personality. She's sophisticated but down-to-earth. She's one of those people who can do anything she sets her mind to."

Over the years he added Bloomberg News, Bloomberg Radio, and Bloomberg Television to his conglomerate, and his empire continued to flourish, although it wasn't always without incidents. Bloomberg was sued several times for sexual harassment, discrimination, and inappropriate remarks; the suits were dropped or settled out of court. When managing the company began to grow stale, Bloomberg came up with four choices of what else he might want to do: president of the World Bank, secretary-general of the United Nations, mayor of New York City, and president of the United States. One down, three to go.

Why He Has a Chance

Bloomberg has succeeded at virtually every professional endeavor, and that gloss of perennial achievement could be immensely appealing to an apprehensive nation.

America is sick of partisan politics. Bloomberg would present himself as a no-nonsense CEO candidate who would take charge of the Iraq War, the budget, and the economy, and who might offer some innovative ideas about taxes, health care, immigration, and the environment.

Five hundred million dollars, give or take, can pay the salaries of the finest strategists and operatives in the country. It can also furnish an unlimited supply of travel, national television ads, direct mail, and infrastructure in every state, all without the grind of fund-raising slogs and budgeting choices. His campaign team is made up of his longtime close advisers, and it has had two test runs with his mayoral races. Political experts credit his operation with spending the money thoughtfully and efficiently, albeit in abundance. Bloomberg's two wins as a Republican in a city in which Democrats outnumber Republicans 5 to 1 were further proof of its proficiency. (Of course, his way was paved by the ramifications of September 11, with voters wishing for a smooth transition from Republican Giuliani to Republican Bloomberg, and a vital endorsement from his hero-predecessor.) Under the radar, Bloomberg has lent his political operation to candidates in states such as Connecticut and Missouri, allowing his team to practice electioneering in different locations, hone their methods, try new strategies, and forge national connections.

He has the ego of a billionaire, and the confidence to match, combined with a gracious, munificent spirit. People seem to like his combination of self-effacing charm and effortless poise. Unlike other well-known billionaires, he has not made a lot of enemies, publicly or privately, and has not encountered much negative press. As a former media baron, Bloomberg has many friends and admirers in the upper echelons of journalism, and knows better than most candidates how the game is played.

Bloomberg Facts and Stories

– Bloomberg's father, William Henry Bloomberg, died in 1963. Bloomberg has since made a number of endowments in Boston and Jerusalem in his honor. (He has also made donations and endowments on behalf of his daughters.) His mother, Charlotte Rubens Bloomberg, just shy of one hundred, lives in the Medford home where he grew up, and gets a phone call from her son nearly every day. He has a sister, Marjorie Tiven.

– He was an Eagle Scout.

– He served as chairman of his alma mater Johns Hopkins from 1996 until 2002, and has given the university more than $300 million.

– His relationship with his ex-wife, Susan Brown Bloomberg, is so close that they spend many Thanksgivings and other holidays together, along with their children. She and her boyfriend volunteered for his mayoral campaign, and she often attends his official events. She has said, "I still love him and I believe he still loves me. The only difference, really, in our relationship now is that we're not married, so that he can have his career and I can have my life without the tensions."

– His older daughter, Emma, born in 1979, has worked in the mayor's office (she accepted the same one-dollar salary as her father). She attended Princeton University, and in 2005 married fellow Princeton graduate Christopher Frissora. Bloomberg performed the ceremony at his Westchester estate. The newlyweds pursued joint master's degrees in business and public administration at Harvard.

– His younger daughter, Georgina, born in 1983, is a student at New York University and is training to compete as an equestrienne jumper in the 2008 Olympic Summer Games.

– He has said he plans to give the bulk of his wealth to charity.

– He is studying Spanish.

– He was named one of *Time* magazine's one hundred most influential people in 2007.

About Bloomberg

"I think [Bloomberg] would make an excellent candidate, because it's all about fixing problems and creating a great vision for the future."   —California governor Arnold Schwarzenegger

Read More About Bloomberg

Michael Bloomberg, *Bloomberg by Bloomberg* (New York: John Wiley & Sons, 2001).

http://www.mike2008.com/

Acknowledgments

My partner in this project was Karen Avrich. The book would not exist without her exceptional writing, ideas, judgment, generosity of spirit, and knowledge of the candidates and of American politics. She knows the way to win, what it takes, and how to decide.

My thanks to Henry Ferris, Lisa Sharkey, Peter Hubbard, and Leslie Cohen of HarperCollins for their excellent ideas and enthusiasm.

At *Time*, Rick Stengel and all my colleagues have been very supportive of the new guy.

Teddy Davis and Adam Nagourney provided invaluable feedback during a busy time—they are great friends.

When the going gets tough, I have come to rely on the sage counsel of Bob Barnett and Gil Fuchsberg, who never let me down and always advise with good humor and realistic appraisals.

Over the years, the presidential candidates and their staffs have answered my questions with good humor.

Laura and Peter Hartmann both assured me that the title and premise were not horrible ideas. During the writing of this book, Hannah and Madelyn Halperin provided invaluable research assistance during three days at Disney World in Orlando (where we ran into Hillary Clinton at the Contemporary Resort hotel).

Mark Halperin
New York City
September 2007

Notes

1. Rudolph Giuliani

10 "Something I learned a long time ago . . .": Eric Pooley, "Mayor of the World," *Time*, December 31, 2001/January 7, 2002.

14 "a quattrocento fresco of an obscure saint": Richard Stengel, "The Passionate Prosecutor, *Time*, February 10, 1986.

15 "frankly, in the Catholic Church the vow of celibacy . . .": David Brody, "The David Brody File," Christian Broadcast Network, June 27, 2007.

16 "The job I have now is important and interesting . . .": "Man in the News; Nominee for U.S. Attorney," *New York Times*, April 13, 1983.

"the most celebrated Federal prosecutor . . .": Todd S. Purdum, "Rudolph Giuliani and the Color of Politics in New York," *New York Times*, July 25, 1993.

17 "If we can prove the existence of the Mafia commission . . .": Michael Winerip, "High Profile Prosecutor," *New York Times*, June 9, 1985.

18 "Damn them . . .": Michael Winerip, "High Profile Prosecutor," *New York Times*, June 9, 1985.

20 He was guided in part by: James Q. Wilson and George L. Kelling, "Broken Windows," *Atlantic Monthly*, March 1982; George L. Kelling, *Fixing Broken Windows: Restoring Order and Reducing Crime in Our Communities*, New York: Free Press, 1998.

21 "The biggest and largest special interest group . . .": John Tierney, "The Holy Terror," *New York Times*, December 3, 1995.

22 "They wanted someone who was going to change this place. . . .": Eric Pooley, "Mayor of the World," *Time*, December 31, 2001/January 7, 2002.

25 "my mother or father said . . .": Don Terry, "Warily, Giuliani Learns to Embrace the Voters," *New York Times*, November 3, 1989.

his father "had a lot of rules . . .": D. D. Guttenplan and Jennifer Preston, "Rudy Giuliani's Roots Show Him as a Man Apart," *Newsday*, October 22, 1989.

It was not until Giuliani's Senate campaign in 1999 that a bombshell was reported: Wayne Barrett, *Rudy!: An Investigative Biography of Rudolph Giuliani* (New York: Basic Books, 2000).

"He would tell me, 'Never take anybody else's money . . . ' ": New York 1 interview with Rudolph Giuliani, August 2000.

27 Giuliani once took a detour: Don Terry, "Warily, Giuliani Learns to Embrace the Voters," *New York Times*, November 3, 1989.

28 "There's obviously a little problem . . .": Russ Buettner and Richard Pérez-Peña, "Noticeably Absent from the Giuliani Campaign: His Children," *New York Times*, March 3, 2007.

"If she wanted to, if they were relevant . . .": *20/20*, ABC News, March 30, 2007.

29 At the ceremony, the two happily described their romance: Ruth La Ferla, "Vows: Judith Nathan and Rudolph W. Giuliani," *New York Times,* May 25, 2003.

39 "It's not Giuliani's tactical sense, but his very nature . . .": James Traub, "The Mayor's Makeover," *New York Times*, August 1, 1999.

41 "I've created a lot of my own stereotype": Todd S. Purdum, "Rudolph Giuliani and the Color of Politics in New York," *New York Times*, July 25, 1993.

"For purposes of ethics and of law . . .": Richard Stengel, "The Passionate Prosecutor," *Time*, February 10, 1986.

"Part of the challenge of life is doing different things . . .": James Traub, "The Mayor's Makeover," *New York Times*, August 1, 1999.

Notes

"I started thinking about Churchill . . .": Eric Pooley, "Mayor of the World," *Time*, December 31, 2001/January 7, 2002.

42 "People ask, 'have you changed a lot since 9/11?' . . .": Eric Pooley, "Mayor of the World," *Time*, December 31, 2001/January 7, 2002.

"It's like you're with Elvis, for God's sake. . . .": Todd S. Purdum, "Rudolph Giuliani and the Color of Politics in New York," *New York Times*, July 25, 1993.

"Nobody believed Giuliani had a heart . . .": Eric Pooley, "Mayor of the World," *Time*, December 31, 2001/January 7, 2002.

Giuliani is "consumed with raw power.": Todd S. Purdum, "Rudolph Giuliani and the Color of Politics in New York," *New York Times*, July 25, 1993.

43 "It's a cult of personality around the great leader. . . .": John Tierney, "The Holy Terror," *New York Times*, December 3, 1995.

"Just exactly how I missed it, I can't describe.": D. D. Guttenplan and Jennifer Preston, "Rudy Giuliani's Roots Show Him As a Man Apart," *Newsday*, October 22, 1989.

44 "I became [a fan]. I had not been to a NASCAR race . . .": RadioIowa interview with Rudolph Giuliani, July 7, 2007.

"The key to this game is you drive for the show . . .": Steven Gaines, "Sunday Brunch Live from the American Hotel," WLIU Radio, July 1, 2007.

2. John McCain

57 "I have faced a lot tougher times than this in my life . . .": Roger Simon, ThePolitico.com, July 16, 2007.

58 "I may not be the youngest candidate in this race . . .": *Meet the Press*, NBC, May 13, 2007.

59 "I had more fun at the Naval Academy than most anybody ever should . . .": *60 Minutes*, CBS, October 12, 1997.

63 "I don't want to be the POW candidate . . .": Nancy Gibbs and John F. Dickerson, "The Power and the Story: Prison Shaped His

Character. Scandal Shaped His Crusade. But is John McCain's Biography Enough to Take Him to the White House?," *Time*, December 13, 1999.

64 "I don't want to be the POW Senator . . .": Susan F. Rasky, "Senator John S. McCain: Two Years in Capital, but Already a Rising Star," *New York Times*, August 9, 1988.

"I got lost on the way to my own rallies": Michael Lewis, "The Subversive," *New York Times*, May 25, 1997.

66 "I believe in duty, honor, and country . . .": Susan F. Rasky, "To Senator McCain, the Savings and Loan Affair Is Now a Personal Demon," *New York Times*, December 22, 1989.

67 "Outside of the prison experience . . .": *60 Minutes*, CBS, October 12, 1997.

"impatience with bureaucratic inertia and ideological purity . . .": Susan F. Rasky, "Senator John S. McCain: Two Years in Capital, but Already a Rising Star," *New York Times*, August 9, 1988.

"This is a very seductive kind of environment . . .": Michael Lewis, "The Subversive," *New York Times*, May 25, 1997.

69 "One of the things that happened . . .": Glenn Frankel, "The McCain Makeover," *Washington Post*, August 27, 2006.

70 "I would have been a man without a country! . . .": Connie Bruck, "McCain's Party," *New Yorker*, May 30, 2005.

72 "If I don't like what you write . . .": John F. Dickerson, "McCain's Mother: 'Johnny, I'll Wash Your Mouth Out,'" *Time*, February 21, 2000.

"I was standing at the hors d'oeuvre table . . .": Nancy Collins, "Cindy McCain: Myth vs. Reality," *Harper's Bazaar*, July 1, 2007.

74 "I have a lot to offer to this country . . .": *Dateline NBC*, NBC, October 10, 1999.

"a remote-control freak . . .": Tom Blair, "Cindy McCain Dialogue with Tom Blair," *San Diego*, August 2007.

75 "He'd be the best president . . .": Nancy Collins, "Cindy McCain: Myth vs. Reality," *Harper's Bazaar*, July 1, 2007.

77 As far back as 2005, some of McCain's friends said . . . : Connie Bruck, "McCain's Party," *New Yorker*, May 30, 2005.

80 "When I got angry I held my breath until I blacked out": John McCain, *Faith of My Fathers* (New York: Random House, 1999).

81 "I'm obviously aware of the enormous responsibilities . . .": Bill Muller, "The Life Story of Arizona's Maverick Senator McCain," *Arizona Republic*, October 3, 1999.

85 "I don't think John McCain had even been associated . . .": Bill Muller, "The Life Story of Arizona's Maverick Senator McCain," *Arizona Republic*, October 3, 1999.

86 "John is seventy going on thirty . . .": Nancy Collins, "Cindy McCain: Myth vs. Reality," *Harper's Bazaar*, July 1, 2007.

87 He reportedly engaged in a vodka drinking contest: Ann Kornblut, "2008 May Test Clinton's Bond with McCain," *New York Times*, July 29, 2006.

   McCain family pets include: Associated Press candidate quiz.

88 his favorite word: Roger Simon, "The Making of the President John McCain," *Washingtonian*, February 2007.

   He owns an iPod: "Scoop," *People*, July 16, 2007.

   McCain keeps a Roosevelt figure: Jennifer O'Shea, "10 Things You Didn't Know about John McCain," *U.S. News & World Report*, February 8, 2007.

3. Mitt Romney

100 "There's nothing like hard work . . .": Neil Swidey and Michael Paulson, "Privilege, Tragedy, and a Young Leader," *Boston Globe*, June 24, 2007.

101 "There are no stick figures in politics . . .": Terry Eastland, "In 2008, Will It Be Mormon in America?," *Weekly Standard*, June 6, 2005.

101 "Some of this anti-Mormonism . . .": Amy Sullivan, "Mitt Romney's Evangelical Problem," *Washington Monthly*, September 2005.

102 "This is a nation that will always welcome . . .": Terry Eastland, "In 2008, Will It Be Mormon in America?" *Weekly Standard*, June 6, 2005.

104 "The Rambler automobile . . .": Mitt Romney announcement speech, February 13, 2007.

105 "It is impossible to be around Romney . . .": Richard Lowry, "A CEO for the USA?—On the Trail with Manager Mitt," *National Review*, April 30, 2007.

108 "I pray that this graduating class . . .": Ben Bradlee, Jr., "Romney Seeks New Chapter in Success," *Boston Globe*, August 7, 1994.

109 "We went home and asked each other . . .": John Powers, "Golden Opportunity," *Boston Globe*, February 3, 2002.

113 "When I was a little kid . . .": *The Charlie Rose Show*, PBS, June 5, 2006.

114 Her mother, however, eventually converted: Neil Swidey and Stephanie Ebbert, "Journeys of a Shared Life: Raising Sons, Rising Expectations Bring Unexpected Turns," *Boston Globe*, June 27, 2007.

120 "You got the feeling you were dealing . . .": Sacha Pfeiffer, "Romney's Harvard Classmates Recall His Quick Mind, Positive Attitude," *Boston Globe*, June 26, 2007.

120 "He was always someone . . .": John H. Kennedy, "Romney vs. Kennedy," *Boston Globe*, November 14, 1993.

121 "If Mitt was wearing the same suit . . .": Andrew Miga, "Battling the Odds, Romney Faces Toughest Fight," *Boston Herald*, August 6, 1994.

"He loves emergencies and catastrophes . . .": John Powers, "Hub's Romney Takes on Salt Lake City Games," *Boston Globe*, February 12, 1999.

"He's gone through all the usual Mitt stages . . .": John Powers, "Golden Opportunity," *Boston Globe*, February 3, 2002.

"If you pay sufficient attention . . .": "A Man with a Mission," *Washington Post*, February 18, 2007.

"I think Mitt's accustomed . . .": Stephanie Ebbert, "Romney Seeks High Office with Confidence, Pedigree," *Boston Globe*, August 11, 2002.

122 "Mitt Romney is a politician . . .": Michael Finnegan, "Turnabouts by Romney Are Fair Game," *Los Angeles Times*, February 1, 2007.

123 "I figured I was at the state park . . .": Frank Phillips, "GOP Hopeful Arrested in 1981; Charge Dismissed in Boating Case," *Boston Globe*, May 5, 1994.

125 "[Seamus] scrambled up there . . .": CNN, June 29, 2007.

127 "I've got an oldies file . . .": "Scoop," *People*, July 16, 2007.

When nervous: Robert Gavin and Sacha Pfeiffer, "Reaping Profit in Study, Sweat," *Boston Globe*, June 26, 2007.

4. Fred Thompson

139 "I have never taken on . . .": Michael Silence, "Senate Candidate Fred Thompson Exudes Intensity," *Knoxville News-Sentinel*, August 28, 1994.

141 "I've often said if I had his voice . . .": *The Situation Room*, CNN, March 2007.

"There's nobody who has to be . . .": Rick Bragg, "Grits and Glitter Campaign Helps Actor Who Played a Senator Become One," *New York Times*, November 12, 1994.

142 "I had the best kind of background . . .": Myra MacPherson, "Fred Thompson, Courting Celebrity; The Watergate Lawyer Takes a Star Turn in 'Marie,' " *Washington Post*, November 4, 1985.

"I barely got out of high school . . .": Myra MacPherson, "Fred Thompson, Courting Celebrity: The Watergate Lawyer Takes a Star Turn in 'Marie,' " *Washington Post*, November 4, 1985.

143 "Watergate was not a monumental shock . . .": Kristin McMurran, "Watergate Lawyer Fred Thompson Is Perfect for His Role in *Marie*," *People*, November 11, 1985.

144 "I'm glad all of this . . .": Michael Kranish, "Not All Would Put a Heroic Sheen on Thompson's Watergate Role," *Boston Globe*, July 4, 2007.

"It wasn't that hard to adjust . . .": Lynn Darling, "The Power of Attorney," *Washington Post*, January 10, 1981.

145 "They were allegedly the bankroll . . .": Myra MacPherson, "Fred Thompson, Courting Celebrity; The Watergate Lawyer Takes a Star Turn in 'Marie,' " *Washington Post*, November 4, 1985.

146 "[I]f a client has a legal and ethical right . . .": Fred Thompson, *Powerline*, July 11, 2007.

"As we get further into . . .": Fred Thompson, *Powerline*, July 11, 2007.

"I thought that standing . . .": Kristin McMurran, "Watergate Lawyer Fred Thompson Is Perfect for His Role in *Marie*," *People*, November 11, 1985.

147 "more like a man who would stuff . . .": Rick Bragg, "Grits and Glitter Campaign Helps Actor Who Played a Senator Become One," *New York Times*, November 12, 1994.

"Regardless of whether you agreed . . .": Frank Rich, "A Star Is Born," *New York Times*, December 22, 1994.

148 "I think we're probably at . . .": William F. Powers, "Fred Thompson, Driving Home a Campaign of Illusion and Disillusion," *Washington Post*, October 21, 1994.

149 "a star is born": Frank Rich, "A Star Is Born," *New York Times*, December 22, 1994.

"a first-class communicator . . .": Tom Shales, "Bill Clinton, Hitting His Stride," *Washington Post*, December 16, 1994.

"I am, in many respects, an average Tennessean. . . .": Rick Bragg, "Grits and Glitter Campaign Helps Actor Who Played a Senator Become One," *New York Times*, November 12, 1994.

150 "I have always looked . . .": Douglas Waller, "10 Questions for Fred Thompson," *Time*, October 28, 2002.

"I have seen the sonograms of my babies": Heidi Przybyla and Catherine Dodge, "Thompson Gains Support from Republican Conservatives," *Bloomberg News*, April 19, 2007.

"He voted the right way . . .": Heidi Przybyla and Catherine Dodge, "Thompson Gains Support from Republican Conservatives," *Bloomberg News*, April 19, 2007.

151 "This is easily the worst . . .": Matthew Rees, "Has Fred Thompson Blown It?," *Weekly Standard*, October 6, 1997.

152 "You know how it is . . .": Elaine Sciolino, " 'Bit Actor' to Star in a New Role: Mr. Chairman," *New York Times*, February 21, 1997.

153 "I've just lost my heart . . .": Rebecca Sinderbrand, "The Mysterious Appeal of Fred Thompson," *New York Observer*, April 9, 2007.

"We just have some other priorities . . .": Bonna De La Cruz, Leon Alligood, and Sheila Wissner, " 'I Simply Do Not Have the Heart for Another Six-Year Term,' " *Tennessean*, March 9, 2002.

154 "As an idealistic teenager . .": Fred Thompson, *Powerline*, July 11, 2007.

"Fred Thompson gives one of the . . .": Janet Maslin, "Spacek in *Marie*," *New York Times*, September 27, 1985.

"the real discovery of *Marie* . . .": Paul Attanasio, "Too-True 'Marie,' " *Washington Post*, October 18, 1985.

155 "Fred Thompson is a very convincing Fred Thompson . . .": Frank Rich, "A Star Is Born," *New York Times*, December 22, 1994.

"If you talk about it, people think . . .": William F. Powers, "Fred Thompson, Driving Home a Campaign of Illusion and Disillusion," *Washington Post*, October 21, 1994.

156 "No one is named Fred except . . .": Kristin McMurran, "Watergate Lawyer Fred Thompson Is Perfect for His Role in *Marie*," *People*, November 11, 1985.

"when they need an old, beat-up . . .": William F. Powers, "Fred Thompson, Driving Home a Campaign of Illusion and Disillusion," *Washington Post*, October 21, 1994.

156 "He has an active social life . . .": Jill Lawrence, "Is White House Next? Don't Bet Against Him, Many Say," *USA Today*, February 14, 1997.

"I was single for a long time . . .": Sarah Baxter, "Old Girlfriends Cast Their Vote for Thompson," *Sunday Times,* June 24, 2007.

157 "I think I'm a pretty good guy . . .": Myra MacPherson, "Fred Thompson, Courting Celebrity; The Watergate Lawyer Takes a Star Turn in 'Marie,' " *Washington Post*, November 4, 1985.

"They just won't leave him alone . . .": "Page Six," *New York Post,* April 27, 2000.

The *New York Times* suggested: Susan Saulny, "Will Her Face Determine His Fortune?," *New York Times*, July 8, 2007.

"babe wife": Ian Bishop, "Babe Wife, 40, Boosts Goper, 64," *New York Post*, June 1, 2007.

"pretty face . . . with a pretty impressive résumé": *Anderson Cooper 360,* CNN, July 4, 2007.

158 the media have scrutinized her past: Holly Bailey, "Not-So-Hidden Power," *Newsweek*, August 13, 2007.

"If he had the drive . . .": Duren Cheek, "Biography," *Tennessean*, March 9, 2002.

"He was smart, but he was lazy . . .": Brade Schrade, "Thompson: How a Small-Town Character Made the Big Time," *Tennessean*, May 6, 2007.

"[Thompson] is not a person . . .": Bill Theobald, "Some Label Thompson a 'Lazy' Senator," *Tennessean*, May 7, 2007.

159 "Fred is a big man . . .": Carl Hulse, "Ex-Senator Seen as Rehearsing for Prime Time," *New York Times,* May 1, 2007.

"It's difficult to see the real drive he has . . .": Jill Lawrence, "Is White House Next? Don't Bet Against Him, Many Say," *USA Today*, February 14, 1997.

"While the Senate is filled with ambitious men . . .": Mark Halperin, "A New Role for Fred Thompson," *Time*, May 24, 2007.

"There's one thing, I think, for certain . . .": *This Week*, ABC, December 25, 1994.

"Yeah, I go to Hollywood . . .": Rick Bragg, "Grits and Glitter Campaign Helps Actor Who Played a Senator Become One," *New York Times*, November 12, 1994.

160 "cool, careful, and conservative": Robert D. Novak, "Thompson Is for Real," *Washington Post*, April 2, 2007.

163 "one advantage you have . . .": *Fox News Sunday*, Fox News Network, March 11, 2007.

164 "We need to think about what . . .": Helen Kennedy, "Role of a Lifetime: Recognition, Charisma Boosting Fred Thompson in '08 Prez Race," *New York Daily News*, June 18, 2007.

166 "I was particularly interested in . . .": Lynn Darling, "The Power of Attorney," *Washington Post*, January 10, 1981.

"Up here, it's a town on the make . . .": Myra MacPherson, "Fred Thompson, Courting Celebrity: The Watergate Lawyer Takes a Star Turn in 'Marie,' " *The Washington Post*, November 4, 1985.

167 "It has to do with lawyers and politicians . . .": Myra MacPherson, "Fred Thompson, Courting Celebrity: The Watergate Lawyer Takes a Star Turn in 'Marie,' " *Washington Post*, November 4, 1985.

"I am delighted he ran for public office . . .": Carolyn Skorneck, "Thompson Gets Lead Role in Fund-raising Probe," *Knoxville News-Sentinel*, January 6, 1997.

"Sometimes you feel he is not working hard enough . . .": Michael Silence, "Attacks Could Spur Thompson to Run," *Knoxville News-Sentinel,* September 23, 2001.

"Fred is a perfect example of chivalry . . .": Sarah Baxter, "Old Girlfriends Cast Their Vote for Thompson," *Sunday Times,* June 24, 2007.

168 "Everybody makes their own luck . . .": Jill Lawrence, "Is White House Next? Don't Bet Against Him, Many Say," *USA Today*, February 14, 1997.

"He's not new at this game . . .": Rebecca Sinderbrand, "The Mysterious Appeal of Fred Thompson," *New York Observer*, April 9, 2007.

168 "Everybody's got a Fred Thompson story . . .": Brade Schrade, "Thompson: How a Small Town Character Made the Big Time," *Tennessean,* May 6, 2007.

I have the greatest affection . . .": Kirk Victor, "Holding Their Applause," *National Journal*, June 27, 1998.

"He has a conservative bearing . . .": Michael D. Shear, "A 'Law & Order' Presidential Candidate?; Actor, Ex-Senator Thompson May Run," *Washington Post,* March 29, 2007.

169 "I just felt like that the work hadn't been done": Eric Schmitt, "For 2 Republican Senators, Signs of an Early Frost over Finance Hearings," *New York Times*, October 22, 1997.

171 "Thompson is a hybrid of good ol' boy and . . .": Jill Lawrence, "Is White House next? Don't Bet Against Him, Many Say," *USA Today*, February 14, 1997.

Thompson's home was filled with: Stephen F. Hayes, "From the Courthouse to the White House; Fred Thompson Auditions for the Leading Role," *Weekly Standard*, April 23, 2007.

5. More Republicans

176 "I'd grown up listening to . . .": Terry Eastland, "Mr. Compassionate Conservative," *Weekly Standard*, August 7, 2006.

177 "being prolife but being . . .": *Morning Edition,* NPR, March 5, 2007.

178 "I did a lot of internal examination . . .": Stephanie A. Salmon, "Ten Things You Didn't Know about Sen. Sam Brownback, " *U.S. News & World Report*, January 30, 2007.

180 "He was just a wholesome . . .": George Diepenbrock and Sophia Maines, "From Farmer to President: Brownback's Ambitions Have Changed, but Family Says He's the Same," *Lawrence Journal-World*, January 15, 2007.

183 "He was the single smartest . . .": James Traub, "Newt at Rest," *New York Times*, October 29, 2000.

187 "I call Newt an experiential conservative . . .": "The Long March of Newt Gingrich," PBS, 1996.

190 "We're dramatically different . . .": Susannah Meadows, "A Would-Be Knight for the Religious Right," *Newsweek*, March 7, 2007.

193 "I need a hard-driving guitar . . .": "Scoop," *People*, July 16, 2007.

194 "Mike's not afraid . . .": Felley Lawson, "Michael Dale Huckabee," *Arkansas Democrat-Gazette*, March 12, 1995.

"[Huckabee] had this dual interest . . .": Felley Lawson, "Michael Dale Huckabee," *Arkansas Democrat-Gazette*, March 12, 1995.

197 "I interpret through the eyes . . .": Danielle Burton, "10 Things You Didn't Know about Ron Paul," *U.S. News & World Report*, March 23, 2007.

198 "The bunching together . . .": Nate Blakeslee, "The Elephant in the Room," *Texas Monthly*, August 2007.

200 His personal finances: Christopher Caldwell, "The Antiwar, Anti-Abortion, Anti-Drug-Enforcement-Administration, Anti-Medicare Candidacy of Dr. Ron Paul," *New York Times*, July 22, 2007.

"Ron Paul is a very charismatic person . . .": Christopher Caldwell, "The Antiwar, Anti-Abortion, Anti-Drug-Enforcement-Administration, Anti-Medicare Candidacy of Dr. Ron Paul," *New York Times*, July 22, 2007.

6. Hillary Clinton

213 "There's that mutuality of respect . . .": Hillary D. Rodham, Wellesley College commencement speech, May 31, 1969.

214 "We sort of feel like . . .": While in Atlanta speaking on "The Politics of Education" at a meeting of education reporters sponsored by the Southern Newspaper Publishers Foundation and the Southern Regional Education Board.

215 "I like having a role as a private citizen . . .": "First Lady Says Her Work for Education Unfinished,"*Arkansas Democrat-Gazette*, January 15, 1985.

216 "Hillary pounds the piano so hard . . .": Michael Kramer, "The Political Interest It's Not Going to Be Pretty," *Time*, April 20, 1992.

217 "It may well be that the time has come to rethink the First Lady model . . .": *Wall Street Journal*, January 22, 1993.

218 "When you work, work hard . . .": Landon Y. Jones, "At Home in Arkansas, the Clintons Talk About Friends, Family, Faith—Pierced Ears," *People*, July 20, 1992.

219 "The paradox: The more . . .": Amy Spindler, "Patterns," *New York Times*, May 18, 1993.

220 "I like Senator Clinton . . .": Raymond Hernandez, "As Clinton Wins GOP Friends, Her Rivals' Task Toughens," *New York Times*, March 6, 2005.

224 "I don't think like that . . .": Dan Balz, "Clinton Is a Politician Not Easily Defined; Senator's Platform Remains Unclear," *Washington Post*, May 30, 2006.

238 "[I would] continue to work . . .": Associated Press candidate quiz.

"I knew that Bill and Hillary were . . .": John Brummet, "Betsey Wright: Aide Part of Circle of 'Strong Women,' " *Arkansas Democrat-Gazette*, September 15, 1985.

"The biggest mistake of the American press . . .": James Bennet, "The Next Clinton," *New York Times Magazine*, May 30, 1999.

7. John Edwards

252 "You have to be yourself . . .": Richard Leiby, "An Answer That's Blowing in the Wind; John Edwards's Political Rise Followed Tragedy, and Much Joy," *Washington Post,* August 7, 2001.

"I don't analyze these issues on . . .": Garance Franke-Ruta, "Mr. Personality: Is That Enough for John Edwards?" *American Prospect*, July–August 2003.

254 "Don't ever start a fight . . .": Julia Reed, "Making His Case," *Vogue*, October 2004.

260 "a constant student . . .": Julia Reed, "Making His Case," *Vogue*, October 2004.

263 "our house was fairly joyless . . .": Richard Leiby, "An Answer That's Blowing in the Wind; John Edwards's Political Rise Followed Tragedy, and Much Joy," *Washington Post*, August 7, 2001.

265 she relayed to *People* magazine: Bob Meadows and Jane Sims Podesta, "Secret Weapon? Elizabeth Edwards, Down-Home Everymom, May Be Her Husband's Greatest Asset," *People*, July 26, 2004.

268 Edwards demonstrated little appeal: Joe Hagan, "Getting Real: Can John Edwards Convince America That He's Got What it Takes to Crush the Red State/Blue State Divide?" *Men's Vogue*, July 2007.

274 "George Bush goes down to . . .": Mark Leibovich, "Getting Personal: John Edwards Tries to Rally His Bid by Going One on One," *Washington Post*, October 22, 2003.

"Why, you lookin' for a haircut? . . .": Richard Leiby, "An Answer That's Blowing in the Wind: John Edwards's Political Rise Followed Tragedy, and Much Joy," *Washington Post*, August 7, 2001.

"I came to genuinely understand . . .": John Edwards, *Four Trials* (with John Auchard), (New York: Simon & Schuster, November 2003).

"You have to see John in action . . .": Robert Lamme, "Edwards Makes Case for Senate Run," *News & Record* (Greensboro, N.C.), August 25, 1998.

275 "I never want him to have another . . .": Richard Leiby, "An Answer That's Blowing in the Wind: John Edwards's Political Rise Followed Tragedy, and Much Joy," *Washington Post*, August 7, 2001.

"It's not every day that you run against a very slick . . .": James Carney, "A Republican Who's Taking His Medicine," *Time*, July 13, 1998.

"I would like to protect innocent people from blind justice": Michael Duffy, "The Natural; Sunny Yet Driven, John Edwards Was Born to Run, But Has He Come too Far too Fast?," *Time*, July 19, 2004.

276 "I'm wipin' my son . . .": Nicholas Lemann, "Senator John Edwards Is This Season's Democratic Rising Star," *New Yorker*, May 6, 2002.

8. Barack Obama

290 "I love to body surf . . .": "Life of the Party: Rising Star Obama Takes the Spotlight at Boston Convention," *Chicago Tribune*, July 27, 2004.

292 "left a very strong mark on me living . . .": Tammerlin Drummond, "Barack Obama's Law," *Los Angeles Times*, March 12, 1990.

"I come from a lot of worlds . . .": Tammerlin Drummond, "Barack Obama's Law," *Los Angeles Times*, March 12, 1990.

"Pot had helped, and booze . . .": Barack Obama, *Dreams from My Father* (New York: Three Rivers Press, 2004).

293 "Some of the problems of adolescent rebellion . . .": David Mendell, "Barack Obama: Democrat for U.S. Senate," *Chicago Tribune*, October 22, 2004.

294 "Chicago politics tends toward polarization . . .": Terry McDermott, "What Is it About Obama?," *Los Angeles Times*, December 24, 2006.

"I have worked and lived in poor black communities . . .": Tammerlin Drummond, "Barack Obama's Law," *Los Angeles Times*, March 12, 1990.

"I feel like I've walked through a door . . .": J. D. Reed, "Class Act," *Time*, February 19, 1990.

295 "When I was in college, I decided I wanted . . .": David Mendell, "Obama Banks on Credentials, Charisma," *Chicago Tribune*, January 25, 2004.

297 "a white man in blackface.": Salim Muwakkil, "Ironies Abound in 1st District," *Chicago Tribune*, March 20, 2000.

"I haven't changed . . .": P. J. Huffstutter, "Skill, Luck Unite to Lift Obama: Young Political Star Straddles Two Worlds," *Kansas City Star*, July 30, 2004.

298 "Obviously, I've got a personal connection to Africa . . .": Jeff Zeleny, "Obama Returns to Africa as Celebrity," *Chicago Tribune*, August 20, 2006.

304 "If politics were my passion . . .": Cassandra West, "Barack's rock: America Was Introduced to Barack Obama at the Democratic Con-

vention. Now Meet His Wife," *Kansas City Star*, September 19, 2004.

Michelle Obama serves as a strong advocate for her husband's candidacy: Scott Fornek, " 'I've Got a Competitive Nature,' " *Chicago Sun-Times*, October 3, 2004.

305 "Chicagoan through and through.": Debra Pickett, " 'My parents weren't college-educated folks, so they didn't have a notion of what we should want,' " *Chicago Sun-Times*, September 19, 2004.

Michelle Obama's college thesis: Rosalind Rossi, "Obama's Anchor: As His Career Soars Toward a Presidential Bid, Wife Michelle Keeps His Feet on the Ground," *Chicago Sun-Times*, January 21, 2007.

306 "I don't lose sleep over it . . .": *60 Minutes,* CBS, February 11, 2007.

"gorgeous, healthy, and mischievous": Barack Obama, *Dreams from My Father* (New York: Three Rivers Press, 2004).

308 "when it comes to Scrabble . . .": Scott Fornek, " 'I've Got a Competitive Nature,' " *Chicago Sun-Times*, October 3, 2004.

312 "By nature, I'm not somebody who gets real worked up about things . . .": Barack Obama, *The Audacity of Hope* (New York: Crown, 2006).

313 "It's interesting that the people who are most hesitant . . .": "Celebrity support," *Chicago Tribune*, January 17, 2007.

314 "I am the first one to acknowledge . . .": "Celebrity support," *Chicago Tribune*, January 17, 2007.

317 "When I'm in rural Illinois . . .": "Life of the party: Rising Star Obama Takes the Spotlight at Boston Convention," *Chicago Tribune*, July 27, 2004.

"In some ways, because it has happened . . .": "Celebrity support," *Chicago Tribune*, January 17, 2007.

"This is something I'm not enjoying . . .": Maurice Possley and Ray Gibson, "The Not-So-Simple Story of Barack Obama's Youth," *Chicago Tribune*, March 23, 2007.

317 "I have high expectations for myself . . .": David Mendell, "Obama Finding Himself Flush With Media Attention," *Chicago Tribune*, July 28, 2004.

"He's very unusual . . .": Tammerlin Drummond, "Barack Obama's Law," *Los Angeles Times,* March 12, 1990.

"The true test comes when . . .": David Mendell, "Barack Obama; Democrat for U.S. Senate," *Chicago Tribune*, October 22, 2004.

318 "I know people might find this hard to believe . . .": David Mendell, "Obama Banks on Credentials, Charisma," *Chicago Tribune*, January 25, 2004.

"Barack is more comfortable without a plan . . .": Cassandra West, "Barack's Rock: America Was Introduced to Barack Obama at the Democratic Convention. Now Meet His Wife," *Kansas City Star*, September 19, 2004.

"He was the kind of [basketball] player . . .": *In Touch*, July 30, 2007.

"Barack is the most unique political talent . . .": William Finnegan, "The Candidate: How the Son of a Kenyan Economist Became an Illinois Everyman," *New Yorker*, May 31, 2004.

"He has restored 'liberal' to the vocabulary . . .": P. J. Huffstutter, "Skill, Luck Unite to Lift Obama: Young Political Star Straddles Two Worlds," *Kansas City Star*, July 30, 2004.

"I know him personally . . .": *Larry King Live*, CNN, May 1, 2007.

319 Obama's family had a variety of pets: Paul Watson, "As a Child, Obama Crossed a Cultural Divide in Indonesia," *Los Angeles Times*, March 15, 2007.

He worked in a Baskin-Robbins: Monica Ekman, "Ten Things You Didn't Know About Barack Obama," *U.S. News & World Report*, January 16, 2007.

As a student in the 1970s: Richard A. Serrano, "Obama's Peers Didn't See His Angst," *Los Angeles Times,* March 11, 2007.

320 According to Obama, his grandfather: Tammerlin Drummond, "Barack Obama's Law," *Los Angeles Times,* March 12, 1990.

321 "dog meat [tough], snake meat [tougher], and roasted grasshopper [crunchy]": Barack Obama, *Dreams from My Father* (New York: Three Rivers Press, 2004).

He told the Associated Press: Associated Press candidate survey.

"I'm old-school, a jazz guy . . .": "Scoop," *People*, July 16, 2007.

"Marvin Gaye is one of his favorites . . .": "Life of the Party: Rising Star Obama Takes the Spotlight at Boston Convention," *Chicago Tribune*, July 27, 2004.

"A Ford Granada . . .": Scott Fornek, " 'Blessed by God,' Rooted in Two Continents," *Chicago Sun-Times*, January 22, 2003.

9. More Democrats

330 "Joe Impedimenta . . .": Joseph Biden, *Promises to Keep: On Life and Politics* (New York: Random House, 2007).

331 "I didn't deserve to be president . . .": Robin Abcarian, "Biden Gets Do-Over 20 Years Later," *Los Angeles Times*, June 18, 2007.

334 "I know most of the world leaders . . .": Jeff Zeleny, "In Iowa Yard, Biden Talks (and Talks) about Experience," *New York Times*, July 7, 2007.

335 "He's a man of immense character and integrity . . .": Robert Draper, "Joe Biden Can't Shut Up," *GQ*, March 2006.

339 "Celebrity and the amount of money you've raised . . .": *Road to the White House*, C-SPAN, August 2, 2007.

340 "Sometimes, I think almost everything Chris Dodd does . . .": David Lightman, "From Father to Son: Dodd Name Passed Along in Senate," *Hartford Courant*, October 12, 1995.

342 "It is great. You always want to be polite . . .": Carl Hulse, "First-Time Fatherhood at 57 Brings a New Perspective," *New York Times*, October 22, 2001.

343 The *Hartford Courant* once referred to Dodd: Miranda Spivak, "Of Blood Politics, the Strangest of Bedfellows, and What the Voters Never See," *Hartford Courant*, June 23, 1991.

344 "Chris Dodd can take you apart and leave you smiling": Jill Lawrence, "Congenial Senator Steers Democrats' Post-'94 Battles," *USA Today*, August 28, 1996.

347 "It's consistent with a desire to help . . .": "Interview with Dennis Kucinich," *Beliefnet*, February 2004.

"Can you imagine what it would be like . . .": Sarah Baxter, "Essex Girl Fills White House Race With Lurve," *Sunday Times*, May 20, 2007.

348 "Throughout high school I've done quite a bit of creative writing . . .": Rudy Maxa, "Dennis Kucinich Is No Joking Matter," *Washington Post*, February 25, 1979.

"I'm going to aim for the very top": Marshall Sella, "The Optimist," *New York Times*, December 21, 2003.

349 He soon acquired less favorable monikers: T. R. Reid, " 'Runt' Mayor: Besieged; Belligerent," *Washington Post*, August 6, 1978.

He refused to sell the city's electric company: Sheryl Gay Stolberg, "Past Defeat and Personal Quest Shape Long-Shot Kucinich Bid," *New York Times*, January 2, 2004.

351 "I'm meditating now . . .": "Interview with Dennis Kucinich," *Beliefnet*, February 2004.

361 "favorite team has always been the Red Sox: *Meet the Press*, NBC, May 27, 2007.

10. Michael Bloomberg

370 "my whole business life has been out in the open": Mark Gimein, "Mayor Mogul: Mike Bloomberg Wants to be New York City's CEO. Too bad he's only mayor," *Fortune*, April 1, 2002.

372 "I just think that the government shouldn't be in certain businesses . . .": *Today*, NBC, July 5, 2007.

374 "I like the theater, dining, and chasing women. . . .": Richard Thomas, "Michael Bloomberg, the Machine-Made Man," *Guardian*, December 28, 1996.

Notes

"She's got beauty, she's got brains . . .": Heidi Evans, "She's Not Just His 'Gal Pal': Diana Taylor Shares a Life With Hizzoner—and Leads a Fast-paced One of Her Own," *New York Daily News*, August 13, 2007.

Bloomberg came up with four choices of what else he might want to do: Dean E. Murphy, "Finding a New Mission: Michael Rubens Bloomberg," *New York Times*, November 7, 2001.

376 "I still love him and I believe he still loves me . . .": Dennis Duggan, "Mike Seems Wed to the Single Life," *Newsday*, July 1, 2003